Elizabeth Pond (photo courtesy of <u>Christian Science Monitor</u>)

Women
War
Correspondents
in the
Vietnam War,
1961-1975

by

Virginia Elwood-Akers

The Scarecrow Press, Inc.
Metuchen, N.J., & London
1988

The author gratefully acknowledges all those who granted permission to reprint material. Full credits appear at the end of each reprinted article.

Library of Congress Cataloging-in-Publication Data

Elwood-Akers, Virginia, 1938-
   Women war correspondents in the Vietnam War, 1961-1975.

   Bibliography: p.
   Includes index.
   Contents: With the paratroops / by Dickey Chapelle -- Saigon summary / by Marguerite Higgins -- Suffer the little children / by Martha Gellhorn -- [etc.]
   1. Vietnamese Conflict, 1961-1975. 2. Vietnamese Conflict, 1961-1975--Journalists. 3. Women journalists--Vietnam. I. Title.
DS557.7.E49   1988   959.704'38   87-23313
ISBN 0-8108-2033-1

This book is dedicated to two very special women:

Eileen Elwood, my mother

and

Edith Wulfestieg, my friend

CONTENTS

Of Vietnam, more than most places, it can be said that there are no experts, only varying degrees of ignorance.

Marguerite Higgins
Our Vietnam Nightmare
1965

AUTHOR'S NOTE

To any woman who was a war correspondent in Southeast Asia between 1961 and 1975, and whose name does not appear in this book, I can only apologize. There are, apparently, no official lists of journalists who covered the Vietnam War. According to Major General Winant Sidle, USA-Ret., formerly with Military Assistance Command, Vietnam (MACV), the lists were lost after being shipped from Saigon to Honolulu. When I completed my thesis on this subject in 1981, I knew the names of seventy-two women correspondents. I have since learned the names of four others.

I would like to thank the women correspondents who were so gracious and generous with their time. Special thanks are due to Georgie Anne Geyer, who lent me her home copier to copy articles directly from her scrapbooks, and to Patches Musgrove, who talked to me almost non-stop for six hours one Sunday afternoon, although she had only recently recovered from a stroke.

I would also like to thank Professors Tom Reilly, Susan Henry, and Richard Camp for their assistance and encouragement.

And I would like to thank my husband, Roy Akers, for cheerful proofreading and constant support.

"Hey, lady, what are you doing here?"

The words were called out to New York Times correspondent Gloria Emerson as she stood watching a platoon of
GIs leave to patrol the jungles of South Vietnam one day in
1970. Emerson did not answer. She simply smiled and waved
a V-for-peace sign to the departing GI. The sight of a woman
correspondent in Vietnam should not, in fact, have been an
unusual one by the time Gloria Emerson arrived to cover the
war. She was one of more than seventy women who reported
on the Vietnam War, beginning as early as 1961, when free-
lance photographer and writer Dickey Chapelle first reported
on the American advisers who travelled with the South Vietnamese forces in the Mekong Delta.

Although women made up a small percentage of the
hundreds of journalists who were accredited as war correspondents during the long years of the Vietnam War, their
role was not unimportant. Women reported for such major
news media as the New York Times, the National Broadcasting
Company, the Associated Press, The Christian Science Monitor, Newsweek, and United Press International. They won
numerous journalistic awards, including a Pulitzer Prize.
They were deeply involved in the controversy which raged--
and still rages--over whether coverage of the war was accurate or distorted to favor one point of view or another. At
least three women correspondents were wounded in action;
four others were taken prisoner. And, in the long corridor
in the Pentagon where the names of American correspondents
killed in action are listed, two of the sixteen names listed for
the Vietnam War are those of women.

And yet, in studies of war correspondence from the
Vietnam War, if mentioned at all, women reporters are usually
grouped together in a chapter with a clever name, such as

"ladies of the front lines," or "femininity at the front." The
women are included more as an amusing footnote than as an
integral part of the study. In fact, a comparison of Vietnam
War accounts written by men and women reporters indicates
that there was little difference between the sexes insofar as
the topics of their reporting was concerned. Women wrote
the so-called "human interest" stories which have traditionally
been expected of the woman reporter, but male reporters in
Vietnam wrote "human interest" stories as well. Both male
and female reporters in Vietnam wrote of the complexities of
the political events that shaped the history of the war. Both
male and female reporters analyzed the effects of the war on
South Vietnamese society. And both male and female reporters covered combat.

Nor is there a clear distinction between men and women
reporters when their attitudes toward American involvement
in the Vietnam War is considered. Despite the cherished belief of many feminists that women are inherently anti-war,
several female journalists fervently supported American involvement in South Vietnam, and went so far as to advocate
escalation of the war and invasion of North Vietnam. When
the "hawks" and the "doves" among the press corps formed
into separate camps, each camp contained both men and women.

What, then, is the significance of these women who
covered the Vietnam War? Is the mere fact that there were
women journalists covering the war of importance? The answer is yes. Aside from the fact that their names have not
been included, for the most part, in histories of Vietnam War
correspondence, their significance lies in the fact that the
experiences and attitudes which influenced their writing were
not the same as those of their male colleagues. It is unlikely,
for instance, that the sight of a male correspondent would
have so astonished the GI who called out to Gloria Emerson.
It is unlikely that a male correspondent would have been confronted with the anger and hostility of military men such as
the career officer who said to Emerson: "Why, for Christ's
sake, didn't they send a man out here? This is no place for
a woman!"[1]

No place for a woman. In the intensely male world of
war, a woman stands out. In the minds of many, and in particular in the minds of many members of the professional military, she simply does not belong there.

General William Westmoreland has been quoted as saying
that a woman who could lead in combat would be a freak;
that it would be impossible for a woman to carry a pack, live
in a foxhole, or go for a week without taking a bath. In
fairness to General Westmoreland, it should be pointed out
that he is not alone in his opinions. Although forced by law
and by reality to admit women into its ranks, the American
military has steadfastly refused women a combat role. With
the exception of nurses, who are obviously necessary in a
combat zone, few military women ever see action. In Vietnam,
even the nurses were usually quartered in heavily defended
areas, but some were under fire, and seven were killed in
action. Even so, the military attitude towards these women
seemingly has been to pretend that they were not there at
all! It was not until 1982 that the needs of women veterans
of the Vietnam War were specifically addressed by the U.S.
Veteran's Administration.

Is it any wonder, then, that the woman war correspondent, even if she is dressed in combat attire and determinedly
carrying her own gear, stands out? According to some women
correspondents, this uniqueness does not always work as a
disadvantage. Some women reported that their high visibility
in press conferences often resulted in their questions being
answered first. Some admitted that helicopter pilots were
often more anxious to offer rides to women journalists. But
more often than not, women correspondents who attracted
special attention from the military because of their sex did
not find the attention especially welcome.

It has been suggested that men consider war a game, a
dangerous and brutal game, but a game nevertheless. Like
a pack of small boys defending their clubhouse from girls,
men do not want women in the game of war. And, because
there is really no coherent reason why they do not want
women there, men frequently explain their attitude in terms
of latrines.

For example, in 1941 a Colonel in the War Department
asked Dickey Chapelle, when she applied for permission to
photograph the training of the Fourteenth Infantry Regiment
in the jungles of Panama: "I presume you realize, Mrs. Chapelle, that troops in the field have no facilities for women?"
Dumbfounded, for she had never given the matter a minute's
thought, Chapelle searched for an answer. "Colonel," she

finally replied, "I'm sure the Fourteenth Infantry has solved much tougher problems than that...."[2] It was apparently the correct answer, because she was granted permission to enter the U.S. military installation in Panama to photograph the training program.

Ten years later, during the Korean War, New York Herald Tribune reporter Marguerite Higgins was confronted with the same excuse as to why she would not be welcome in a combat area. Told that she would have to leave Korea because there were no facilities for ladies at the front, Higgins curtly replied, "There is no shortage of bushes in Korea."[3]

The same obsession with latrines was reported by Gloria Emerson during the Vietnam War. She wrote: "Women reporters who go into the field make professional Army officers nervous, for these men must immediately explain that no, repeat, no toilets exist for us."[4]

Even if they were not specifically involved in military latrine fixation, women who were war correspondents in the Vietnam War often reported that the military were overprotective towards females. For reasons which usually had nothing to do with chivalry, officers fussed over the women reporters, assigned them bodyguards, and ordered them away from the front lines. According to free-lance reporter Beverly Deepe, who spent ten years as a correspondent in South Vietnam, the reason that she was often provided with bodyguards and told to be back from the front lines before dark had less to do with concern for her personal safety than it did with the officers' own self image. A Marine Captain later explained to her that men were killed all the time, but if a women were killed it would be an insult to the commander. For Deepe the custom of assigning bodyguards to women reporters had an unexpected benefit. Marine Lieutenant Colonel Charles Keever, her escort at Da Nang, later became her husband.

In fairness to the officers, it must be admitted that the presence of a woman correspondent in their midst probably did cause unwelcome distraction among the troops. One woman reporter wrote that Marines in the field were always doing "cute" things like flinging themselves over her to protect her from mortar fire. It is easy to understand the furious officer who roared at a woman correspondent, "You'll wear fatigues all the time. We don't want women with legs down here!"[5]

The GIs, or "grunts" as they were called in Vietnam, usually had no objections to a woman correspondent accompanying their patrol. They enjoyed having a woman to talk to, and to look at, and they also enjoyed the fact that the woman's presence caused such discomfort to the officers. As Associated Press reporter Kelly Smith Tunney pointed out, "The officers are there to fight a war; it's their job. If I were a man I wouldn't have wanted a woman along either."[6]

In general, however, women like Tunney, who worked for wire services such as United Press International and Associated Press, rarely reported having experienced problems associated with their sex while covering the war. Tunney, although she believed that the officers were usually unamused by the presence of women reporters, has stated that this attitude had little effect on Associated Press reporters. She stressed that wire service reporters work long hours, usually in an atmosphere of teamwork, and are too concerned with a reporter's performance to worry about his or her gender. Although she was the only woman on the AP staff during the four months she was in South Vietnam, she experienced no discrimination. She has said that it was like having twenty brothers. But she has also said, significantly, that although she travelled many miles throughout South Vietnam, she "didn't have to be with"[7] the military very often.

Similarly, Kate Webb of United Press International has also stated that she experienced no discrimination as a woman reporter covering the war. Webb, who was promoted to Bureau Chief after only three years with UPI, said, "If you're reasonable, people will be reasonable back."[8] Webb's UPI colleague Margaret Kilgore did experience one incident directly associated with her sex, however. Ironically, the situation concerned a latrine. Determined to be "just one of the guys" while travelling on a troop plane, Kilgore refused to ride in the cockpit. Finally the Colonel told her discreetly that her presence in the back of the plane was inhibiting the use of the open hose latrine by the 115 men aboard! But Kilgore did not mention what, if any, facilities were provided for <u>her</u> during the trip.

It is possible that the protective atmosphere of the
wire service "family" insulated these women from the hostile
attitudes and paternalism reported by other women correspondents in South Vietnam. It is also possible that their
own attitudes, which stress the work-a-day, matter-of-fact
atmosphere of wire service reporting, simply caused them to
interpret their experiences differently. It has been said that
no two people have the same experience of the Vietnam War.
This is no less true of the women war correspondents than
it is of others who were involved in the war.

The women correspondents had little in common, at
first glance. The subjects of their writing ranged from cool
reports of battle to sentimental accounts of civilian tragedy.
Their personal styles ranged from the tomboyish Dickey Chapelle, determined to be one of the Marines, to the elegant
Michele Ray, trudging through the jungle in clouds of "Miss
Dior" perfume. Their politics covered the spectrum from
Philippa Schuyler's fervent anti-Communism to Madeleine Riffaud's equally fervent Marxism. Some were advocates of a
style of journalism which allows for no personal opinion; others
wrote in a highly emotional and dramatic style which bordered
on fiction. Yet, in some ways, they were alike.

As women, they brought to the Vietnam War attitudes
and life experiences which were different from those of their
male colleagues. They shared the experience of being a
woman in a "man's world." Even women correspondents who
insisted that they personally never experienced antagonism
due to their sex admitted that such antagonism did exist.
In some cases, being the only or first woman in a situation
was a matter of pride; in some cases it was a matter of indifference; but it was difficult to ignore. Even when dressed
in combat boots and fatigues they could not deny the fact
that they were women. Some put ribbons in their hair under
their helmets; some dodged behind trucks to dab on a little
makeup. Even Dickey Chapelle, who thought like, talked
like, and marched like a Marine, wore pearl earrings and her
hair in a pony tail. Even Gloria Emerson, who wrote angrily
that she was "weary of feminists who think that women have
special qualities in war reporting,"[9] also wrote, "women reporters also ask why? and what for? with something in their
voices that also asks, is it worth it?"[10]

Gloria Emerson's caustic reference to feminists reflects

an intriguing attitude common to many of the women who
were war correspondents in Vietnam. Although Jurate Kazickas has called herself a "born feminist,"[11] none of the
women war correspondents credited the women's movement
with their success--in fact quite the opposite. While most
of the women correspondents did not mention the women's
movement at all in their Vietnam war reporting or in subsequent writing, those who have written about the movement
were decidedly unfriendly to it.

Gloria Emerson, for instance, attacked the women's
movement in her 1976 book Winners and Losers. Emerson
was furious when feminist Germaine Greer visited Saigon in
1971 and announced that the worst thing she had seen in
Vietnam was a group of Vietnamese women filling sandbags
at Long Binh near a sign which said "Men at Work." With
that frivolous remark Greer killed Emerson's "early excitement" over the women's movement. Emerson wrote that she
could not cope with feminists who refused to join the anti-
war movement because it did not stress the crime of rape
(although, of course, it did) as if violence against women
were the only recognizable form of violence. It was not that
Emerson did not realize that women were often not treated
as equals by men, but simply that she thought that the problem of male chauvinism paled when compared to the horrors
of war. "Men may be condescending to women," she wrote,
"but they do not send us out to die for them. The real
victims of men are other men."[12]

No less caustic in her attitude towards the women's
movement was Italian journalist Oriana Fallaci. Fallaci's attitude towards women is ambivalent at best--she has often
stated that she prefers the company of men--but she did not
turn her full wrath upon the women's movement until an interview in Playboy in 1981. She stated that she disliked
what she perceived as a tendency among feminists to view
women as victims. Feminists wanted her to say that she had
risen above male oppression to success, said Fallaci, but that
was not so. "It helped me to be a woman," she insisted,
"It helped a lot!"[13]

Other women correspondents who were in Vietnam did
not mention the women's movement at all in their writing, with
the exception of Margaret Kilgore, who wrote that she viewed
it with amused detachment because she herself had never felt

oppressed. Kilgore's remark helps to explain why these women, who certainly believed in equal rights for women, were either disinterested in, or annoyed by, the organized women's movement. Strong women who had made it on their own, they had spent a great deal of energy in proving that women should have equal opportunities in journalism. Several of them had already come to a point of conflict between marriage and career early in their lives and had chosen their careers. Small wonder that they would have little inclination towards a movement to "liberate" women. As journalists, and as war correspondents specifically, they were determined to cover the war in Vietnam in spite of any barriers which might be placed in their way because they were women.

It is certainly true that barriers to women correspondents were fewer in the Vietnam War than in previous wars. In World War II, for instance, although dozens of women reported from all over the globe, strict military regulations usually prohibited them from witnessing combat. In a few cases, such as the women who were present in London during the Blitz, the war came to them. But, for the most part, women reporters were not assigned to cover military action. When they circumvented the rules to reach the front lines, as Dickey Chapelle did when she sneaked ashore during the battle for Okinawa, they risked the righteous anger of the military.

During the Korean War, only Marguerite Higgins managed to break down the barriers for women reporters, at least partly due to her friendship with General Douglas MacArthur. Higgins was rewarded with a Pulitzer Prize for her combat coverage of the Marine landing at Inchon in 1950. But the fact that Higgins, a woman, was covering combat was in itself a news event.

In Vietnam, however, there were no military barriers aside from the hostility of individual officers. Indeed there were no "front lines." Easy access to the war, rather than changed attitudes towards women, was probably the major reason such a large number of women reported from Vietnam. Aside from obtaining a visa, no permission was required to go to South Vietnam during the war. Commercial airliners flew into Saigon's Tan Son Nhut Airport throughout the years of the war. One had only to buy a ticket to Saigon. Several women correspondents paid their own fare to Vietnam and arrived with no official status as correspondents. Once there, they established contact with agencies or produced letters from hometown newspapers in order to apply for accreditation. Application for accreditation was made both to the Saigon government and to MACV (Military Assistance Command, Vietnam.) Apparently the red tape was minimal. Forms were filled out, letters from news agencies were verified, photographs were taken, and the applicant became an accredited war correspondent.

A MACV press card gained one admission to the official briefing of JUSPAO (Joint U.S. Public Affairs Office). This daily briefing, held at 4:45 p.m., became known as the "5 o'clock follies," a name apparently coined by the military, not by the journalists. It was possible, and was indeed the custom of some journalists. to "cover" the war merely by attending the "5 o'clock follies." If, on the other hand, the correspondent chose to leave Saigon to travel in the provinces or to go to the site of a reported battle, she or he could hitch a ride on military transport, if that was available, or could travel on commercial airliners or buses, or could rent a car or a bicycle. Official military permission to travel about looking for the war was not required.

In Saigon, throughout the war, life went on as it always had. Correspondents with long-term assignments often rented apartments and settled into a comfortable life in a city that had been called the "Paris of the East." Other correspondents stayed in hotels such as the Caravelle or the Continental. There was a weirdness about the contrast between life in Saigon and the war that was being fought in the countryside that affected not a few. Oriana Fallaci tells of returning to her hotel, tired and bedraggled after a day in the field, and riding up in the elevator with a woman in tennis whites, fresh from a game on the hotel's courts.

And yet, even in Saigon, there was danger, there were terrorists, there was war. The war in Vietnam was the major event, the biggest news story of its time. If you were a journalist, and if you were adventurous, sooner or later you went to Vietnam. And the mere fact that you were a woman surely could not stand in your way.

CHAPTER I

In 1961 Dickey Chapelle, at the age of forty-three, was covering her sixth battleground. Her career as a war correspondent began during World War II on the island of Iwo Jima, and seventeen years later she was one of the first correspondents to cover the American involvement in Vietnam. One evening in Khanh Hung, a town on the southernmost tip of Vietnam, Chapelle was approached by three young Marines, each on his first overseas duty. As she listened incredulously, the Marines confided that, although they had never met her, she was well known to them. Their fathers had met her during the battles for Iwo Jima and Okinawa during World War II. With a shock, Chapelle realized that she was now covering her second generation of combat Marines.

To Dickey Chapelle the war in South Vietnam was a simple matter. Communists were attempting to take over South Vietnam. Anti-Communists, assisted by Americans, were attempting to stop the invasion. Chapelle's opposition to Communism was total; her patriotism was unquestioning. Early in 1959 she had undergone paratrooper training with the 101st Airborne Division on Okinawa because she hoped to "link up with Asian freedom fighters one day."[1] In 1961 she made her first trip to South Vietnam, believing that she had found those "freedom fighters" when she was introduced to Father Augustin Nguyen Lac-Hoa, leader of a commando group called the Sea Swallows. Father Hoa was a refugee from North Vietnam and before that from China. He was as outspoken in his opposition to Communism as was Chapelle herself.

Airlifted by helicopter over 530 miles of jungle from Saigon, Chapelle was greeted warmly by Father Hoa and invited to stay with him in the village of Binh Hung. She remained in the village for five weeks in 1961, accompanied nine

Sea Swallows' operations, and wrote with open admiration of
the priest and the village in which it seemed to her every
man had become an aggressive fighter in the offensive against
Communism.

One moonlit night Chapelle accompanied the Sea Swallows as they surprised a Viet Cong raiding party. She wrote
proudly that the raiding party had retreated, leaving behind
four dead. On another night she participated in an ambush
of Viet Cong "tax collectors" who supposedly came to extort
the villagers in exchange for protection. Chapelle was certain
tain that the Sea Swallows' operations were keeping the village safe from Communist takeover. She wrote of Father Hoa
and his men: "They have tasted slavery and found it bitter.
Now they are enlarging the area of freedom in the world.
Who can serve a greater cause?"[2]

There were few Americans fighting in South Vietnam
in 1961. The total number of American advisers to the South
Vietnamese forces was then about 700. Some of the Americans
were helicopter crews assigned to airlift South Vietnamese
troops in and out of battle and some were Special Forces
(Green Beret) units or intelligence officers. A few were
stationed in remote villages where their assignment was to
"counsel" the local South Vietnamese regimental commander.
The war at the time was a series of brief jungle skirmishes,
as South Vietnamese troops and Viet Cong guerrillas wrestled
for control of villages. The American press, and the American public, had scant interest in the war. In 1961 only the
New York Times had a regular correspondent in Saigon, veteran war reporter Homer Bigart. All other American newspapers and magazines relied on the four wire services: Associated Press, United Press International, Reuters, and
Agence France Presse.

Why then was Dickey Chapelle, a middle-aged, nearsighted American woman from the Midwest, scrambling through
the jungles of South Vietnam? The answer is that she was
led by two forces--uncompromising hatred of Communism, and
her long-standing love affair with the United States Marines.

Georgette Meyer Chapelle, who was always called Dickey,
was already a well-known war correspondent when she arrived in South Vietnam in 1961. Her career had begun in
the South Pacific during World War II, when she was sent by

Fawcett Publications to Iwo Jima to photograph wounded Marines as publicity for the Red Cross blood drive. She first
came under fire when she boldly stood up on an Iwo Jima
ridge to take a photograph. When she later told her tent-
mate, Barbara Finch of Reuters News Agency, that she had
been bothered on the ridge by the sound of wasps, she was
told that the sound she had heard was the zing of rifle bullets. It was a heady experience for a twenty-three year old
from Milwaukee, Wisconsin, and she remembered the thrill of
typing the words "under fire" on her by-line.

Born in 1918 to pacifist parents who taught her that
violence in any form was unthinkable, Chapelle later admitted
that because it was unthinkable, violence became as attractive
a mystery to her as sex was to other teenagers. When she
was fifteen, having seen a film on Admiral Byrd's expedition
to the South Pole, she decided to become an aerial explorer.
She was prepared for the fact that being a girl might prove
a handicap to her ambitions, but she was unprepared for the
absolute opposition of her mother to her plan. A compromise
sent her to the Massachusetts Institute of Technology to become an aircraft designer.

Unfortunately for her academic record, Chapelle had
little interest in study. It was to avoid taking a chemistry
test that she decided to cover a flood in Worchester, Massachusetts for the Boston Traveler, an assignment for which
she received $3.85 from the Traveler, a C+ in Journalism,
and her first airplane ride. Within a short time she had
flunked out of MIT and returned to Wisconsin and to her
plan to become a pilot. But she was extremely nearsighted,
and was forced to abandon this ambition when she nearly
crash-landed a training plane. Still the danger and thrill
of flight continued to attract her. Instead of a pilot she
became a publicist for the Miami All-American Airshow and
later for Transcontinental and Western Airlines, then called
TWA. A course in photography from TWA's publicity photographer Tony Chapelle led, in 1940, to marriage.

When her husband volunteered for Navy duty after
Pearl Harbor, Chapelle applied to Look magazine as a news
photographer in order to join him in Panama. In 1944, when
it seemed imminent that Tony Chapelle would be ordered overseas to China, Dickey Chapelle also applied for an overseas
assignment, with Fawcett Publications. It seems never to

have occurred to either husband or wife that she could, like
most wives during World War II, have waited at home.

Ironically, Dickey Chapelle's orders came through before those of her husband. She found herself on her way to
Iwo Jima, assigned to the hospital ship <u>Samaritan</u>. She was
acutely aware of the importance of her assignment as part
of the Red Cross blood drive. She later wrote:

> The shapeless dirty bloody green bundles being lifted
> and carried before me were not repeat not human as
> I was human. Some part of my mind warned me that
> if I thought of them as people just once I'd be un-
> able to take any more pictures. Then the story of
> their anguish would never be told.[3]

In spite of her assertions of detachment, however,
Chapelle's compassion for the wounded Marines was evident
in both her writing and in her photographs. She learned
each Marine's name, talked to him, shared cigarettes. Often
she sent copies of the photographs to the man's family.

Ultimately Chapelle was sent back to the United States
in something like disgrace, having disobeyed Rear Admiral
Miller's orders not to go ashore on Okinawa. But her assignment in the South Pacific had made a deep impression upon
her. She ever thereafter thought of herself as a Marine,
and she remembered the war in the South Pacific not in terms
of blood and death, but in terms of valor and commitment.
She wrote:

> As Iwo (Jima) set a standard of valor, I think Oki-
> nawa set one of commitment. I cannot forget, nor do
> I want to, that I once was part of a group of almost
> a million Americans who in one time and place shared
> a single aim.[4]

Just as her experiences in the South Pacific led to a
lifelong attachment to the Marine Corps, Chapelle's experiences
in Europe in the years immediately following World War II led
to her deep hatred of Communism. With her husband she
had taken an assignment photographing refugees for the American Friends Service Committee, CARE, the United Nations
Childrens Emergency Fund and other relief agencies. In
Hungary in 1948 the Chapelles had their cameras and photographs

confiscated by the Communist government. Enraged, Dickey
Chapelle said to the official who had taken the cameras, "Young
man, you know I'm not a spy. But if you ever see me in
Hungary again, you'd better shoot first. Because I will be."[5]
The words were ironically prophetic.

In 1956 Dickey Chapelle returned to Hungary alone.
Her marriage had ended in an amicable divorce in 1955 and
she accepted a double assignment in Austria as Life magazine's
photographer for a story on refugees from the Hungarian
revolution, and as publicist for the International Rescue Committee. Penicillin was being smuggled to the revolutionaries
by people who were re-entering Hungary in order to lead
other refugees out. On December 5, 1956 a small group
entered Hungary on such a mission. Dickey Chapelle was
with them. Within a few hours the group had been captured
by a Russian sentry patrol.

Chapelle spent fifty-two days in Budapest's Fö Street
Prison, thirty-eight of them in solitary confinement. Hunger
turned her mood sullen, and the cold froze her breath in
the air. Once when she was not being interrogated she went
for eight days and nights without communication with another
human being. Finally, on January 27, 1957 she was brought
to trial, found guilty of illegal border crossing rather than
espionage, and sentenced to the fifty-two days she had already served and expulsion from Hungary. "Thank God I'm
an American," she said as she arrived at New York's Idle-
wild Airport.[6]

Thereafter, her intense hatred of Communism and her
zeal to proselytize what she considered the American ideal of
freedom led Chapelle from conflict to conflict. In her own
words she had become an "interpreter of violence."[7] In 1958
Algerian rebels, impressed by her conduct during her im-
prisonment in Hungary, invited her to cover their side of
the war in Algeria. Smuggled through the Algerian underground from Spain to North Africa, sometimes blindfolded
and sometimes disguised as a veiled and robed Arab woman,
Chapelle finally joined the rebels. While with them, she
learned how to survive on very little food and water, how to
sleep on hard rock, and how to walk for five hours without
a break, abilities she would later use with the Marines in
Vietnam.

After Algeria Chapelle covered the U.S. Marine landing in Lebanon in 1958, and had no sooner returned to the apartment in New York which was her nominal home when she was sent to Cuba to cover the revolution there. She entered Cuba wearing spike heels, dangle-earrings, and a pale blue fluffy blouse. Into a sequin-trimmed wallet she had tucked a photograph of a Marine she had once met. Questioned by Cuban authorities at the airport, she played the part of a woman seeking an illicit rendezvous with a Marine at Guantanamo Base. The Cubans, apparently deciding that romance was more important than international politics, waved her through.

On her way to interview Fidel Castro, Chapelle covered four actions in Oriente Province and was painfully, but not seriously, injured when her jeep overturned as the driver tried to avoid a mortar attack. Limping back to Santiago after the interview, again wearing her tourist costume, she was once again forced to dive into a ditch during a B-26 strafing attack. Chapelle had little respect for Castro, whom she considered a psychopath, but she had respect for his revolution. She particularly admired the women who fought with Castro. "I was never more proud to be a woman," she wrote, "than when I marched with Fidel Castro's Cuban guerrillas."[8]

Late 1959 found Chapelle on the island of Quemoy, off the coast of China. The little island and its neighbor, Matsu, were under bombardment from the Chinese mainland. Interviewing Father Joseph Bernard M. Druetto, a missionary on Quemoy, Chapelle asked him why he refused to leave during the bombardment. Father Druetto responded by asking her how she had felt when she was imprisoned by the Communists in Hungary. "I intend to spend my life making them sorry they let me go," she told him.[9]

So it was that she came to South Vietnam with a mission of telling the people in the United States the "real" story of the war. When she returned home after her experiences with the Sea Swallows she took to the lecture circuit under the auspices of the University of Minnesota, telling American audiences that the war in South Vietnam was "their war." "South Vietnam today is even in my mind almost as much 'my' real estate as Minnesota," she wrote a friend in 1962.[10]

Chapelle returned to South Vietnam in 1962, this time
to accompany the helicopter patrols in Ba Xuyen Province in
the southernmost part of the country. She wrote of South
Vietnam that it was the place

> where the fate of millions of people was being de-
> cided in blood--the blood of the men around me. If
> their battles were won, Southeast Asia might remain
> free; if the battles continued to be lost, the Com-
> munists would surely dominate all Vietnam and strike
> for the rest of the Indochinese peninsula.[11]

On a typical helicopter mission in 1962 Chapelle wrote
of huddling nervously with a squad of South Vietnamese infantrymen in a helicopter flying to the village of Ap My Thanh,
once a hideout for river pirates, and now thought to be the
headquarters for Viet Cong guerrillas. When the helicopters
landed, Chapelle ran under fire (which turned out to be
American) behind her squad leader Corporal Nguyen, into
the village. Patient villagers greeted them, but they found
no Viet Cong. An unsuccessful operation, but to Chapelle
the significance was that the villagers were being made aware
of their government's efforts to defend them from the Communists. To Chapelle it was unthinkable that the villagers
would find such defense unwelcome.

On another helicopter mission, Chapelle wrote of an
attack by what she determined had been North Vietnamese
regulars on the village of Vinh Quoi. She noted that among
the twenty-seven dead were six women and children.

In the "strategic hamlet" of Kha Quang, Chapelle talked
to Major Henry McCurley, who served as adviser in this isolated and dangerous outpost. "Strategic hamlets" were, in
fact, artificial villages, into which peasants were moved--
often against their will--to protect them from the Viet Cong.
But Chapelle saw only the courage of the Major, and his two
radiomen, M/Sgt. James Horne and Sgt. William Riley, who
were maintaining this outpost in constant danger of guerrilla
attack. When she left Kha Quang, Chapelle felt as if she
were leaving a theater before the final curtain, and she hoped
to return for the rest of the show.

By this time Chapelle had jumped with Vietnamese airborne units six times. She proudly wore the wings she had wo:

for her jumps pinned to the slouchy Australian bush hat she
habitually wore while on patrol. She was proud of the fact
that she asked for no special favors because she was a woman.
She carried her own pack, ate C-rations from the can, and
kept up with the men on the march. In 1961 and 1962, when
few Americans were giving any thought to the war in South
Vietnam, Dickey Chapelle trudged more than 200 miles, sometimes in 100° heat and torrential rain, following South Vietnamese troops and their American advisers on operations
which sometimes lasted as long as six days. She did it because she believed that an American outside of the military
should have firsthand knowledge of what was going on in
South Vietnam. She was convinced that, with American help,
the South Vietnamese would be able to defeat Communism in
their country. And she saw it as her special mission to drum
up support for the war when she returned to the United
States.

In July, 1963 a second woman war correspondent, one
who was at least as outspoken a foe of Communism as Chapelle, arrived in South Vietnam. She was Marguerite Higgins,
also a veteran correspondent, winner of the Pulitzer Prize
for her coverage of the Korean War, and "an old Asia hand."
This was Higgins' seventh visit to Vietnam, a country she
had first seen as an infant. Born in Hong Kong in 1920 to
an American businessman and his French wife, Higgins had
been taken to the mountain resort of Dalat in central Vietnam at the age of six months to recover from an attack of
malaria.

With her decidedly anti-Communist point of view, and
speaking in the voice of an expert on Asian politics and
Asian society, Higgins almost immediately incurred the wrath
of correspondents in Saigon who were critical of the Saigon
government, such as David Halberstam, who had succeeded
Homer Bigart as the New York Times Saigon correspondent,
Neil Sheehan of United Press International, and Charles Mohr
of Time magazine.

Higgins arrived in Saigon at a time of great crisis.
Although American involvement in the war had been increasing steadily to over 11,000 military personnel by the end of
1962, the government of South Vietnam, led by President Ngo
Dinh Diem, had begun to crumble. In May 1963 Buddhists,
led by a monk named Thich Tri Quang, began to demonstrate

against alleged repression by Diem's government. There
were dramatic incidents in which Buddhist monks and nuns
committed suicide by fire. Higgins, whose concept of Vietnamese Buddhism was that of a spirit of non-violence and
compassion, found the situation difficult to comprehend.
Briefing by the U.S. State Department before she left for
Vietnam told her only that the U.S. government was annoyed
with Diem for stubbornly insisting on running his country
his own way. In Saigon, U.S. Ambassador Frederick Nolting
told Higgins that Diem was maligned and misunderstood and
far from the narrow fanatic described by his enemies.

Determined to seek her own truth, Higgins spent four
weeks during the summer of 1963 traveling in the Vietnamese
countryside, interviewing Buddhist monks, Montagnard and
Cham tribal leaders, Vietnamese peasants, and American military personnel. The religious leaders she interviewed claimed
no knowledge of religious persecution. Furthermore, one
Buddhist monk she interviewed told her firmly that no true
Buddhist would commit suicide. Higgins became convinced
that the Buddhist agitation was actually Communist inspired.

Higgins interviewed General Paul Harkins, chief of the
American military mission in the Mekong Delta, who told her
that the war in Vietnam was beginning to be won. She interviewed President Diem, whom she described as a man torn
between loyalty to the Americans and the conviction that the
Buddhists were stirring up trouble in order to topple his
government. She interviewed Diem's brother Ngo Dinh Nhu,
who believed himself to be the scapegoat for all that went
wrong in his country. She interviewed Nhu's beautiful and
outspoken wife, Madame Nhu, who tried, unsuccessfully, to
enlist Higgins' sympathies for the cause of Vietnamese women's
rights. But her most remarkable interview was with the Buddhist monk Thich Tri Quang.

Misinterpreting Higgins' White House accreditation as
a direct contact with President John Kennedy, Thich Tri
Quang gave Higgins a message for the American President.
She quoted the monk as saying:

> We the Buddhists have good information that Presi-
> dent Kennedy sympathizes with our anti-Diem efforts
> ... the time is coming when President Kennedy will
> have to be more outspoken because it would be hard
> to get rid of Diem without explicit American support.[12]

The astonished Higgins realized that the aims of the
Buddhists were nothing less than the overthrow of Diem, and
that they wanted, and expected, American help in accomplishing their aims. She concluded that the suicides by fire and
supposedly spontaneous street demonstrations which had turned
the American correspondents and public against Diem were
in fact carefully planned and staged "media events."

In a series of articles, "Viet-Nam Fact and Fiction,"
which appeared in the New York Herald Tribune in the late
summer of 1963, Higgins wrote: "What did the Buddhists
want? Diem's head ... and not on a silver platter but en-
veloped in an American flag."[13] Higgins tried in the series
to present both the pros and cons of Diem's government.
While clearly opposed to any change in the Saigon government, Higgins admitted that Diem was, by western standards,
a dictator. She noted Diem's alienation from the intellectuals
in his country, although he himself was an intellectual. She
conceded that Diem's brother Nhu and his wife were almost
universally hated by Saigon's dissidents, and that hatred of
the Nhus was almost the only thing that the factionalized
opponents of the Saigon government could agree upon. But,
she pointed out, it was unrealistic to expect that Diem would
fire his brother. Insisting that the war really was going
well for the Americans, and believing firmly that the fate of
Southeast Asia was at stake, Higgins concluded that the overthrow of Diem's government would be a mistake and a major
setback for the South Vietnamese and American cause.

Like Dickey Chapelle, Marguerite Higgins had developed
her strong opposition to Communism while in Europe immediately
after World War II. Also like Chapelle, Higgins' career as a
journalist began during World War II. In 1942 she was hired,
partly because so many male reporters had gone to war, by
the New York Herald Tribune. She would remain with the
Herald Tribune for more than twenty years.

Less than three years after she was hired by the Herald Tribune, Higgins was in Paris, sauntering into the Hotel
Scribe, headquarters of many war correspondents. She affected what she hoped was a knowing air, but could not conceal her elation when she was introduced to Ernest Hemingway and realized that she was actually his colleague. Within
a few weeks she was allowed to go on assignment to the front
lines when another journalist was unable to leave Paris. In
the group which left Paris for the front lines with Higgins

were three other woman correspondents: Margaret Bourke-
White of Time and Life, Lee Miller of Vogue, and Helen Kirk-
patrick of the Chicago Daily News.

Higgins spent eight weeks at the front, interviewing
top Nazis, including Reich Marshal Hermann Goering, and
German resistance leaders. Her first journalism prize was
the result of her having casually accepted a ride in the jeep
of Stars and Stripes reporter Peter Furst. She and Furst,
who spoke German, decided to cut across territory still held
by the Germans in hopes of being the first reporters to reach
the concentration camp at Dachau. They had decided they
would be safe, considering the prevailing atmosphere of surrender. In fact, they reached Dachau before the army of
liberation. Much to the surprise of the two reporters, the
SS men guarding the camp offered to surrender to them.
For her story of the liberation of Dachau, Higgins received
the New York Newspaper Women's Club award for best foreign correspondence of 1945. Higgins believed that the story
was inadequate in light of the natural drama of the situation,
and blamed the inadequacy on her hurry to make a deadline.

After the war, spurred by a broken romance, Higgins
turned to her work with the intensity of a fanatic. As a
result she began what she called "the most educational years
of my career"[14] spent behind the Iron Curtain in Europe,
culminating with her appointment as Berlin Bureau Chief
for the Herald Tribune in 1947. Her strong anti-Communist
beliefs were the result of the experience of watching the
Communist takeover of Poland and Czechoslovakia and the
blockade of Berlin. Her absolute opposition to Soviet-style
totalitarianism was the result of her horror and disgust in
seeing how even proud, brave, people can "disintegrate into
groveling specimens of humanity when they are subjected to
organized, relentless fear."[15]

Because of her interest and involvement in what was
happening in Europe, Higgins was dismayed when she was
transferred to Tokyo in 1950. But her journalistic luck held
out and exactly twenty-five days after her arrival in Tokyo
the Korean War began. Higgins saw in the invasion of South
Korea the manifestation of her fear of Communism. She was
beginning to take what she referred to as "Russian pushing
around"[16] very personally.

On June 27, 1950, two days after the Communist invasion of South Korea, Higgins was in Seoul, Korea. She had scarcely arrived in the city when it was attacked, and she joined in the retreat, on foot, to the south. Her fellow correspondents Frank Gibney of Time and Burton Crane of the New York Times were wounded when the bridge they were crossing exploded under them. When General Douglas MacArthur flew from Korea to Japan a few days later he offered Higgins a ride in his private airplane, which infuriated the bureau chiefs of Associated Press, United Press International, Reuters, and International News Service. These four, called by other newsmen "the palace guard" because they always accompanied MacArthur, resented the intrusion of Higgins into their private domain. It did not help that MacArthur invited Higgins to his cabin for a private interview during the flight.

After three weeks with the troops in Korea, Higgins was suddenly informed that she must leave the country immediately by order of General Walton Walker. The reason given was the usual "there are no facilities for ladies at the front." The stated reason was ridiculous, countered Higgins. She pointed out that nobody in Korea, including Koreans, worried much about powder rooms. There were plenty of bushes. But the ban held, in spite of Higgins' pleas that her banishment was unfair to the Herald Tribune, until General MacArthur himself stepped in. "Ban on women in Korea being lifted," the General cabled. "Marguerite Higgins held in highest professional esteem."[17]

Higgins re-joined the troops in mid-July and on September 15, 1950 was in the fifth wave of U.S. Marines who made an amphibious landing at Inchon, near Seoul. For her account of the landing she received the Pulitzer Prize for international reporting in 1951. Because of this and of the media coverage of her banishment and subsequent reinstatement in Korea, Higgins was probably the best-known reporter of the Korean War.

Higgins saw the Korean War as a warning to the Free World of the aggressiveness of the Communist threat. She issued warnings that Korea had shown the United States to be unprepared for Communist aggression. "Korea has shown how weak America was," she wrote. "It was better to find this out in Korea and in June of 1950 than on our shores and possibly too late."[18]

n 1951 Higgins received an assignment from the Herald
e to travel the world as a "roving reporter." It was
ın ˍˍ that she visited Vietnam for the first time since her
infancy. She interviewed the Emperor, Bao Dai, who told
her that it was impossible for his country to compromise with
Communism, and she visited the front lines of the French-
Indochinese War. She visited countries on the edge of the
Communist world, interviewing Shah Reza Pahlavi of Iran,
Marshal Josip Broz Tito of Yugoslavia, and Queen Frederika
of Greece, among others. She also visited the Soviet Union, interviewed Premier Nikita Kruschev, and sounded the warning
when she returned that the Soviet "game" was to pursue a
conciliatory policy with the "gullible" Americans, leading
eventually to victory for the Communists.

Marriage in 1952 to General William Hall, and the birth
of two children, did not slow down her traveling. In 1961
she was in the Congo where she turned in an exclusive story
of Indian troops arriving in Leopoldville, and conducted an
interview with rebel leader Antoine Gizenga. Higgins wrote
at that time that she considered Vietnam to be "as much a
front line of freedom as Hawaii or San Francisco."[19] It is
not surprising then that she accepted immediately when asked
in July 1963 if she would go to Saigon to cover the so-called
"Buddhist crisis."

When she returned from her September 1963 trip to
South Vietnam, Higgins found herself in the middle of a battle
within the press corps. On September 20 Time magazine
carried a story about the Saigon press corps, insinuating that
a "club" of correspondents was projecting its own ideas about
what was going on in South Vietnam, and was deliberately
confusing readers at home. This story caused Charles Mohr,
chief Time correspondent in Southeast Asia, to resign in protest over his magazine's accusations. Columnist Joseph Alsop
then took up the cause, accusing resident U.S. reporters in
Saigon of a crusade against the Diem regime. The resident
journalists, including David Halberstam of the New York Times,
Neil Sheehan of United Press International, Malcolm Browne
of Associated Press, and Beverly Deepe of Newsweek, fought
back. They insisted that they had only been reporting facts,
and that news reporters had not invented the Buddhist crisis,
nor had they told Diem how to handle it.

Marguerite Higgins entered the battle on the side of

Alsop and Time magazine. She agreed with Alsop that the
war was going well for the Americans at that time. She believed the American major who told her that he believed the
Vietnamese trusted the Americans more every day. She believed that the Americans actually wanted to win the trust of
the Vietnamese people as much as they wanted military victory. Most importantly, she believed that the fate of Southeast Asia was at stake, and that the Americans had to win
in Vietnam in order to hold back the progress of Communism.
What enraged her about the attitude of the resident press in
Saigon was that she believed that they would have rather
seen the United States defeated in Vietnam than to have been
proven wrong.

Halberstam later attacked Higgins, Alsop, and other
"visiting reporters" to Vietnam in his book The Making of a
Quagmire. He accused them of naïveté based upon their short
tenure in the country, pointing out that he had been in Saigon
since 1962. When he dismissed Higgins for being naïve about
Vietnamese politics, he was of course disregarding the fact
that her 1963 trip to Vietnam was her seventh visit to that
country, and that she had been an observer of the war in
Southeast Asia since the early 1950's. In a curious incident,
Halberstam is supposed to have shown Higgins a photograph
of dead bodies and asked her if she had ever seen a dead
man before. If the incident actually occurred, it would seem
that Halberstam had seriously underestimated the woman who
had been at both Dachau and Buchenwald.

It should be remembered that Halberstam and Higgins
did not disagree on whether or not Americans should be in
Vietnam, but only as to whether or not the American strategy
was succeeding. Whatever may have been the correct military
strategy in South Vietnam in 1963 (and twenty years later
it was still being debated) Higgins' analysis of the situation,
given her emotional bias against Communism, was still astute.
As was later confirmed by the publication of the so-called
"Pentagon Papers," she was correct in her assessment of the
extent of U.S. government involvement in the plots against
President Diem. As early as September 1963 she wrote:

> The State Department's apparent attempt to set the
> Vietnamese Army at the throat of the Diem regime in
> the middle of a war will be the subject of bitter con-
> troversy both inside this government and around the
> world for an unpredictable period of time. [20]

On November 2, 1963 a military coup with the tacit
support of the United States overthrew President Diem. Both
Diem and his brother Ngo Dinh Nhu were assassinated. Madame Nhu, who was traveling in the United States with her
eldest daughter, telephoned Marguerite Higgins for assistance
in rescuing her three small children, who were still in Saigon.
Higgins called the State Department and was successful in
arranging to have the children flown to Rome to join their
mother.

After twenty-one years with the New York Herald Tribune Higgins resigned in late 1963 to become a columnist for
the Long Island newspaper Newsday, which syndicated her
column. In November 1963, shortly after the coup against
Diem, she was back in Saigon writing her column "On the
Spot," and maintaining her stance that the South Vietnamese,
with American aid, were winning the war. She firmly believed that the fact that there were more South Vietnamese
than ever before who were free of Viet Cong harassment was
a sign of progress, if not imminent victory. But she had to
admit, on leaving Saigon after her second visit in one year,
that she had gained the impression that the United States in
Vietnam had "no real idea of the forces they had unleashed.
They had opened a kind of Asian Pandora's Box--and didn't
even know it."[21]

Although Marguerite Higgins and Dickey Chapelle were
in South Vietnam at the same time, neither made mention of
having met the other. There were two other women correspondents covering the war at the time, however, both of
whom were at least acquainted with Higgins. One was Suzanne Labin, a French journalist who was even more anti-
Communist than Higgins and Chapelle. The other was Beverly
Deepe, who had opposed Higgins in the press controversy.

Beverly Deepe had arrived in Saigon in February 1962
and remained there, except for two home leaves, as part of
the Saigon press corps until 1969. Born in 1936, Deepe was
graduated with honors from the University of Nebraska and
the Columbia School of Journalism. After a round-the-world
tour in 1961 she settled in Saigon, took an apartment, and
worked as a stringer for the London Daily Express, the
Christian Science Monitor, and Newsweek.

In late 1962 Newsweek's Saigon correspondent François

Sully was expelled by President Diem for allegedly writing
articles which were unflattering to the Diem government.
Deepe then took over the role of Saigon correspondent for
Newsweek. Much of her work in Newsweek in 1962 and 1963
is uncredited but she is occasionally listed in the index as
the author of an article. Although based mainly in Saigon,
Deepe occasionally visited front line positions, as in October
1962 when she reported from a South Vietnamese base at A
Chau, north of Saigon near the Laotian border. Deepe sympathized with the American advisers at A Chau, who lived
in rat-infested huts. The Americans told her that it was
not possible to tell the friendly Vietnamese peasants from
those who were aiding the Viet Cong. In this strange war,
they told her, everyone must be considered an enemy. "It
is a shadowy war," she wrote. [22]

Deepe's articles in Newsweek chronicled the events
which led up to the overthrow of President Diem in November
1963. She wrote in August 1963 that it was in Hue, the
hometown of the President, that the Buddhist crisis was the
most tense. She admitted that the crisis had gone beyond
religious grievances and that the Buddhists now sought to
overthrow the Diem government.

On August 21, 1963 troops, described by Deepe as
ruthless Catholics from the President's hometown of Hue,
attacked several Buddhist pagodas. The raids of government
troops against Xa Loi pagoda in Saigon and other pagodas
were undoubtedly a strong factor in Diem's fall. On the one
hand, Newsweek reported that at least thirty Buddhists had
been killed. On the other hand, a United Nations mission
investigating the raids three months later reported no evidence that anyone had been killed. Whatever the reality,
President Diem singled out Newsweek for "systematically"
turning American opinion against his government. Deepe
was accused of echoing the line that the Catholic President
was oppressing the Buddhists. In his 1973 book Report or
Distort? former Vietnam correspondent Glenn MacDonald went
further, and accused Deepe of having "sympathies with the
Buddhists." [23]

Whatever her sympathies, Deepe was on the scene when
the Diem government fell. According to Newsweek, her Saigon apartment was gutted by a stray shell. When the white
flag of surrender was raised over the presidential palace,

Deepe reported that "thousands ran to the palace, screaming
'freedom' and 'long live the junta.'"[24] Deepe entered the
palace shortly after the troops, climbing through a shell hole
in the six-inch thick wall. She noted such details as a pink
marble washbasin, and family photographs scattered in the
deserted quarters of Nhu and his family. She wrote that
Diem's style of government was reflected in his room--musty
and dank. Deepe concluded that Diem's isolation had ultimately proven his undoing, cutting him off from the people
and even from his own military commanders.

At the same time that Deepe was reporting on Diem's
fall in words that were decidely unflattering to the fallen
president, Suzanne Labin, a French writer and photographer,
was viewing the scene from exactly the opposite point of view.
Like Marguerite Higgins, Labin believed that the anti-Diem
demonstrators were organized and Communist-inspired. The
anti-Diem campaign, she wrote, "aims to discourage and if
possible put an end to American support of the Saigon government in its life-and-death struggle against the red guerrilla
offensive."[25]

Suzanne Labin's anti-Communism was the more fervent
because she was a convert from Marxism. Born in Paris in
1913 of working-class parents, Labin had been a Marxist when
she entered the Sorbonne. She was repelled however, by
what she felt to be the immoral tactics of the campus Communists, and refused to join their party. When she met
fellow student Edouard Labin, he had also recently resigned
from the Young Communists. The two were married and
joined a moderate non-Marxist faction of the Socialist Party.
For her Master's degree at the Ecole des Hautes Etudes So-
ciales et Internationales, Suzanne Labin undertook an in-depth
study of Soviet Communism. It was this research which led
to her deep abhorrence of Communism, but she always insisted that her attitude was not emotional. "I claim that I
have studied Communism with total objectivity," she said,
"and that this very objectivity leads me to a total condemna-
tion. I am objective but not neutral."[26]

Sought as members of the anti-Nazi resistance during
World War II, the Labins were forced to flee to Argentina.
When they returned to France after the war, Suzanne Labin
continued to write and lecture in opposition to Communism.
She became chair of the French chapter of the World Anti-

Communist League.   In 1962, after several trips to South
Vietnam, she made a trip to America to lecture on her belief
that the campaign against President Diem was Communist-
inspired.   In five weeks she gave twenty-six lectures, a
dozen press conferences, and eighteen radio and television
appearances, winding up with two addresses to members of
Congress in Washington, D.C.

     In the fall of 1963 Labin was back in South Vietnam,
watching with horror the fall of the Diem government.   She
had talked with President Diem, and believed that in
him lay America's best hope to control Communism in Southeast Asia.   Wandering the streets of Saigon during the coup,
Labin observed what she determined to be disciplined groups
attacking buildings which had no connection with Diem, but
were connected with anti-Communism, such as the headquarters
of the Asian People's Anti-Communist League.   She reported
that the demonstrators shouted "Communist slogans."   The
"thousands" of demonstrators reported by Deepe as celebrat-
ing the downfall of Diem and Nhu were dismissed by Labin as
"not more than a few thousand people."[27]

     In her 1969 book Vietnam Assessment, Labin accused
the U.S. State Department of complicity in the Diem coup and
accused western journalists of partiality for refusing to re-
cognize the true nature of the Buddhist movement.   Unfortunately the strength of Labin's argument was undermined by
her tendency to write such unsubstantiated statements as:

          If Americans and South Vietnamese ground forces
          entered North Vietnam and occupied the land ... then
          immediately the population living there would rise and
          hang the Communist bureaucrats....[28]

     As early as 1963, then, the conflict within the press
corps in South Vietnam had appeared.   Like the old legend
of the blind men "seeing" the elephant, the war in South
Vietnam was perceived differently by different people, colored
by the biases they had brought with them to the conflict.
Women reporters were on both sides of the controversy.   As
the reporters bickered and the public--those who were paying
any attention at all to the war--looked on in confusion, the
war itself began to change.   Between 1961 and 1963 a crucial
difference in American commitment to South Vietnam took place.
The number of American forces in South Vietnam had grown

from less than 1,000 in the beginning of 1961 to more than
15,000 by October of 1963.   There was conflict within the
U.S. State Department and the American military as to whether
the American role in South Vietnam should remain advisory or
become more active.   Americans were demoralized and numb
from the shock of the murder of President John F. Kennedy
in November 1963, and were giving scant thought to a small
war many thousands of miles away.   And major portions of
South Vietnam, in the wake of the coup against President
Diem were, according to Beverly Deepe, in a "state of total
insecurity."[29]

WITH THE PARATROOPS _____ Dickey Chapelle

It is deep night, and for a long minute, opening my eyes in
the guttering candlelight, I don't know where I am. Then
I see the orderly's small brown hands fixing the candle up-
right on the top of the olive drab jerry can--familiar American shape, symbol of clean water and good gasoline!--and it
all comes back.

The high wall with gunports across from the army cot
where I have been sleeping is not part of a medieval fortress
or a Hollywood movie set. This is the command post of a
modern fighting force, the Vietnamese Airborne Brigade. A
very good fighting force and very modern, with U.S. equipment and training.

I sit up on the edge of the cot in my rumpled fatigues
as the orderly begins to talk, low and a little hoarse, the
way men at war talk in the middle of the night. He is speaking his language, not mine, but I do understand one syllable.
He repeats it. "hai, hai." It means "two." (Whenever I
jump with these paratroops, the final commands are Moat ...
hai ... ba! One ... two ... three ... go!)

It must be two-o-clock in the morning. Time to get up,
time to pretend as everybody else will that a few hours are
enough rest, to make believe I am not hungry, to remind
myself that we will all feel better when we get moving.

This is not a game. We--two battalions of Vietnamese
paratroopers and their two American military advisers from
the U.S. 101st Airborne Division--are not waking up in the
humid darkness just to prove that we can. Here, near the
Cambodian border in the heart of southeast Asia, we are
going out to hunt down live human beings. Human beings
who otherwise, tonight or a decade from now, will hunt us
down here or perhaps somewhere closer to home.

I button my pocket flaps, fasten my web belt. As I
do so, the question rises in my mind once again: What am
I doing here?

And another question: How can it be that in this nu-
clear age, with all the disarmament negotiations, all the arts
of modern diplomacy, and all the world's will for peace, the
real course of history is still being written by strong young
men betting their lives at hide-and-seek on foot in darkness?

I check my canteen (full), my cameras (loaded), my
boot laces (square-knotted). I try to walk erect out into
the courtyard to take my place in the operation.

We are not jumping tonight. Under our orders from
the high command in Saigon the paratroopers are, as often
happens, being used as infantry. What my Vietnamese friends
call the new elephants of Asia--U.S. six-by-six trucks--will
carry us over the first lap of our patrol, the short green
pencil mark on the map that means ten miles of movement.

I remember from my briefing that I must mill around
the crowded courtyard in the starglow, lit only by flashlights
flicked on and off in the hands of other people similarly
briefed, until I find a truck marked "014." Being a woman
and a guest, I won't have to crowd with 40 troopers into its
bed but may ride the lonely splendor of the high cab, brac-
ing my own gear with one hand and the driver's carbine,
muzzle up, with the other. We've all been told we probably
will be ambushed, whether on the road or on one of the two
river crossings, and we've all been drilled on what to do about
it.

I repeat it to myself. If you hear firing, get out of
the truck--out of the truck. And you'll be cut off from the
troops unless you move toward the fire--toward the fire, not
away from it. I'll be on the right side of the truck, so if
I have to go out in a hurry, the easy way is over my right
shoulder in a somersault. And, I mentally add with a grim-
ace, don't do what you did the last time in Cuba; leave your
right foot behind. You'll sprain your knee again--remember?

In a moment some incisive voices are heard. Then the
low, rising thunder of truck engines. The mission shoves
off, on time. It is just three o'clock.

We grind through a shuttered village in which not a
candle or lantern glows. I wonder: What do the Vietnamese
farmers feel when we roar by through their dreams? Are we
freeing them from Red terror and "taxation?" Or are we
bringing our own kind of fear? Are we just another military
force in the parade of centuries of soldiers that have moved
across Asia, neither better nor worse, only truck-borne?

Then comes a long stretch of plain, cut into mirror
squares under the starlight by the low dikes which hold
water on the rice fields. No ambush here, we can see for
miles. But there is the reminder that later in the day we
may move for hours on foot through the clinging mud of
paddies like this.

Now there is a tree-line ahead. I stare at it, waiting
for the pinpoints of light that will mean the vehicles ahead
of us are under fire. No light comes, no popping noise. Is
there no ambush from the trees--or is the enemy waiting for
the tail of the column?

No--I see now why the stretch of road here is probably
clear of the enemy. These trees are not jungle but those of
a rubber plantation. No undergrowth to hide a Viet Cong
(communist) gunner; only geometrically perfect rows of trees
standing like sentinels. The trucks are slowing and stopping.
We have not come ten miles. Why the halt?

The driver jumps down to walk forward and ask. When
he comes back, he takes his carbine and motions me down
from the truck. The road ahead has been freshly cratered.
From here on we have to walk.

The craters are hard to see in the dim light, but I do
not need to see them. They were the first evidence of real
enemy force that I learned to know in Vietnam, and they can
be found on almost every road in the country. They are
not just round holes, but a wicked complex of U-shaped
crags ten feet deep dug in from the road shoulders in a
systematic pattern so that a foot or two of the center of the
pavement remains intact. This means that the villagers' bicycles can continue to use the road surface; only four-wheeled
vehicles like those driven by the military and the moneyed
people are effectively stopped.

Almost without command, the troops have formed two
lines side by side.   Then the echo of a grunt--the word was
"Tiens!" or "Move!"--passes back along the double column.
Now as the column surges forward the miracle of willed silence
seals out the world; no cough or boot scrape can be heard,
even though we are hundreds strong.

The silhouette before me is easy to follow because it
is the tallest, Texas born Captain Sam Jeffers, long-time
company commander from the 101st Division and now mentor
to the Vietnamese airborne troops.   The man behind me I
know, too.   He is the heavy-shouldered first sergeant of
the 32nd Company, Tong Si Bong, 15 years a freedom fighter
(against the Japanese, the French, the Reds.)

We have reached the first river crossing now, but
here, too, the enemy has been before us.   The bridge we
expected to use no longer stands.   So a crossing is impro-
vised.   In the starlight two steel beams, each four inches
wide and long enough, are manhandled across the gap above
the rushing water.   Without a handgrip and with no footway
but the beams themselves, the men carrying their knapsacks
and ammo belts and weapons start to feel their way across.
I would fall but for Captain Jeffers' rock-like balance; as
I cross I rest one hand on his pack.

We are across--and still no ambush.

The next river crossing is wider; we make it aboard
a vehicle as familiar to me as the trucks were--old LCM's
(Landing Craft, Medium) from World War II, now operated
by the Vietnamese Navy.   In a few minutes the LCM's decant
us into waist-deep swamp water on the side.   I flounder and
exhaust most of the unladylike words I know, gasping until,
at last, firm earth rises under my sodden boots.

Still we have not been ambushed.

Now the sun is edging over the horizon, and we are
on a wide, dry, straight path.   Just ahead of me strides the
wiry company commander, Lieutenant Phung Si Thanh, sixteen times decorated for bravery since 1940.   He speaks no
English, but I see him gesture to Captain Jeffers; he is pointing to a collection of huts a hundred years to the right of
the trail.

His eyes are narrowed, and he is grunting speculatively,
"Ah ... ambuscade ici." This is where they'll hit us.

In ten seconds his guess is proved right.

There are three loud detonations, a little pall of smoke
before us, a scattering of shots rising to a stuttering hail,
and two clear shouts. The Viet Cong gunners have our range.

From flat on my stomach in the ditch, I see First Sergeant Bong, waving his heavy shotgun, lead a score of men
in a splashing charge across the rice fields towards the huts.
Over the barrel of the machine gun talking next to me, I
watch the man carrying the .57 recoilless fire steadily time
and again into the huts. Lieutenant Thanh calls over the
radio for the big artillery behind us--a .155 mm. howitzer
battery--to fire an adjusting round on the target area. His
face breaks into a huge grin as in less than a minute the
shell strikes almost where he wanted it. After that only the
over-and-over utterly authoritative crack! of the .57 can be
heard. Except for a few rifle shots, it is the final sound
of the fight.

Sergeant Bong is striding back. His men are carrying
the two enemy mortars that fired on us (homemade but lethal)
and the piece of the mine which made the third of the explosions signaling the ambush.

We have neither dead nor wounded, but Sergeant Bong
tells one of his men, Pvt. Hong Nuoc Cu, to escort me into
the hamlet so I can photograph the body of the one communist
attacker who has been killed.

Private Cu, his brown eyes huge in the frame of his
helmet rim, gestures me after him. In a clearing among the
stunted palms from which the fire on us had first come, I
take the pictures to document what I have seen. The dead
man is not old, and his flat features are composed as if the
fatal bullet had taken his life without his having had time to
be aware of it.

Unthinkingly, I drop to one knee to close his unseeing
eyes, and I reach to check his stilled pulse. Then I realize
from the expression on my Vietnamese paratrooper-escort's
face what I have seemed to do. To Private Cu, it appears

that I have expressed intolerable sympathy for his enemy.
For a minute he is puzzled about how to communicate his
disapproval. As I step back from the body, he solves his
dilemma. His hand moves to his hip.   There are two sharp
detonations almost at my ear; he has fired his .45 twice into
the body of his foe.

As we walk back toward the command group, he seems
to think his impulse needs explanation. He searches out the
French-English words for it. "Mama, Papa, Tires, Hanoi."
Later I check and find I have interpreted them correctly.
As a child, Private Cu was forced to watch the murder of
his own mother and father by the Communists in Hanoi. In
South Vietnam there are thousands of men who have an equiva-
lent reason to hate the communists.

Now I knew what I was doing here, and I carried that
knowledge with me on every mission I went on in Vietnam.

I jumped with the Vietnamese airborne troops six times
onto drop zones which had to be cleared of enemy snipers
and held secure within a ring of infantrymen each time we
landed on them. On operations with the brigade, I walked
more than 200 miles, photographed enemy dead, their own
dead and wounded, the Reds they took prisoner and the
suspects they freed. I followed them in 100° plus heat and
torrential rain, once for six days and nights without returning from the field. I did this out of a conviction that some
American outside the military ought to know and report at
firsthand what our allies against communism are doing, what
they are able to do.

What I saw convinces me that we can win in Asia if
we will. With help, Vietnamese fighting men can be full allies
of the West. They are intelligent, soldierly and better able
to fight on their soil than our own troops. They have the
will to win, but we must have the will to help them.

If I have learned one lesson about warfare, it is that
technical details are not the deciding factor in the battle,
large or small. During my coverage of the front in southeast Asia I saw again and again that rural Asians are capable
of fighting for freedom as hard as ever it has been fought
for anywhere including Lexington and Concord--or, for that
matter, at Iwo Jima and in the streets of Budapest. This,
I know, is what really matters.

This is the story I have been writing, episode by episode, for 20 years: the story of men brave enough to risk
their lives in the defense of freedom against tyranny.   To
me it has always been the most important story in the world.

Where, I wonder, will I next have the chance to go on
observing it and telling of it?

Reprinted by permission from <u>The Reader's Digest</u>, February
1962.

The coup against President Diem did not bring South Vietnam the political stability which the United States had sought. Instead, in January 1964, the government of South Vietnam changed again, with General Nguyen Khanh leading a bloodless coup against the generals who had overthrown Diem. Khanh was ousted in turn by September 1964, and after a politically chaotic period which was later described by Frances Fitzgerald as having the "pace and style of a Marx brothers movie,"[1] power was seized by Generals Nguyen Cao Ky, Nguyen Van Thieu, and Nguyen Huu Co in June 1965.

This tumultuous period was covered by Beverly Deepe, still established in Saigon, and by Marguerite Higgins, who made several more trips to South Vietnam in 1964 and 1965. Meanwhile, Dickey Chapelle continued to cover the first line of battle, Elaine Shepard arrived to concentrate on the air war, and Susan Sheehan ignored the American efforts altogether and concentrated instead on the effect the war was having on the Vietnamese people. At the same time, French reporter Madeleine Riffaud was traveling through the jungles of South Vietnam with the Viet Cong, and was reporting on the war from the opposite side.

Marguerite Higgins continued to be positive on the subject of American military victory. In March 1964 she wrote of "overwhelming evidence that the tide was beginning to turn our way in the Spring and Summer of 1963,"[2] and predicted that the tide would soon turn that way again. In the more than four hundred columns she wrote for Newsday, Higgins stressed the importance of an American and South Vietnamese victory, and deplored the overthrow of Diem. When coup followed coup in Saigon, and even U.S. Secretary of Defense Robert McNamara had to admit that the unsettled conditions in South Vietnam were allowing the Viet Cong to make

progress, Higgins observed that, before agreeing to the
ouster of Diem, the American government ought to have recalled politician Al Smith's advice that it was unwise to change
barrels going over Niagara Falls.

If the perspective of twenty years makes Higgins' insistence that the United States could and would win in Vietnam seem somewhat starry-eyed, it is also true that she was
not blind to the mistakes that the Americans were making
there. She suggested that the South Vietnamese government
needed a strong man who would take firm control and force
the many squabbling national factions into line. She was
aware that such a strong man might not necessarily fit into
the American plan, and she was aware that the American expectations for South Vietnam were naïve. In late 1964 she
wrote:

> The good Americans had acted on the very false as-
> sumption that somehow an Oriental country that had
> never experienced nationhood or known peace could
> none the less develop 'instant democracy' and operate
> responsibly in the middle of a war ... such a false
> assumption is a bungle that history does not lightly
> forgive. [3]

Higgins continued to stress her belief that the Buddhist
unrest in South Vietnam was Communist-inspired. In 1964
she found that Thich Tri Quang had been expelled from the
Xa Loi Pagoda, which had become the tranquil meditation
center which she had expected a Buddhist temple to be. Un-
daunted, however, Thich Tri Quang had established a Buddhist Institute five miles away from the pagoda, from which,
Higgins insisted, he still stage-managed riots. Higgins found
that the techniques of the riots had changed little, and she
recognized many of the old "professional agitators," and waved
at them. One waved back.

In 1965 Higgins wrote in an article about the U.S. diplomatic corps about the "total breakdown of communications
between the American embassy in Saigon and the Vietnamese." [4]
She felt that the breakdown was due to the American lack of
experience in dealing with people like the Vietnamese, who
she described as "Asians with a touch of French culture." [5]
She pointed out that few of the Americans in South Vietnam
spoke French, and hardly any had bothered to learn Vietnamese.

Thus disconnected from Vietnamese reality, the Americans
made mistakes, according to Higgins, such as misunderstanding the conflict between President Diem and the Buddhists.
She wrote:

> As the months, years, coup d'etats, and crises went
> by it became appallingly evident that the United
> States simply did not know who its friends were in
> that tormented country or how to distinguish them
> from its foes.[6]

In September 1965 Higgins made her tenth visit to South
Vietnam. She found Saigon depressing and unreal. Her
Newsday columns continued to argue against the American
hypocrisy which precluded a full-scale war effort. After the
Viet Cong beseiged the American camp at Plei Me, she argued
in favor of the use of chemical defoliants as a means of preventing infiltration of the enemy from the North. "This war
won't even start coming to an end until those border points
used by Ho Chi Minh's troops are finally cleared and, at the
very least, open to surveillance,"[7] she wrote.

Convinced that the United States could and would ultimately win in South Vietnam, Higgins continued to push for
acceleration of the United States effort. She insisted that,
if it were vital to American interests, the United States could
keep up its operations in South Vietnam for decades. She
feared the loss of American determination to win the war, and
dreaded the swing of American public opinion against involvement in South Vietnam. "The American people should remember," she wrote, "that there is no conceivable way in which
the Viet Cong can win if we remain determined to do whatever is necessary to prevent it."[8]

Higgins returned to the United States in late 1965
feverish and ill. On November 6 she was admitted to Walter
Reed Army Medical Center in Washington D.C. Ill as she
was, she continued to write her column for Newsday. She
contrived with her children's nurse to be smuggled out of
the hospital and flown to New York to appear on television
promoting her newly published book Our Vietnam Nightmare.

It became obvious that Higgins was seriously ill, but
doctors could not determine the cause of her illness. Baffled
doctors thought at first that she had contracted a drug-

resistant form of malaria that is common in Vietnam. Next
they feared that she had cancer, but an exploratory operation found no evidence of the disease. By the time that the
doctors concluded that she had fallen victim to a rare para-
sitic disease called leishmaniasis, she was too weak to fight
the complications. She died on January 3, 1966 at the age
of forty-five and was buried in Arlington National Cemetery.
Because she had contracted the disease while on duty in
Vietnam, M.L. Stein wrote in his book Under Fire that she
was a "combat casualty just as certainly as if she had been
felled by a bullet on the front line."[9]

Higgins' obituaries were unanimous in their assessment
of her as one of the greatest of war correspondents. Personally, however, she had been an enigma. She was invariably ladylike and feminine, even when wearing Army fatigues
and covered with mud, but her detractors soon discovered
that the ladylike exterior covered a strong, tough woman who
did not hesitate to put up a fight for something she wanted.
Rival reporters found that she could be ruthless when in
search of a story.

She had been aware that her good looks were sometimes
a disadvantage. She wrote:

> As a foreign correspondent my biggest disadvantage
> in being both young and a woman was the resulting
> tendency of some male officials to associate the com-
> bination of feminity and blonde hair with either dumb-
> ness or slyness, or both.[10]

Still, the combination of youth and beauty with evident
talent as a war correspondent led to a great deal of media
coverage during the Korean War and undoubtedly was a factor in her success. Strong, ruthless, ladylike, talented, always feminine, Marguerite Higgins baffled many of her colleagues. In 1950, when she was at the height of her popu-
larity as a correspondent in Korea, her colleague Carl Mydans,
who knew her quite well, described her as a "small slight
blonde, sometimes described as winsome."[11] In reality she
was five feet, eight inches tall, cool, and totally professional.

Although admittedly biased in favor of American involvement in South Vietnam because of her unwavering hatred of
Communism, Higgins was still not uncritical of American policy

there. Many of her opinions have been proven correct, according to the 1979 study on Vietnam War coverage done at
the U.S. Army War College. She was correct in her assessment of the Buddhist movement as being politically motivated;
in her statement that the Diem government, whatever its de-
fects, would be replaced by governments equally defective;
and in her belief that the United States, by becoming a party
to the overthrow of Diem, would irrevocably commit itself to
full-scale intervention in the war. And she could almost be
credited with the gift of prophecy when she wrote, in 1965:

> The only way that the Communists could make the
> United States welsh on its commitment to Vietnam is
> if American public opinion in the 1960's were to be-
> come as demoralized as French public opinion in the
> 1950's.[12]

While Higgins had been reporting on the political situation in South Vietnam in late 1964, Dickey Chapelle had returned to cover combat. In December she joined a River Assault Group (RAG) patrol in the Mekong Delta. RAG 23,
with which Chapelle traveled, was responsible for safeguard-
ing three delta provinces, Vinh Long, Vinh Binh, and Kien
Hoa. The little gunboat was commanded by Vietnamese Lieutenant Hoa and American Lieutenant Meyercord. Many of
the people in the delta provinces under the "protection" of
RAG 23 owed little allegiance to the Saigon government, having long been under the control of local warlords and river
pirates. The murky waters of the rivers were mined.

Chapelle recognized that the war in Vietnam was unlike any other conflict she had covered. For one thing,
neither side seemed to be winning. There seemed to be no
rules, and Chapelle had been warned that civilians were
treated as spies if captured by the Viet Cong. For the first
time in more than twenty years of reporting wars, Chapelle
carried a gun. Leaving the gunboat for a patrol in the
jungle, Meyercord teased Chapelle about his nervousness in
being followed by a woman carrying a loaded carbine. Chapelle admired Meyercord and men like him. She wrote:

> And why were Americans like Meyercord here? They
> had brought all their expertise and dedication and
> raw nerve from the security of their home towns to
> the ultimate insecurity of guerrilla warfare as far from

home as it was possible to go. Was that the American
idea of global leadership? I know it was at least one
American's idea--mine.[13]

Chapelle also travelled with the "junk" fleet of small
boats which patrolled the seacoast. Coming in one day from
a sea patrol, she had taken off her combat boots to relax
and sort film, when she heard the sound of gunfire. The
base was under fire from a nearby village. According to
Chapelle, the Viet Cong often fired from a village, as they
knew that the sailors did not like to fire blindly into huts.
When the frantic skirmish was over the American lieutenant
burst into laughter because Chapelle, who had run several
miles to the village with the troops, was still wearing her
rubber thonged shower shoes. But, she later wrote sadly,
laughter seldom lasted long on the Delta. Shortly after she
returned to the United States early in 1965 Chapelle learned
that Lieutenant Meyercord was dead from a sniper's bullet
in South Vietnam.

Like Marguerite Higgins, Dickey Chapelle did not let
anti-Communism and her support of the Vietnam War blind
her to reality. When she returned from her 1964 trip she
wrote, "We are losing the war."[14] Like Higgins she tried
to drum up support for the war, writing with admiration of
the quality of leadership being provided by the American advisers, and reminding her readers of the American treaty
with South Vietnam which pledged whatever help was needed
to win their battle against Communism. She concluded that
the reason the war was "being lost" was because the United
States government had not provided enough leadership. She,
like Higgins, called for a total American commitment to winning the war.

Chapelle travelled throughout the United States lectur-
ing on campuses and debating vigorously with anti-war pro-
testors. Wherever she went she tried to convince people of
the importance of American support of the South Vietnamese.
"The one factor that can significantly alter the balance of
bloody anguish in Vietnam," she wrote, "is the will of the
American people."[15]

In November 1965 Chapelle returned to South Vietnam
on assignment for the National Observer, pausing enroute on
Okinawa to cover Marine guerrilla warfare training. She

called the training a "grim rehearsal" for the war. The
Marines were trained for "search and clear" operations, in
which they entered villages suspected of harboring Viet Cong.
Included in the training was a simulated silent manuever in
which all commands were given by hand signal, instructions
on the best methods of talking to village leaders, and advice
on the avoidance of booby traps such as pointed sticks hidden
in the ground behind a fallen log. By this time American
troops in South Vietnam were no longer being called "advisers"
but were recognized as active participants in the "search and
clear" missions.

Arriving in South Vietnam Chapelle met Elaine Shepard,
an old friend who was covering the war for Mutual Broadcasting. According to Shepard the two talked late into the
night, discussing the dangers of their chosen profession.
"Oh I suppose my luck will run out someday," Chapelle told
Shepard, "But if you're scared, really scared, you don't
belong over here."[16]

In the press billets in Da Nang Chapelle learned that
Marines were going on "search and clear" operations through
a dozen miles of coastal mountain terrain between Da Nang
and Hue. She asked one squad leader if she could go along.
"They say nothing that can happen in the field shakes up a
professional Marine sergeant," she wrote, "and the idea that
his outfit would suddenly include a middle-aged woman reporter did not furrow the sergeant's brow."[17]

That night Chapelle began the first combat patrol she
had seen in South Vietnam with all American troops. The
mission was called Operation Black Ferret. The unit was
the 1st platoon of the F Company of the 2nd Battalion of the
3rd Marine Regiment. Chapelle suspected that this patrol
might be different from the many others she had made because of the professionalism of the U.S. Marines. The word
"professionalism" occurs over and over in Chapelle's writing
on the Marines. She believed that the professionalism of the
U.S. combat troops would be the factor which would tip the
scales in South Vietnam over the fanaticism of the Viet Cong.
In the cover letter she submitted with the story, she wrote:

> Here is a report on what is probably the character-
> istic Marine operation here, the search and clear ef-
> fort. I think it makes the one point about these that

I've not seen in print: the fact that they are such
grinding bull labor, sheer physical labor either in
movement or in withstanding discomfort.   And that
as this observer saw them, they are being done with
such professionalism. [18]

On the morning of November 4, 1965, the second day
of Operation Black Ferret, Chapelle left with a Marine patrol
near Chu Lai.   As was her custom, she was wearing her
Australian bush hat, decorated with the paratrooper's emblem
she had earned jumping with the 101st Airborne Division.
She was also wearing the glove and anchor Marine emblem
given her by Marine Corps Commandant General Wallace M.
Greene, Jr. just before she left on her latest Vietnam assignment.   She had stuck a flower in the band of her hat.
As she and several Marines moved through the low brush,
someone's foot brushed a concealed wire, triggering a booby
trap made of a grenade wired to an 81mm mortar round.
Struck by shrapnel in the throat, Dickey Chapelle died within
minutes.   She was forty-seven years old.

As the stunned Marines stood by, a Navy Chaplain ad-
ministered the last rites of the Catholic Church.   Correspondent Ernest G. Ferguson of the Baltimore Sun, who was
also along on the patrol, wrote that one of the Marines handed
him Chapelle's hat, with the sprig of pink flowers still in the
hatband.

In an unusual tribute to a civilian, Chapelle's body was
sent back to the United States accompanied by a six-member
Marine honor guard, the casket draped in an American flag.
She was the fourth U.S. correspondent to be killed in action
in South Vietnam.   In May 1965 free-lancer Pieter van Thiel,
and in October 1965 two Associated Press photographers,
Bernard Kolenberg and Huynh Thanh, had been killed.

Chapelle's obituaries recalled her courage and her often
salty language, her insistence on carrying her own gear and
being "one of the Marines," and using the word she herself
favored, her complete professionalism.   On her grave in Milwaukee her former husband Tony Chapelle placed a lone rose,
next to a bouquet of roses sent by former Hungarian Freedom
Fighters.   The following year she was honored with a ceremony dedicating the Dickey Chapelle Memorial Dispensary in
Chu Lai.   With Lieutenant General Lewis Walt, USMC, and

members of the 3rd Marine Amphibious Forces in attendance,
correspondent Jim Lucas of Scripps-Howard Newspaper Alliance spoke in tribute, saying of Chapelle:

> Dickey Chapelle was a Marine ... she was a patriot.
> She loved her country and served it well ... Dickey
> Chapelle was one hell of a girl.[19]

News of Chapelle's death reached her friend Elaine
Shepard at Clark Air Force Base in the Philippines. Shepard
wept when she saw the wirephoto of the chaplain administer-
ing last rites to Chapelle's crumpled body. But like Chapelle
and Marguerite Higgins, Shepard was passionately committed
to the American mission in South Vietnam, and believed that
American involvement in the war was the only hope of withstanding Communism in Asia. An unrepentant hawk, she
wrote in 1981 that she was first motivated to go to Vietnam
in 1965 when she began to see in the American press the
first hints of public disapproval of the war. "I would have
gone to Vietnam if I'd had to swim over with my typewriter
between my teeth," she said.[20] She was spared the swim
when she received an assignment from the Mutual Broadcasting System. In addition, Sid Goldberg, editor-in-chief of
North American Newspaper Alliance, asked her to file stories
for NANA.

Elaine Shepard came to the field of war correspondence
in a roundabout fashion, by way of Hollywood. Born in Olney,
Illinois in 1923, she traveled to California on a cross-country
bus with her brother and, being a beautiful blonde, soon
found herself in the movies. After doing several "darkest
Africa" serials with animal trainer Clyde Beatty and some
lions, Shepard was offered her first major role and promptly
turned it down in order to marry an Air Force colonel. When
her husband was sent overseas during World War II, she
spent nineteen months selling War Bonds on tours with other
celebrities and taking her turn at the famous Hollywood Canteen. After the war Shepard settled into the life of an Air
Force wife and foster mother to her brother's daughter, who
had come to live with her.

When Shepard's marriage ended in divorce several years
later, she moved with her niece and mother from her elegant
Georgetown home into a one-room New York apartment and
embarked on a career as a journalist. Her first overseas

assignment sent her to Moscow in conjunction with Vice President Nixon's 1959 tour.   Later the same year, with a hatbox of food under her arm, she was the only female reporter to accompany President Dwight Eisenhower on his eleven-nation peace tour.   Highlights of that assignment included an exclusive interview with India's Prime Minister Nehru, and a visit to the aircraft carrier Essex in the Mediterranean.   The ship's officers were distressed at having a woman aboard but could hardly refuse her, since she was traveling with the President.

In 1960, once again traveling with President Eisenhower's entourage, Shepard was in the Far East.   She organized a group of reporters to fly to the island of Quemoy, then being shelled by the Chinese.   She was effusive in her praise of the Nationalist Chinese on Taiwan and Quemoy and adamant in her opposition to Communism.   Like Chapelle and Higgins, Shepard never wavered in her hatred of Communism.   Like them also, she was convinced that the war in Vietnam was America's last stand against Communism in Southeast Asia, and she never lost her belief in the rightness of the war.

Shepard traveled widely as a foreign correspondent, covering riots in Cairo and London, and the bloody civil war in the Belgian Congo in 1961.   In the Congo she encountered Marguerite Higgins in what Newsweek reported as a somewhat less than civil meeting.   Introduced by a man who thought the two female reporters should get to know one another, Higgins was reported to have looked Shepard over coolly and asked, "Who's she?   Is she a reporter?"[21]

When Shepard arrived in Saigon in 1965 she checked into the Caravelle Hotel, where many members of the press corps stayed.   Her first move was to hitch a ride with photographers Tim Page and Paul Schutzer to the black market, where she could buy such essentials as a canteen, waterproof poncho, and combat boots.   "The irony is," she wrote, "that some of the gear is available only in the black market."[22] Then came accreditation and getting used to life in Saigon, which she found "weird," a place where life went on as if oblivious to the war.   Americans, she wrote, alternated between a casual attitude and attacks of paranoia over the danger of Viet Cong terrorists.

Operation "Rolling Thunder," the plan for a sustained
air war against North Vietnam, had begun in March 1965.
Shepard covered the story of the night-bombing missions
from Bien Hoa, near Saigon. She wrote of her experiences
in her book The Doom Pussy. The book's title refers to the
emblem worn only by pilots who have flown the dangerous
night missions. According to Shepard, the emblem was em-
broidered with a large yellow cat with a patch over its right
eye and a twin engined airplane in its teeth. The motto on
the badge, written in Vietnamese, translated into "I have
flown into the jaws of the cat of death." Shepard wrote
that the pilots translated the phrase "cat of death" as "doom
pussy."

"The granite facts are not easy to come by in Vietnam,"
Shepard wrote.[23] To do a thorough job she believed that a
reporter must go on patrols in the jungle, get shot at, accompany airmen on strikes, and sleep on the wet ground.
She herself traveled the entire time she was there, from Bien
Hoa to Da Nang, where she went on a mission with a combat
crew called "Harry's Hog Haulers;" from Da Nang to Qui
Nhon, where she photographed the disembarking of troops;
from Qui Nhon back to Saigon, where she interviewed Ambassador Henry Cabot Lodge. She visited a Montagnard village,
where she removed her blouse to gain the confidence of the
bare-breasted women she wanted to photograph. She flew on
a helicopter mission to Dong Xoai with pilot Chuck Honour,
who was killed in action three months later. She was the
only foreign reporter to accompany Prime Minister Nguyen
Cao Ky and his wife on a state trip to Malaya.

Believing strongly that a united home front supports
fighting men, Shepard railed against the anti-war demonstrations that had begun back in the United States, culminating
in a November 27, 1965 march of 35,000 war protesters to
the White House. Shepard saw herself as the top publicity
agent of the men she met in Vietnam. She took pride in her
rapport with tough pilots with unlikely names such as "Nails,"
"Smash," and "Moose." Although she received two citations
from the 145th Aviation Battalion for her participation in helicopter assault missions, she was proudest of a gift given her
by "Nails" and "Smash" when she left Vietnam. It was a
cigarette lighter engraved with the words, "Last of the great
broads."

Shepard returned to the United States in January 1966 to write her book and continue her campaign for home front support of the men in Vietnam.   Meanwhile Beverly Deepe remained in Saigon, where she continued to write for the Christian Science Monitor and the New York Herald Tribune. By 1965 she had developed valuable contacts among the Vietnamese which she used to good advantage.   "I try to make friends with people on their way up," she said, "and they remember me later."[24]   One such friend was Nguyen Khanh, whom she had earlier interviewed in August 1964, shortly after he had been ousted as Premier.   Later that year Deepe asked Khanh to give her a second interview.   Three weeks later she was called to his elegant Saigon townhouse, where she interviewed him for more than half an hour, hardly believing what she was hearing.   Khanh's attack on U.S. Ambassador Maxwell Taylor in the interview made headlines all over the United States.

The interview with Khanh was not the first time Deepe had angered the American Embassy in Saigon.   In 1964 Ambassador Taylor had challenged the accuracy of one of her stories, saying that the story was based on inaccurate leaks. It is not surprising that the Embassy was annoyed with Deepe's story.   In it she had reported that Taylor, at a news conference from which she had been excluded, had stated that some of the generals who had taken over power within the South Vietnamese government "bordered on being nuts."

Deepe was the only U.S. reporter who was regularly excluded from official U.S. briefings.   By 1965 she had her own contacts and resources for obtaining information, however, so she was unruffled by the exclusion.   "They don't like me because I won't say what they want me to say," she reported.   "They accuse me of giving the Vietnamese line, when in fact what I do is listen to them and then go out and find out for myself."[25]   Deepe "found out" with the assistance of two Vietnamese informants, one of whom was later discovered to have been a high-ranking Communist spy.   It is possible that this man, Pham Xuan Anh, did plant inaccurate stories with Deepe.   If so, she was in good company, as Anh also worked for Time magazine.

Although Deepe's reporting in late 1963 had been accused of sympathy to the Buddhist cause, she was clear by

early 1965 that the Buddhist movement was anti-American
and opposed to any U.S.-backed government in South Vietnam. She wrote in the <u>New York Herald Tribune</u>:

> The Communist-oriented militant Buddhist movement
> is in a warming-up phase of its campaign to overturn
> the government of Premier Tran Van Huong. Its
> potential power over the masses has yet to be tested.[26]

In July 1965, Neil Sheehan, now with <u>The New York</u>
<u>Times</u>, returned to Saigon with his wife Susan and set up
housekeeping in the Hotel Continental. Susan Sheehan was
also a writer, and she wanted to write about the effect the
war was having on the people of South Vietnam. "Since I
was fortunate enough not to have to cover daily stories,"
she wrote, "I could spend my time roaming the countryside
seeking out the people I wanted to interview...."[27]

Accompanied by an interpreter, Nguyen Ngoc Rao,
Sheehan traveled throughout South Vietnam for several months,
interviewing Vietnamese from all levels of society. Ten of
the interviews were later collected into a book, <u>Ten Vietnam-</u>
<u>ese</u>. In the book are interviews with a peasant woman who
told Sheehan that she didn't care how the war ended, just
so long as it ended, a landlord who specialized in renting
to G.I.'s and their Vietnamese girlfriends, a man living in
a refugee camp, a politician, a Montagnard tribesman, a
thirteen-year-old war orphan, a Buddhist monk, a South
Vietnamese soldier, a member of the Viet Cong, and a North
Vietnamese prisoner-of-war.

Sheehan had met resistance from the American military
when she sought to interview a North Vietnamese prisoner-
of-war. Finally she was able to obtain an interview through
the assistance of a South Vietnamese friend who was a high-
ranking government official. "Our war is a people's war and
a war for a just cause,"[28] the prisoner-of-war proudly told
Sheehan. Since the official American line at the time was
that North Vietnamese morale was low, Sheehan was not surprised that the Americans had declined to cooperate with her.

While the political situation in Saigon continued to be
unstable, and the bombing of North Vietnam continued to
stir up angry anti-war protest in the United States, the
guerrilla war against the Viet Cong continued in South Viet-

nam. In fact, despite increased American intervention, the
number of Viet Cong guerrillas in South Vietnam had actually
increased. In 1964 a group of western journalists and photographers, led by British writer Wilfred Burchett, spent
several weeks traveling with the guerrillas through the jungles
of South Vietnam. With the group was a woman journalist,
Madeleine Riffaud.

Riffaud was a reporter for L'Humanité, the official
organ of the French Communist Party. In the book she later
wrote of her travels with Burchett's party during December
1964 and January 1965, it is obvious that Riffaud equated
the Viet Cong with the French Resistance during World War
II. The book is called Dans Les Maquis "Vietcong" (With
the Maquis "Vietcong"). Members of the World War II French
Resistance had been called "Maquis," and Riffaud later referred to her months with the guerrillas as "my small experience in the resistance movement of Vietnam."[29]

Riffaud's Communism and her identification with resistance movements was born during World War II, when the
Nazis conquered her country. A high-school girl at the
time, she became a member of the Resistance with the Groupes
de Combat des Facultés. Arrested in July 1944, she was
seriously wounded when she attacked a German officer. She
was tortured and condemned to death, but was rescued during the Paris uprising as France was being liberated by Americans. But huddled in a jungle shelter twenty years later
as American planes dropped bombs on Burchett and his party,
Riffaud saw the Americans as the enemy. To her, the war
in Vietnam was clearly a war of Communist guerrillas fighting
to liberate their country from foreign oppressors.

There was already polarization of opinion about the war
in South Vietnam by the end of 1964. On the one hand such
hawks as Marguerite Higgins and Dickey Chapelle were calling
for an all-out war effort to defeat the Communists. At the
other extreme doves were demanding American withdrawal
from the war which they, like Madeleine Riffaud, saw as a
popular revolution against an oppressive government. Although it stopped short of the total commitment to victory
demanded by the hawks, the American government increased
its commitment to the war. Even as Lyndon Johnson was
elected U.S. President in November 1964 as a peace candidate,
U.S. officials had come to a general consensus to begin bombing

North Vietnam.   In August of 1964 an incident had occurred
which encouraged them in their plan.

On August 2, 1964 the United States destroyer <u>Maddox</u>
was attacked by North Vietnamese PT boats in the Gulf of
Tonkin off the coast of Vietnam.   On August 5 President
Johnson asked Congress to approve a joint resolution calling
for full support of U.S. forces in Vietnam in order to "promote the maintenance of international peace and security in
Southeast Asia."   The Tonkin Gulf resolution, which opened
the way for full-scale American involvement in Vietnam, was
approved by the house of Representatives 416 to 0 and by
the Senate 88 to 2, with only Senators Wayne Morse and
Ernest Gruening dissenting.   There was little public outcry
in the United States when the bombing of North Vietnam began in March 1965.   And the number of U.S. forces in South
Vietnam rose steadily until it reached nearly 150,000 by the
end of 1965.

What is the meaning of the five tragic self-immolations that took place in Vietnam in the six weeks following the November coup d'etat against Diem? How did it come to pass that under the military junta, which seized power in the name of an end to "persecution," there have been more suicides by fire over a short period than had ever been the case under President Diem and his brother Ngo Dinh Nhu? Even though virtually ignored by the Western press, will this latest spate of suicides by fire--without clearly stated reason--destroy at last the false notion that the repeated acts of self-immolation in Vietnam were indisputable proof of massive persecution of the Buddhist religion by President Diem, a Roman Catholic?

Will historians be more equitable with President Diem than his contemporaries were?

On two trips in Vietnam in 1963, one before and one after the coup d'etat, this writer was never able to find an instance of repression on religious grounds. Under Diem, there were repression of Buddhists, Catholics, Confucianists, etc., when--in defiance of clearly stated laws--they took to the streets to demonstrate against the government. But Diem's repression was not directed against a religion. It was aimed at overt political opposition. There were deplorable police excesses in Vietnam, but there is no sign that they were desired or condoned by Diem any more than police excesses in Alabama are condoned or desired by Washington.

There was, for a long time, a clear double standard in Vietnam, in which accusations against Diem gained, in most cases, giant headlines, but attempted refutations received only perfunctory notice. For instance, last summer Thich Duc Ngiep, the Xa Loi pagoda spokesman, told reporters dramatically that 365 persons in a Saigon suburb had been arrested "because they were Buddhists." That figure was headlined throughout the world. But when I went to

the suburb in question, I found that a routine check was
being made of a neighborhood through which the Viet Cong
often infiltrated. I stayed for two hours to talk with those
rounded up as they emerged from the police compound after
questioning. I talked to twenty persons--ancestor worshipers,
Catholics, Confucianists, Taoists, Caodaists, etc.--before I
finally found a genuine Buddhist among those picked up. So
the charge of 365 persons arrested because of being Buddhists
was invention.

There is no doubt that the overwhelming majority of
the American press corps in Saigon thought--out of the most
idealistic and patriotic motives--that they were serving a
good cause in arousing world opinion against Diem. Whether
his strengths and faults were greater or less than those of
his junta successors remains to be seen.

It is certain that under the military junta, Vietnamese
have been jailed for far less than was necessary to send a
person to prison under Diem. Said a European observer:
"Under Diem, a Vietnamese had to do something specific
against the regime to get into trouble. Under the military
junta, a Vietnamese can be jailed without charge, simply under
the suspicion that he was loyal to the Diem regime, when it
was the legally constituted authority."

Sanche de Gramont, of the New York Herald Tribune,
has estimated the number of arbitrary arrests right after the
coup as around five hundred. So far, Mr. de Gramont and
this reporter are the only ones who have written with any
detail about the junta's reversion to some of the police-state
tactics the Saigon press corps so bitterly criticized in Diem.

Nowadays, some of the most ardent anti-Diem writers,
such as David Halberstam, Saigon correspondent of the New
York Times, acknowledge that the Buddhist agitation of last
summer and fall was politically motivated. In an admiring
magazine article written by his close friend George J.W. Goodman, Mr. Halberstam is quoted as saying: "I always said it.
The Buddhist campaign was political.... I thought I always
emphasized that this was a political dispute under a religious
banner--the only place an opposition had found to gather in
an authoritarian regime...."

Whatever Mr. Halberstam's intentions, his and other

press dispatches last summer and fall did create the impression in the outside world that some kind of religious crisis
was going on inside Vietnam. And it was the image of religious persecution--false as it was--that paved the way for
Diem's downfall. Without the embarrassment of being the pa-
tron of a country suspected of battling Buddhists, it is doubt-
ful that the United States would ever have reached the decision to try to get rid of Diem. The authorities in Washington knew, of course, that the conflict in Vietnam was political, not religious. But they were reluctant to speak out lest,
in the process, they attract to Washington some of the onus
being poured--with hardly any contradiction--on Diem.

By staying silent, Washington acted as if it thought
Diem guilty. And this helped to complete the vicious circle.

Or, as Roger Hillsman, Assistant Secretary of State
for Far Eastern Affairs, put it: "After the closing of the
pagodas on August 21, the facts became irrelevant." So,
evidently, did a sense of perspective. What, for example,
about the fact that President Diem was far more lenient to
his political opposition than President Sukarno of Indonesia
or Premier Sarit Thanarat of Thailand, both recipients of
American aid? Whereas some three hundred political prisoners, at most, were found in Diem's jails, the prisons of
Thailand, Indonesia and Burma were filled--and are still
filled--with tens of thousands of political victims.

"But," explained a pro-coup State Department officer,
"the world spotlight is not on those countries, and it is on
Vietnam."

At the State Department there have been some attempts
to rationalize the coup d'etat by describing it as necessary
to save the Vietnamese war efforts from going to pieces.
One difficulty with this argument is that it makes liars out
of Secretary of Defense McNamara, Chief of Staff Maxwell
D. Taylor and General Paul Harkins, who testified under oath
to Congress in October that the war was making reasonable
progress. If the State Department ever took seriously the
argument that the disturbances in the cities would affect
morale in the countryside, it betrays a regrettable lack of
understanding of the structure of Vietnam and of the gap
between the countryside, where the war will be won or lost,
and the cities, where less than ten per cent of the Vietnamese
live.

For the Buddhists, intellectuals and students who
marched the streets in anti-Diem demonstrations could not
have cared less about the war--before the coup, or after the
coup. Vietnamese students in particular tell you quite frankly
that one reason they prize admission to a university is that
it enables them to avoid the draft. Vietnam's intellectuals
have narrow horizons, are excessively inward-turning, and
make constant and factional criticism their specialty. Except
for a handful of terribly militant leaders, Buddhist monks
are rather passive. If the success or failure of the war
were to depend on these groups, Vietnam would have been
lost from the start. As to the effects in the countryside of
the critical clamoring by Vietnam's spoiled young intellectuals
in the cities, it was virtually nil. The American attitude
seemed to be that if a Vietnamese student demonstrates, virtue
is on his side and the government is wrong. But in the
countryside there were many peasants and plain soldiers who
disapproved of the defiance of the regime--in those rare
places where anyone knew anything whatsoever of what went
on beyond the next village.

If there was any slowdown in the war in September
and October of 1963, it was because the Vietnamese generals--
under American prodding--were concentrating on thoughts of
a coup d'etat, while Diem and Nhu, out of fear of America,
were concentrating on how to prevent a coup.

It was not until after the coup d'etat that the Vietnamese war took a decidedly downward turn. The military
junta with its uncertain leadership, after purges of key (and
scarce) officials, finally plunged much of the countryside
into the confusion from which it purportedly was trying to
save Vietnam.

No wonder the Viet Cong took advantage of the situation to seize the military initiative for the first time in many
months. No wonder that, in the two months after the coup
d'etat, the military junta lost more real estate, lives and
weapons to the Viet Cong than at any previous time in the
war.

It was precisely out of fear of such predictable con-
sequences of trying to change regimes in midwar that Secretary of Defense McNamara and Central Intelligence Agency
Director John McCone opposed a coup d'etat. But they were

overruled by the pro-coup d'etat faction led by Ambassador
Henry Cabot Lodge, Undersecretary of State Averell Harri-
man, and Assistant Secretary of State for Far Eastern Affairs Roger Hillsman.

The Diem-must-go decision came shortly after the tem-
porary closing of about a dozen (out of 4,000) pagodas on
August 21, which outraged Washington. Diem said that his
only aim was to get the Buddhist leaders out of politics and
back to religion. The Vietnamese leader insisted that unless
he shut down the propaganda machinery of the pagodas and
put a halt to the glorification of suicide by burning, public
disorder in the cities would mount and world misunderstanding would deepen. Washington disagreed. Further, it felt
that Diem had not only humiliated it and flouted its advice,
but had broken a promise to be conciliatory. Washington's
anger was heightened by horrendous stories of killings and
brutalities during the pagoda raids. (There were no such
killings, as the monks themselves later said.)

In any case, on August 24, the State Department sent
out word--without the knowledge of Secretary McNamara or
of C.I.A. Director John McCone--instructing Ambassador
Lodge to "unleash" the Vietnamese generals with a view to
toppling the Diem government if they could. Plotting among
educated Vietnamese, including the generals, is a kind of
national pastime, as chess is to the Russians. Until lately
it had been a pretty harmless pastime, because everybody
knew that real action was dependent on an American green
light--and until August such a green light had been with-
held.

But on Sunday, August 25, Washington publicly gave
the generals a green light in a Voice of America broadcast
that virtually called on the Vietnamese military to take over.
At the same time, Ambassador Lodge asked the C.I.A. to
poll the Vietnamese generals and see when and if they were
ready to translate revolt talk into action.

Diem's shock at the Voice of America broadcast and
the C.I.A. poll of the Vietnamese generals can only be imagined by turning the tables around. Suppose the United
States were engaged in a war against Communists in which
we depended almost totally on aid from Vietnam; suppose, in
the middle of the war, Vietnam issued a broadcast calling for

the American Joint Chiefs of Staff to overthrow the American
government?

The miracle is that the Diem regime survived as long
as it did the virtual declaration of political war served on it
that August by Washington.

What, after many months of hesitation, finally decided
the generals (in mid-October) to stage the coup? In separate
interviews with this correspondent, members of the military
junta spoke of these factors:

1. The late President Kennedy called, at a press conference, for "changes of policy and maybe personnel" in Vietnam.

2. Washington announced the withdrawal of 1,000 American soldiers by the end of 1963, and possible total withdrawal
by 1965. (Said one general: "That convinced us that unless
we got rid of Diem, you would abandon us.")

3. The economic aid was cut. Many generals agreed
that this cut was psychologically the most decisive goad to a
coup d'etat. "It convinced us," a key plotter explained,
"that the United States was serious this time about getting
rid of Diem. In any case, this was a war we wanted to win.
The United States furnished us with the jeeps, the bullets,
the very guns that made the war possible. In cutting economic aid, the United States was forcing us to choose between your country's help in the war and Diem. So we chose
the United States."

Ironically, President Diem did make some important con-
cessions to the United States in September and October.
For example, in mid-September President Diem agreed to
every point put forward by the United States in a program
to reform and consolidate the strategic hamlet program in
the Mekong Delta. Many Americans had long felt that this
program had been overextended. At last President Diem
agreed with the diagnosis and decided to do something about
it. Why was this move toward the American position never
publicized? One Western diplomat put it this way: "Ambassador Lodge and his deputy, William Truehart, were so determined to get rid of Diem that they were opposed to putting
him in a conciliatory light. They were afraid this would

strengthen the hands of those in Washington against a coup d'etat."

Even at the eleventh hour, Ambassador Lodge could, of course, have turned off the revolt if he had chosen to give the slightest sign that the New Frontier and President Diem were even beginning to move to heal their rent. As one member of the military junta put it: "We would never have dared to act if we had not been sure that the United States was giving us its moral support."

In the last hours before his death, President Diem was stripped of any doubt whatsoever of Washington's hostility. Telephoning the American Embassy from the Palace at 4:30 p.m. on November 1, after the bombardment had started, President Diem asked Ambassador Lodge: "What is Washington's attitude toward this?" Lodge replied: "I don't know Washington's attitude. After all, it is four-thirty in the morning there."

"But you must have some idea," Diem said.

Whereupon Lodge turned the conversation to the matter of Diem's safety, offering him an airplane to take him out of the country. Could anything have indicated more clearly that in American eyes the success of the coup d'etat was a fait accompli?

The only certain thing about the murder of President Diem and Counselor Nhu is that they were shot in the back (Diem in the neck, Nhu in the right side) with their hands tied behind them. Nhu also had a dagger or bayonet wound in the chest, which was apparently indecisive.

These facts were established beyond all doubt by this reporter through photographs and through talk with military eyewitnesses, attendants at St. Paul's Hospital (where the bodies were first taken) and from information given by two relatives, a niece and nephew who handled the preparations for the burial.

In the light of the way Diem and Nhu died there is a strong possibility that the shootings were ordered by some or all members of the military junta. Would a junior officer take such a responsibility on himself?

Now for the Buddhist leaders who started it all: have
they got what they wanted? I use the word "leaders" ad-
visedly, for of the Buddhists in Vietnam, who form about
thirty per cent of the population of fourteen million people,
the overwhelming majority are largely nonpolitical. Buddhist
monks tend to be somewhat passive. They would never have
dreamed of resorting to violent demonstrations had they not
been subjected to the skillful and inflammatory propaganda
that poured from the humming mimeograph machines of the
Xa Loi pagoda. By the end of last summer, the original
grievances of the Buddhist leaders in Hue--matters of property rights, flag flying, etc.--had largely been met by the
Diem regime.

In the midst of the anti-Diem ferment I wrote an article
asking: "What do the Buddhists want? They want Diem's
head--not on a silver platter, but wrapped in an American
flag."

You have to hand it to the Buddhist leaders that they
got what they wanted. But will this satisfy the more militant
Buddhist leaders? It is heady stuff, even for Buddhists, to
have the attention of the entire world focused on you, and
to exercise the kind of political power that can topple governments. Will, for instance, the venerable Thich Tri Quang,
the mastermind of the Buddhist campaign and by far the most
intelligent and militant of all, be satisfied to take a political
back seat?

Thich Tri Quang is a Buddhist leader from Hue who
was granted asylum at the American Embassy even though
his past is in some controversy. According to records of
the French Colonial Office, he had twice been arrested during the postwar French occupation of Indochina for dealings
with Ho Chi Minh. By his own admission, he was a member
of the Vietminh Communist Liberation Front. He claims to
have fallen out with the Communists later. Again according
to the French, who still have representatives at Hanoi, Thich
Tri Quang's brother is currently working for Ho Chi Minh
in the Communist Vietnam's Ministry of the Interior. The
duties of Thich Tri Quang's brother are the direction of sub-
version in South Vietnam.

None of this, of course, proves anything about Thich
Tri Quang's current attitude toward the Communist Viet Cong

What does seem clear is that he learned a lot from the Communists about organization and propaganda. He ran his emergency headquarters at the Xa Loi pagoda like a company command post. Orders were barked out, directing a demonstration here, a protest meeting there. Messengers scurried in and out, carrying banners with their newly painted slogans. Respectful monks brought in the last anti-Diem propaganda blast for Thich Tri Quang to review word by word.

In my discussion with Thich Tri Quang I was somewhat taken aback at his indifference about the war against the Communists. When I asked whether the occasional outburst of turmoil might not offer the Viet Cong the opportunity to infiltrate among the demonstrators, Thich Tri Quang shrugged his shoulders and said: "It is possible that the current disorders could lead to Communist gains. But if this happens it will be Diem's fault, not ours."

In the same interview in the Xa Loi pagoda, Thich Tri Quang told me that his preferred solution for Vietnam was "neutralism," adding: "We cannot get an arrangement with North until we get rid of Diem and Nhu."

The Viet Cong are suspected of having led several of the attacks against property on November 1, the day of the coup d'etat. For instance, a small but violent gang of young people attacked and demolished the newly opened headquarters in Saigon of the Asian Anti-Communist League. This league had no connection, financial or otherwise, with Diem. Yet the coup-day rioters systematically removed its anti-Communist literature onto the streets, burned it, then wrecked the headquarters.

Whether the new military junta's government by committee can do any better than Diem and Nhu remains in doubt. The junta is ripe for further coups and countercoups. In any case, it was not because he enjoyed being condemned by world public opinion that President Diem engaged in repressive measures (mild as they were by Asian standards). The new Government will be faced by similar problems, because the fundamental situation has not changed. For example, the change of government has not altered the tendency of Vietnam's citified intellectuals to take to the streets.

Within two weeks after the coup d'etat, 10,000 students

at Hue demonstrated noisily against the military junta because it had not dismissed several professors who had been
loyal to Diem.   This is but one example of pressure by mob.
Can the military junta long tolerate decisions enforced by
street mobs, or justice by demand of the newly "freed" and
utterly irresponsible Vietnamese press?   Three newspapers
have closed--and rightly--already.   The smut and sheer
mendacity of the post-coup "free press" of Vietnam is one
of the blackest marks of recent months in the annals of Vietnam's so-called "intellectuals."   In view of the indiscipline,
factionalism and irresponsibility of citified Vietnamese, can
the military junta long escape resorting to the same tight
rein held by President Diem?

        The only sure thing in Vietnam today is that the United
States has set an extremely controversial precedent by en-
couraging, for the first time in our history, the overthrow
in time of war of a duly elected government fighting loyally
against the common Communist enemy.

CHAPTER III

1966

The winter of 1965-66 marks a change in the reporting of women correspondents in Vietnam. Two of the older generation of professional correspondents, Dickey Chapelle and Marguerite Higgins, were dead within weeks of one another. For the most part the women correspondents who began to arrive in South Vietnam in 1966 were in their twenties and early thirties. Few were as fervently anti-Communist as their older colleagues. Some were decidely leftish in their philosophy. Keyes Beech, who covered the war for the Chicago Daily News, has written:

> To a very large extent, the Americans in Vietnam were a reflection of American society in the '60's. There was a generation gap in Vietnam as well as the U.S.[1]

In 1966 the escalation of the war continued, with nearly 400,000 American forces in South Vietnam by the end of the year. The number of correspondents also increased to more than 400 by the end of 1966. There were enough women among these 400 to attract the attention of Time magazine, which devoted an article to the female correspondents in October 1966. Time reported that at that time there were nearly a dozen women correspondents in South Vietnam, and at least as many had visited on short term assignments.

Beverly Deepe, now working as a freelance correspondent since the demise of the New York Herald Tribune, was cited by Time as the woman who had been in Saigon for the longest period. Deepe told the Time interviewer that her biggest problem was facing the expectations of American troops that she be a living symbol of the wives and mothers they had left at home. "They expect me to be typically American, despite cold water instead of cold cream, fatigues instead of frocks," she wrote. "Always it's more important to wear lipstick than a pistol."[2]

Some of the women who had joined Deepe in the Saigon press corps had come to South Vietnam to join men who were there. Ruth Burns, a journalist student at Rutgers University, was one such woman. She had come to Saigon to join her husband, a helicopter pilot. The war in South Vietnam was unique in that women could follow their men to war. One can only imagine General Eisenhower's reaction if male reporters had expected to bring their wives and girlfriends with them to the invasion of Normandy. Burns, with accreditation from the North American Newspaper Alliance and from various magazines, interviewed village chiefs, peasants, soldiers, and shopkeepers. Her husband acted as her cameraman. Eventually she returned to the United States at the request of her husband, who decided that worrying about her safety was interfering with his ability to pilot his helicopter. Burns' articles earned her a William Randolph Hearst journalism award.

Two other women who came to South Vietnam with their husbands were Betsy Halstead and Pat Schoendoerffer. Halstead was only twenty-four years old, and was accredited by UPI. Halstead was the first reporter to witness and photograph a B-52 raid, according to Time, and the first to interview the mayor of Danang after Premier Ky called him a Communist and erroneously stated that he had fled the city. In describing her success as a reporter, Halstead told Time, "I've learned to keep quiet and not to argue. You can always sweet-talk someone into doing something for you."[3] Schoendoerffer was from France, the wife of a television cameraman. Wearing a blue straw hat with her khaki fatigues, Pat Schoendoerffer attracted attention wherever she went. Reporting for a Parisian daily, Schoendoerffer also seemed to attract adventure. While her husband was actively looking for action and she was not, it was she who was in an ambushed convoy.

Twenty-five year old Denby Fawcett, a former swimming champion, arrived in South Vietnam with her boyfriend, also a reporter, and remained even after he had returned home. Fawcett reported for the Honolulu Advertiser. She described life in Saigon as "harsh," adding that as an American woman she was a "curiosity, followed by stares"[4] wherever she went.

Fawcett wrote in the Advertiser of the everyday problems of
life in Saigon, where water in the shower, if it ran at all,
often ran red with rust, and where the nightly curfews and
uncertain electrical system made "normal city life" almost impossible. Blonde and attractive, Fawcett also noted that it
was impossible to sit down for a drink without attracting
lonely American servicemen who wanted to talk about their
own wives and sweethearts back home. Yet Fawcett had
little time for social life in Saigon, according to Time. She
covered both political stories and battle stories. When she
was under fire once at Danang, Time reported, Fawcett "took
pictures first, cover second."[5]

While many of the younger women reporters who were
covering the war in 1966 had little or no previous experience
as correspondents, forty-six year old Esther Clark had already jetted through the sound barrier, been the first woman
reporter to spend a day at sea aboard a submarine, and received an award from the U.S. Air Force for outstanding
service by a civilian when she arrived in South Vietnam.
Clark, who reported for the Phoenix Gazette, had come to
South Vietnam because she felt that she had to try to explain
to the people back home what was going on in the war. Clark
based herself in Danang. "I detest Saigon," she said, "The
war seems so remote there."[6]

Another correspondent who brought the experience of
years, if not of reporting, with her to South Vietnam in 1966
was Helen Musgrove, who would come to be known as Patches
Musgrove. Musgrove was a widow in her late forties when
she came to Saigon on what was to have been a brief visit,
and remained to work as a journalist for the next six-and-
a-half years. Musgrove became a substitute mother to the
hundreds of young servicemen she met during her career as
a war correspondent, even going so far as to dress up as
Santa Claus for Christmas parties at the various bases. In
return, the young men gave her shoulder patches represent-
ing their various units. It was from these patches that she
took her new name.

Born in Nebraska in 1918, Musgrove became a registered
nurse and joined the Coast Guard during World War II. She
was the first woman to be sworn into the Women's Auxiliary
of the United States Coast Guard. Stationed in Alaska, she
wrote radio scripts and broadcast to military men in the Pa-

cific Theater as "GI Jill." After the war she was married to
a surgeon with whom she planned to work in a clinic in Hong
Kong. When her husband's sudden death intervened, Musgrove went to Hong Kong alone to "fulfill a promise."

In Hong Kong, besides working in the clinic, Musgrove
established a dressmaking business, calling herself "Madame
Cheung." It was as Madame Cheung that she stopped in
Saigon in 1964 on her way to Thailand to purchase silk. From
the roof of the Embassy Hotel in Saigon she looked across
the river one evening and admired "the most beautiful coils
of rubies in the sky."[7] She was told that what she was
watching was a firefight from "the war across the river," a
phrase that was to haunt her when she returned to Hong
Kong.

In 1966 Musgrove was invited to place her line of
clothing in the Saigon PX. She opted out of the PX deal,
but decided to spend ten days in South Vietnam to learn
about the "war across the river" and to write about it.
Dressed in a pink silk suit, high-heeled shoes, and a picture hat, she went to JUSPAO and asked, "Where do I go to
cover combat?" After recovering from their astonishment,
the officers at JUSPAO accredited Musgrove as a freelance.
She picked up fatigues, a bush hat, and boots so large that
they had to be stuffed with padding, and went out on her
first patrol. Musgrove's first assignment was with a combat
tracking team which used dogs to hunt mines and hidden
snipers.

A few days later Musgrove flew to Chu Lai. She was
met in Chu Lai by a major who commented that he had seen
few correspondents in I Corps area, and that one of the
others had also been a woman, Dickey Chapelle. On the final
day of the ten she had scheduled as a war correspondent,
Musgrove was on her way to a hospital tent when she was
dropped off by a helicopter in the wrong place. "I didn't
know where I was," she recalled many years later, "but it
was colder than blazes."[8] She heard cries for a medic and
found a group of seven wounded men, their medic dead and
their radioman in shock. Musgrove took the most seriously
wounded serviceman in her arms. He was very young. The
man opened his eyes and, seeing a middle-aged woman,
gasped, "Mama, I'm so glad you're here," and died in her
arms. Horrified, Musgrove shook the radioman out of his

shock, crying "Get that dustoff (helicopter) here!" Back
at the MEDIVAC base she wept and told the officer in charge
that she was too old for this war and wanted to go home.
As Musgrove tells the story, the officer startled her out of
her hysteria by telling her, "God needed you on that hill."
It was all she needed to hear to make her desert Madame
Cheung for the life of a war correspondent.[9]

Back in Saigon, Musgrove rented an apartment and
settled in. Her apartment, a "little two-room hootch," was
near the Third Field Hospital. As an experienced nurse,
Musgrove would rush to the hospital when heavy casualties
arrived. As a journalist she wrote for seventy papers, but
especially for the Jacksonville (Florida) Journal. She spent
twenty days each month in the field and scorned the "five
o'clock follies." Musgrove preferred to see the war herself.
"I wasn't going to take any briefer's briefing," she said.[10]
On one patrol, a man pulled the patch off his shirt and handed
it to Musgrove. "You look like a grunt," he said. It was
the first of what was to become a collection of hundreds of
patches.

The escalation of the war was beginning to attract
correspondents to Vietnam from many parts of the world.
From Holland came Hendrika (Henny) Schoute, who wrote a
weekly column for De Telegraaf. Schoute, who had dreamed
of being a journalist since she was fourteen years old, had
worked for the Dutch news agency ANP and the Haarlems
Dagblad, one of the largest papers in Holland. She decided
to go to Vietnam in December 1966 after reading the Time
article on women war correspondents. She saved enough
money for a one-way ticket to Saigon, and settled into an
apartment. Schoute became the second woman--the first
having been Dickey Chapelle--to graduate from the South
Vietnamese Army's Airborne Training School. She made nearly
fifty paratroop jumps during the next four years in Vietnam,
Laos, and Cambodia. The closest she came to death in Vietnam was the day she jumped with ARVN paratroopers near
Bien Hoa and was blown off course by the wind. "I fran-
tically tugged at my harness as I slowly descended into a
huge roll of concertina wire," she recalled. "But I was lucky.
Just ten feet more and I would have landed in a minefield."[11]

From France came Michele Ray, a twenty-eight-year-old
former fashion model for the House of Chanel. Born in Nice,

France, Ray had supported herself and her son from a teen-
age marriage as a fashion model, until boredom set in. An
amateur racing car driver and a confirmed daredevil, she
organized an expedition on which four women were to drive
40,000 kilometers from Alaska to Tierra del Fuego. The Renault company provided automobiles and financial backing,
and Ray wrote of the adventure for the French magazine
Elle.

It was while she was driving from Alaska to Tierra
del Fuego that Ray began to develop an interest in going to
Vietnam. She decided, as she drove through country after
country, that it would be more interesting to go to one country only, to learn about it, and to write about it. She decided on Vietnam, she later wrote, because it was "the most
interesting place ... and also the most difficult to understand."[12]

Arriving in Saigon with no accreditation and no visa,
Ray took care of the first problem by going immediately to
Agence France-Presse, and the second problem by entering
the country on a 72-hour visa which she intended to extend.
Like other women correspondents, Ray first made a trip to
the Saigon black market, where she outfitted herself with
boots, fatigues, and other equipment. The Americans told
her that anything that could not be found at the American
PX could surely be found at the black market. Camera in
hand, Ray rode around Saigon in a cyclo pousse, trying to
ignore her terror at the wild traffic. She dutifully attended
the "five o'clock follies," where she was impressed by the
number of women correspondents. "Long hair was seen more
and more frequently," she wrote, "and the scent of perfume
or make-up mingled with that of cigarettes."[13] She longed
to go to the front, but wanted to go with another correspondent because of her hesitant English. Finally she had
her opportunity, when she joined a childhood friend, Christian Simonpietri, who was also a reporter for AFP.

On her first patrol Ray was chagrined to learn that
her major problems would not be snipers and land mines so
much as boredom and mosquitoes. Another, more delicate,
problem, she solved by drinking little. That way, she wrote,
she only had to find a private bush once a day.

Ray credited the influx of women correspondents for

the U.S. Navy's changed policy regarding women aboard
ships. After having been refused permission at first to visit
an aircraft carrier, Ray was asked two months later if she
would like to visit the Coral Sea. With a group of correspondents, of which she was the only female, she was taken
on an extensive tour of the gigantic carrier. That evening
she was surprised with a huge cake decorated with the words
"Welcome Michele," and an hour-long film featuring herself.
Apparently television cameras had covered her every move
during the day. That night she was the first woman ever
to sleep on board the carrier.

Ray's solution when faced with discrimination against
a woman correspondent was simply to ignore it. When a commander of the Special Forces refused to allow her to go along
on a mission, she went over his head. As a result, she
spent eight days with the Green Berets on a mission they
called "Operation Michele." The result of "Operation Michele"
was the burning of forty or so houses, and the collection of
sixty-three refugees, mostly women and children. This time
Ray was not bored, but still the major enemies she faced
were heat, rain, mosquitoes, and leeches, which had to be
burned off her arms and legs with a cigarette.

For a time Ray travelled with Pat Schoendoerffer. The
two French women created excitement among the lonely servicemen wherever they went. When they arrived in Danang to
cover a rumored visit by President Lyndon Johnson, they
were greeted with cheers of "Two French girls! We're the
luckiest unit of all!"[14] Ray and Schoendoerffer were in a
convoy of gasoline trucks going from Pleiku to Ankhe when
it was ambushed. In Ankhe they had an adventure of another kind when they wandered into a compound of prostitutes. The prostitutes were delighted to meet the two European women, insisting that they stop for drinks in one of
the little bistros, hugging them, and bombarding them with
questions. But Schoendoerffer eventually went home to Paris,
leaving Ray to bewail the boredom, bugs, and heat, and the
fact that the press camp smelled like wild animals and damp
wool in spite of the "Miss Dior" perfume which she sprayed
conscientiously twice a day.

Michele Ray was not the only daredevil French woman
to arrive in South Vietnam in 1966. In February Catherine
Leroy bought a one-way ticket in France and arrived in Saigon

with two hundred dollars and one Leica camera. Leroy was
only twenty-one years old and only five feet tall, but she
was determined. With photographers in fierce competition to
have their work bought by UPI and AP, Leroy decided she
would have to cover areas where there were no other photographers at work and, as a result, she was usually in the
thick of battle. She held the record, according to Michele
Ray, for numbers of operations followed by a woman correspondent. "A Frenchwoman," enthused Ray, "The youngest
of us all, too! Because she was so short, knee-high to a
grasshopper, they nicknamed her "hedgehopper." Her height
... no doubt made it easier for her to escape bullets."[15]

Leroy was born near Paris to parents who had hoped
that she would become a musician. But their adventurous
daughter, who had taken up parachuting as a sport, left
the Conservatory of Music, and saved enough money to make
the trip to Vietnam. Her professional experiences as a photographer was minimal, but she progressed from being barely
competent to being a first-rate combat photographer in a
short time, and was soon selling her photographs to UPI and
AP for fifteen dollars apiece. Coming in exhausted from combat operations, she would watch anxiously as Horst Faas,
picture editor for Associated Press, scrutinized her work.
From time to time Faas would clip one of the negatives as
acceptable. "Each clipping meant $15 for me," Leroy said.
"Sometimes he would clip a lot and I would come out $200
richer. I felt great then."[16]

These women were part of the so-called "permanent
press corps" of Saigon, reporters whose tours of duty in
South Vietnam lasted one year or longer. In 1966 there were
approximately 400 members of this permanent press corps,
but MACV had accredited eleven hundred journalists in six
months of 1966. Those who were not part of the permanent
press corps were classed as "tourists," who sometimes came
in organized groups with guides and interpreters and sometimes came alone. Some stayed for a week or less; others
stayed for one month or two.

One such "tourist" was Jill Krementz, who spent several
months in South Vietnam as a photographer. Krementz' book
The Face of South Vietnam, with text by NBC correspondent
Dean Brelis, includes scenes as varied as children in orphanages, crapshooters at the NCO club of an American airbase,

air strikes, and memorial services for dead Americans. Krementz, born in New York in 1940, began her career in the
fashion industry. In 1961 she took up photography and was
hired by the New York Herald Tribune as their first female
staff photographer. She resigned this position in order to
go to South Vietnam.

Another reporter who made an even briefer trip to
South Vietnam was Marlene Sanders of ABC, who spent three
weeks in South Vietnam in 1966. A veteran reporter, Sanders was thirty-five years old and was already anchoring the
afternoon news on ABC in New York when she was asked if
she would go to South Vietnam. She said yes with only the
briefest hesitation. She was the first woman correspondent
to be sent to cover the Vietnam War by a major television
network.

Born in 1931 in Cleveland, Ohio, Sanders grew up with
the idea that a woman could and should be a competitor and
an achiever. She attended the one year of Ohio State University that she could afford and then left for New York to
pursue a career in acting. In 1955 she was hired as a producer's assistant in television, and ten years later she joined
ABC as an anchorwoman.

Sanders' goal in South Vietnam was not to cover combat, but rather to tell the story of how the Vietnamese people
were going about their daily lives, how the troops lived in
the field, and what kinds of medical care was available to
civilians. Nevertheless, she had her share of exciting mo-
ments on the tour. She was tear-gassed twice while covering
mob demonstrations in Saigon and was often close enough to
combat to hear the sound of mortar shells. Besides, as she
observed, "You could get killed by just riding down the
road in a jeep."[17]

Sanders travelled from Saigon to Danang to Pleiku,
sometimes by jeep, sometimes stuffed in the back of a C-130
aircraft, and sometimes in a helicopter with open sides. She
sent film and commentary daily back to the United States.
She felt apprehension, but she says no real fear once she
was at work. She found her experience both fascinating and
upsetting. She had not been prepared for the poverty of
the Vietnamese people nor for the enormous suffering inflicted
upon them by the war. She came back to the United States

deeply disturbed by American involvement in what she considered the destruction of Vietnam.

Another veteran journalist who made a short, but memor-
able, visit to South Vietnam in 1966 was Martha Gellhorn.
The redoubtable Gellhorn had covered her first war thirty
years earlier, when she went to Spain during the civil war.
Born in Missouri in 1908, Gellhorn had been a novelist when
the Spanish Civil War broke out. In Spain she fell in love
with fellow correspondent Ernest Hemingway, returned with
him to Cuba, and married him. But when World War II began
Gellhorn was not content to remain in Cuba; by 1943 she was
back in London as an official war correspondent. In early
1944 Gellhorn was in Italy, writing from a press camp near
a ruined village outside Cassino, and travelling in a jeep
near the Italian front lines. Hemingway, in Cuba, fumed.
Gellhorn returned in March 1944 to Cuba and when she returned to London in May, Hemingway went also. However,
he had deliberately signed to write for Collier's, the magazine
for which Martha Gellhorn also wrote. Since he was the more
famous writer, and since a magazine was allowed only one
front-line correspondent, Gellhorn was blocked from any
chance of covering the fighting war in any official capacity.
Not surprisingly, the marriage did not survive.

Gellhorn did manage to scoop Hemingway once more,
however. Both covered the D-Day invasion of Normandy on
June 6, 1944. Hemingway, on a landing craft, was not allowed to go ashore. Neither was Gellhorn, who had covered
the landing from a hospital ship, but she managed to sneak
ashore with the stretcher bearers to collect wounded men.
When he heard that his soon-to-be ex-wife had actually gone
ashore on D-Day when he had not, Hemingway was so infuriated that he insisted ever after that the incident could
not possibly have happened.

After World War II Martha Gellhorn remained in Europe
until 1946 with the occupation troops in Berlin, and then
from March to May 1946 she covered the war in Java. For
the next twenty years she returned to her pre-war career
of novelist, living first in Mexico and then in London. In
August 1966 she returned briefly to the field of war reporting in South Vietnam.

Before coming to South Vietnam Gellhorn had formed

an opinion of the war based upon news reports and speeches
of American leaders. She expected Saigon to be a city paralyzed by fear and danger. She expected snipers, grenades,
and Viet Cong raids at any moment. Instead, she found a
small, efficient, and courageous fighting force engaged in
dirty jungle warfare, a great many servicemen doing dull
everyday jobs, and a population which was oppressed mainly
by poverty. Gellhorn challenged the American propaganda,
which she called the "fear-syndrome," and which she believed
demeaned the bravery of the actual fighting men, and glossed
over the country's real problems. She insisted that one result of the false propaganda was that it discredited both the
American and South Vietnamese governments in the eyes of
the Vietnamese people, who were certainly capable of seeing
the reality of the situation.

       Gellhorn spent a month travelling in South Vietnam,
visiting a provincial hospital in Qui Nhon, an orphanage on
the outskirts of Saigon, camps for refugees, and camps for
Viet Cong defectors. Introductions from the London friends
of Vietnamese citizens led her to private discussions with
newly-impoverished members of the Vietnamese middle class
who spoke cynically of the motives of both the Americans and
the North Vietnamese and who expressed longing for a peace
that they were sure would never come. "Unfortunately we
are between two great power blocs," one man told her. "Vietnam is the waiting room for the next war."[18]

       At Qui Nhon hospital Gellhorn pointed out that most
of the injured children had been injured by American bombs,
shells, and napalm. She appealed to Americans to help the
children. "We cannot give back life to the dead Vietnamese
children," she wrote. "But we cannot fail to help the wounded
children as we would help our own."[19]

       Gellhorn wrote that in all of her years of covering wars
she had never seen one quite like the one in South Vietnam.
It was not the actual brutality of the war which appalled her
so much as the hypocrisy. Taking from the indoctrination
lecture given new military arrivals in Vietnam the sentence
"to really and truly and finally win this war we must ... win
the hearts and minds of the people of South Vietnam," Gellhorn pointed out:

       We are not maniacs and monsters; but our planes

range the sky all day and all night and our artillery
is lavish and we have much more deadly stuff to kill
with. The people are there on ground, sometimes
destroyed by accident, sometimes because Viet Cong
are reported to be among them. This is indeed a
new kind of war, as the indoctrination lecture stated,
and we had better find a new way to fight it. Hearts
and minds, after all, live in bodies. [20]

In an interview with Phillip Knightley, Gellhorn told
him that the angry articles had placed her on some kind of
blacklist, and that she was not allowed to report from Vietnam again. If so this was hardly fair, as the tone of Gellhorn's articles was not unlike that of material being written
by other correspondents at that time. In fact one of the most
outspoken and well-known critics of American policy in the
Vietnam War also made her first trip to South Vietnam in
1966. She was Frances (Frankie) Fitzgerald, young, brilliant,
well-connected, and convinced that the war in Vietnam was
being seriously bungled by the Americans.

From the beginning Fitzgerald's articles from South
Vietnam stressed the negative aspects of American involvement
in the war. Like Gellhorn, she was not interested in battlefield action, but in the effect of the war upon the Vietnamese
people. Fitzgerald went to Vietnam as a free-lance writer in
February 1966, intending to stay only one month. The month
turned into a year and the beginning of a commitment which
would plunge her into an in-depth study of Vietnamese culture, and result in the publication of Fire in the Lake, a book
which has been called "one of the best descriptions and analyses of Vietnam ever published in English." [21]

Fitzgerald was born in 1940 to a family committed to
political involvement and intellectual achievement. Her father
was Desmond Fitzgerald, one-time Deputy Director of the
CIA; her mother, the elegant Marietta Tree, served as United
States Representative to the Trusteeship Council of the United
Nations. Her grandmother, Mary Elizabeth Parkman Peabody,
wife of a Bishop, was arrested at the age of seventy-two for
taking part in a civil rights demonstration and spent a night
in a Florida jail.

With such antecedents it is hardly surprising that Frances Fitzgerald brought to Vietnam a highly developed political

consciousness. She went with the intention of writing a few
articles but with, she insists, no preconceived opinions about
the war. She perceived almost immediately that "something
was dreadfully wrong"[22] with the war. En route to Vietnam,
traveling with her mother's friend William Blair, who was then
Ambassador to the Philippines, she visited the site of a dam
being built with Agency for International Development funds
in Laos. An AID official had made the dam sound like an
impressive accomplishment, and Fitzgerald was taken aback
to discover that the "dam" was in reality a pile of stones
being placed one by one by an old man against some chicken
wire. "That's when I started writing about language," she
says, "about the incongruity of what Americans were saying
with what actually existed out there."[23]

In Saigon Fitzgerald rented an apartment and set herself apart from the rest of the journalists because, she says,
she was interested in the politics of the war rather than
following American units around. Instead of covering combat,
she searched for documents, interviewed officials, and visited
hamlets outside of Saigon. The articles she wrote concentrated on the war's devastating effect on the structure of
Vietnamese society. She wrote of the refugees who had
swelled the population of Saigon, of people clinging to habits
of their no longer existent society. The question of who
was winning the war was absurd, she wrote. No one was
winning, nothing was happening, except that little by little,
the society was disintegrating.

Fitzgerald sounded the warning that the American failure to understand the Confucian-based politics and psychology
of the Vietnamese would prove disastrous. When she returned
to the United States after a year in Vietnam she immersed
herself in the study of Vietnamese history and culture. She
was contacted by Paul Mus, a French anthropologist who in
1952 had written a book on Vietnam, Sociologie d'une Guerre.
Mus' theory that Ho Chi Minh's revolution would eventually
prevail because it was harmonious with the essentially Con-
fucian nature of Vietnamese society had influenced Fitzgerald.
Mus in turn had admired Fitzgerald's articles from Vietnam.
He became her mentor over the next few years as she studied
Vietnamese history and culture and worked on her book.

As intellectual as Fitzgerald, and almost as well connected socially, Philippa Schuyler also made her first trip

to Vietnam in 1966 as the guest of Ambassador Henry Cabot
Lodge. A gifted pianist, she had made her concert debut at
the age of four and had performed with the New York Phil-
harmonic Symphony at the age of fourteen. Schuyler had
been invited to perform a concert for wounded soldiers at a
hospital in Saigon. What Lodge apparently did not know was
that Schuyler had plans beyond her concert performance.
For several years she had been combining her concert career
with one as a professional journalist, and her plan was to
see as much of South Vietnam as was possible and to report
her experiences to the Manchester (New Hampshire) Union
Leader.

        Philippa Schuyler was no ordinary journalist. In fact,
there was nothing at all ordinary about Schuyler. Born in
1932, she was almost immediately recognized as a genius.
By the time she was two and a half years old she could read,
spell 500 words, and recite from The Rubiyat of Omar Khay-
yam. Her father was George Schuyler, a distinguished black
novelist, and her mother was Josephine Duke, an artist,
writer, and dancer. These two talented people carefully
nurtured the genius of their only daughter, whose musical
abilities were early apparent. Her composition Manhattan
Nocturne was written when she was only twelve years old.
Her first book, Adventures in Black and White, published
when she was nineteen, described her travels as a concert
pianist, and also her insights as an American of racially mixed
background. She would use these same insights in Vietnam
to understand the failure of many Americans to communicate
with the Vietnamese.

        Educated at New York's Manhattanville College and
Convent of the Sacred Heart, Schuyler was baptized a Roman
Catholic at the age of seventeen. It is important to understand the depth of her religious conviction when considering
her attitude about the Vietnam War. Schuyler was politically
conservative and wrote for a conservative newspaper, but
she was too intelligent to be blind to the mistakes being made
by the Americans in Vietnam. Like Frances Fitzgerald, Schuyler could see clearly that the inability of the Americans to
understand the Vietnamese and their culture was dooming
them to failure in Vietnam. Unlike Fitzgerald, however, she
could never have accepted the ultimate success of Ho Chi
Minh's revolution as a solution. Because of her ardent Ca-
tholicism, she was intensely anti-Communist. "Communism is

our implacable enemy, and the greatest enemy of freedom in
our time," she wrote. [24]

At Tan Son Nhut airport in Saigon in September 1966
Schuyler was met by the mysterious Mrs. Dorian, ostensibly
an employee of JUSPAO, the Joint United States Public Affairs Office. Mrs. Dorian attached herself to Schuyler as an
official, and unwelcome, escort. Mrs. Dorian whisked Schuyler
to the Ambassador's residence where Lodge cordially but
firmly told her that it would be unwise to stay in Vietnam
after her concert the next day. Lodge pointed out that there
would surely be increased terrorism since it was a time of
elections in Saigon. Schuyler assured him that she could
handle terrorism, as indeed she could, having spent time as
a journalist in the Belgian Congo during the civil war in 1960.
Her dramatic articles from the Congo had been compiled as
a book, Who Killed the Congo?, in which she wrote, "I have
tried to present the whole bitter truth." [25] It was perhaps
knowledge of Schuyler's penchant for honesty which was behind Lodge's unwillingness to allow her to remain in Vietnam.

With Mrs. Dorian firmly attached, Schuyler attended
the "five o'clock follies," and received her copy of the official MACV news release. The release was dimly mimeographed
and nearly illegible, and Schuyler noted that several Australian
and British newspapermen around her were snickering with
open contempt as the JUSPAO officer droned on about structures damaged and air strikes, obviously unaware of what he
was talking about. Like Frances Fitzgerald, Schuyler immediately perceived the gap between reality and what was
being said. One of the British correspondents asked if the
geographical distance indications on the release were correct.
If they were, he pointed out, the target would have to be
somewhere in the Middle of Burma.

The audience laughed and the embarrassed JUSPAO officer had to admit that maybe the numbers were not correct,
and in fact he didn't know where the target was located.
Finally one of the correspondents volunteered that maybe the
target was in a certain location, the officer agreed that maybe
it was, and all of the correspondents duly noted the information on their reports like Schuyler said, "jurors in Alice in
Wonderland." [26]

Schuyler began to notice that Mrs. Dorian, though

uninvited, was always with her. Mrs. Dorian screened Schuyler's appointments, insisted on mailing her letters, and tried
to keep her away from "undesirables," which apparently included taxis, pagodas, and all Vietnamese people. Furthermore, Mrs. Dorian was vague about her own background, insisting that she was an American although she spoke English
with an accent, and telling Schuyler only that she had previously worked in public relations for "professional people in
Asia." Schuyler concluded that Mrs. Dorian was a CIA agent,
the first of several who were to keep an eye on her in Vietnam whenever they could find her.

        "I'm going to keep you right under my wing, just like
a little mother hen," Mrs. Dorian assured Schuyler.[27] This
was too much for Schuyler, who left Lodge's house to escape
surveillance. She had determined that she would stay in
South Vietnam as long as possible and see as much of the
country as possible. She decided to travel in disguise, partly
so that she would be able to mingle with the people, and
partly to escape her watchdogs.

        After leaving Lodge's home and finally receiving her
MACV press card, Schuyler adopted what she called her
"Through the Looking Glass" strategy. Every Monday she
promised Mrs. Dorian that she would take the next plane out,
which would be on Thursday. On Thursday she would suddenly delay until Saturday, and on Saturday she would post-
pone until Monday, when she would begin the cycle over
again. No doubt Mrs. Dorian was not fooled, but open con-
frontation was avoided, and the strategy worked.

        In Saigon Schuyler interviewed President Nguyen Van
Thieu, in spite of the efforts of a Tunisian woman correspondent who placed herself firmly between Schuyler and the
President. The Tunisian woman moved to block Schuyler's
access every time Schuyler moved to try to attract the President's attention. Finally the resourceful Schuyler sat on the
floor to catch the President's eye. She was impressed with
him, both by his good looks and by his firm opinions. Thieu's
anti-Communism naturally appealed to Schuyler, who concluded
that it was American intervention which was preventing him
from taking strong military action against North Vietnam.

        Schuyler flew to Hue on a military transport. On the
flight she met another mysterious character, who wore civilian

clothes but told her he was an American Captain. Curiosity
overcame her suspicions about him and she accepted his offer
of a tour of Hue, during which he asked her questions which
she evaded and she asked him questions which he evaded.
When she told him she thought that he was in intelligence,
he did not deny it. Eventually Schuyler and the Captain
reached an understanding based upon a mutual interest in
Asia and a mutual admiration of each other's courage. She
sympathized with the loneliness of his profession, which she
believed he had entered out of idealism. She shared many
of his views, and thought him the "kind of fighting man who
deserves a war strategy whose goal is victory."[28]

Returning to Saigon from Hue, Schuyler determined
not to leave South Vietnam until she had visited Chu Lai,
Danang, and other strategic positions in the northern part
of the country. Still playing cat and mouse with Mrs. Dorian,
Schuyler told her that she was too ill to take that day's flight
to India, but would surely catch the next one. Then she
went immediately to the U.S. Information and Press Center,
had her press card extended, and caught the afternoon military flight to Chu Lai. She wanted to visit the Korean base
in Chu Lai, and to interview some of the nearly 50,000 Koreans
who were fighting for South Vietnam. Schuyler admired and
respected the Koreans, whose anti-Communism matched her
own. The Koreans were clear on the issues, she wrote; they
knew it was "freedom versus Red slavery, truth against
lies."[29] She also felt that the participation of the Koreans
in the war disproved the theory that the conflict in Vietnam
was a white, imperialist war. However, she noted that at
least one American Marine was offended when Schuyler referred to the Koreans as "colored." He wanted to think of
them as "white," she reasoned, so that he would not be psychologically bound to be prejudiced against them.

Racism was a recurring theme in Schuyler's articles.
She noted it in the attitude that some Americans held towards
the Asian costume which she habitually wore. She had pur-
chased a traditional Vietnamese ao dai, the graceful long
dress of Vietnamese women, and she wore a conical hat and
sandals so that she could mingle freely with the Vietnamese
people. When she wanted to be totally in disguise, she added
a straight wig to cover her curly hair. She had been made
to understand more than once that it was "incorrect" for her
to wear Vietnamese clothing. An American Colonel exploded

in rage when he discovered that she was an American. Schuyler concluded that his anger was because he could not stand
for his comfortable prejudices to be challenged by a blur in
the lines of demarcation between races. Another American,
an intelligence agent, told her that wearing an ao dai discredited American prestige, which she concluded was an "obvious attitude that anything Asian is inferior to anything
American."[30]

Schuyler also believed that incipient racism was behind
the inability of many Americans to communicate with the Vietnamese. She was told again and again by Americans that it
was difficult to get to know the Vietnamese people. Since
she had experienced no difficulty in getting to know Vietnamese people, Schuyler concluded that it was the Americans'
own racial attitudes which were inhibiting communication.

Another recurring theme in the articles which Schuyler
was sending back to the Union Leader was the failure of the
Americans and South Vietnamese to take aggressive action in
the war, a failure which she blamed on the Americans. Seemingly all of the Vietnamese she encountered, from President
Thieu down to the humblest villager, let it be known that the
lack of American initiative was hampering the victory over
Communism. Schuyler believed that a show of strength would
earn the Americans more respect in Asia. In her first article
from Vietnam to the Union Leader, she wrote that the South
Vietnamese did not want peace at any price, but wanted victory over Communism. "If we do not help them gain that
victory," she wrote, "we will be betraying their cause and
our own."[31]

Schuyler's travels in South Vietnam in 1966 took her
as far north as the Ben Hai River. On the other side of
the river was North Vietnam. Gazing across the river, she
felt great sorrow for people she believed to be imprisoned
by Communism. Her biases were reinforced by the Roman
Catholic priests and nuns who provided hospitality to her as
she traveled. They in turn introduced her to other Vietnamese people of like mind, such as the woman in a hospital
ward who asked her why there were so many peace demonstrations in the United States. "Do the American people hate
us?" Schuyler reported the woman asked.[32]

For several weeks Schuyler traveled by bus, plane,

and bicycle. Her ao dai began to disintegrate under the
strain of a particularly vigorous bicycle ride and she held
the pieces together with hairpins. "The worn look made my
costume more authentic," she wrote. "Few peasants had
brand-new clothes in this part of the I-Corps area."[33] The
dark-skinned Schuyler blended easily into the crowd. She
had the look of a French-Vietnamese half-caste, and because
she spoke French fluently, no one suspected that she was
an American. Her ability to mingle with the Vietnamese pleased
Union Leader publisher William Loeb, who called her reports
the most authentic he had seen come out of Vietnam. Less
pleased were the American officials, particularly those who
were in intelligence. There is no doubt that her ability to
become one of the crowd worked to her advantage as a journalist. In a cafe in the fly-infested market in Thua Thien, she
sat silently drinking tea with a Vietnamese friend, listening
to others in the cafe tell stories of American atrocities. She
was aware that some of the young men and women in the cafe
might be Viet Cong. The atrocity stories disturbed her, but
she attributed them to Vietnamese misunderstanding of the
United States and its motives. She believed that the atrocity
reports were National Liberation Front (Viet Cong) propaganda
and that the photographs of atrocities were faked.

        Schuyler left Vietnam in late 1966 under what she des-
cribed as "inauspicious circumstances." Having offended
JUSPAO by her persistence in avoiding both protocol and
surveillance, she was left to find her own way to Tan Son
Nhut. In a driving rainstorm, she rode in a tiny car driven
by a friend, crushed among her bags. Reflecting ruefully
on the difference between her arrival as Ambassador Lodge's
honored guest and her somewhat humbler departure, Schuyler
tried to draft a thank-you note to JUSPAO Director Barry
Zorthian, but was unable to achieve the correct tone between
distress and diplomacy. She was depressed by the situation
in Vietnam. It seemed to her that few of the Americans she
had met had any understanding of the country or its people.
An exception, Jolynn Cappo, was a young woman who worked
as a translator for the Viet Nam Press. To Schuyler it seemed
that people like Cappo, one of the few who "knew anything
scholarly or substantial about Vietnam,"[34] should have been
involved in important intelligence work. The fact that Cappo
was instead doing routine work seemed to Schuyler to be
symbolic of the mistakes being made by the Americans in Vietnam.

The bleakness of Tan Son Nhut, darkened by a power failure, did little to improve Schuyler's mood. Amidst the din of shouting passengers and the outside noise of artillery shelling, she reflected that Vietnam seemed to her to be an "idealogical frontier, where the battles that are waged will affect men's minds throughout the earth."[35]

At almost the same time that Philippa Schuyler was traveling in South Vietnam, Madeleine Riffaud was traveling in North Vietnam. When Riffaud arrived in Hanoi in July 1966 it was her second visit to North Vietnam. In 1955 she had been in Haiphong witnessing the departure of the French. Although on the opposite side, Riffaud was as passionate in her beliefs as Philippa Schuyler. Just as Schuyler idealized the people of South Vietnam as noble crusaders against Communism, Riffaud likened the people of North Vietnam to the members of the French resistance with whom she had fought twenty years earlier. She believed that American bombing was consolidating the people of North Vietnam rather than demoralizing them. "Millions of people," she wrote, "are thus ready to sacrifice everything as we ourselves (the French) did at the time when we faced the Nazis."[36]

In October 1966 Riffaud interviewed captured American flyers, one of whom told her that he sincerely regretted the acts he had committed against North Vietnam. She talked to civilians who had survived bombing attacks and who told her that they were determined to continue the war until the Americans had been driven away. "Our country is determined to fight ten, twenty years if necessary for its independence," one farmer told her.[37]

To Riffaud, as to Philippa Schuyler, the issues were clear. But what was also clear to Riffaud in the North and was becoming increasingly muddied in the South was the war's ultimate goal. To some Americans, like Frances Fitzgerald and Martha Gellhorn, it was ridiculous to destroy a country in order to "save" it from Communism. To others, like Philipp Schuyler and Patches Musgrove, the only error was in not taking a stronger stand against North Vietnam. Journalists were beginning to look at the war from the point of view of the Vietnamese people, rather than that of the Americans or even the Saigon government. And, although their politics were as far apart as is possible, journalists like Fitzgerald and Schuyler were arriving at the same conclusion. The war was going very wrong.

SUFFER THE LITTLE CHILDREN _____ Martha Gellhorn

We love our children. We are famous for loving our children,
and many foreigners believe that we love them unwisely and
too well. We plan, work and dream for our children; we are
tirelessly determined to give them the best of life. "Security"
is one of our favorite words; children, we agree, must have
security--by which we mean devoted parents, a pleasant,
settled home, health, gaiety, education; a climate of hope
and peace. Perhaps we are too busy, loving our own children, to think of children 10,000 miles away, or to understand that distant, small, brown-skinned people, who do not
look or live like us, love their children just as deeply, but
with anguish now and heartbreak and fear.

American families know the awful emptiness left by the
young man who goes off to war and does not come home; but
American families have been spared knowledge of the destroyed
home, with the children dead in it. War happens someplace
else, far away. Farther away than ever before, in South
Vietnam, a war is being waged in our name, the collective,
anonymous name of the American people. And American weapons are killing and wounding uncounted Vietnamese children.
Not 10 or 20 children, which would be tragedy enough, but
hundreds killed and many more hundreds wounded every
month. This terrible fact is officially ignored; no government
agency keeps statistics on the civilians of all ages, from babies
to the very old, killed and wounded in South Vietnam. I
have witnessed modern war in nine countries, but I have
never seen a war like the one in South Vietnam.

My Tho is a charming small town in the Mekong Delta,
the green rice bowl of South Vietnam. A wide, brown river
flows past it and cools the air. Unlike Saigon, the town is
quiet because it is off-limits to troops and not yet flooded
with a pitiful horde of refugees. Despite three wars, one
after the other, the Delta peasants have stayed in their hamlets and produced food for the nation. Governments and

armies come and go, but for 2,000 years peasants of this
race have been working this land. The land and their families
are what they love. Bombs and machine-gun bullets are changing the ancient pattern. The Delta is considered a Viet Cong
stronghold, so death rains from the sky, fast and indiscriminate. Fifteen million South Vietnamese live on the ground; no
one ever suggested that there were more than 279,000 Viet
Cong and North Vietnamese in all of South Vietnam.

The My Tho children's hospital is a gray cement box
surrounded by high grass and weeds overgrowing the peacetime garden. Its 35 cots are generally filled by 55 little patients. One tall, sorrowing nun is the trained nurse; one
Vietnamese woman doctor is the medical staff. Relatives bring
their wounded children to this hospital however they can,
walking for miles with the children in their arms, bumping
in carts or the local buses. Organized transport for wounded
civilians does not exist anywhere in South Vietnam. Once
the relatives have managed to get their small war victims to
the hospital, they stay to look after them. Someone must.
The corridors and wards are crowded; the children are silent,
as are the grown-ups. Yet shock and pain, in this still
place, make a sound like screaming.

A man leaned against the wall in the corridor; his face
was frozen and his eyes looked half-mad. He held, carefully,
a six-month-old baby girl, his first child. At night, four
bombs had been dropped without warning on his hamlet.
Bomb fragments killed his young wife, sleeping next to her
daughter; they tore the arm of the baby. As wounds go,
in this war, it was mild--just deep cuts from shoulder to
wrists, caked in blood. Yesterday he had a home, a wife,
and a healthy, laughing daughter; today he had nothing left
except a child dazed with pain and a tiny mutilated arm.

In the grimy wards, only plaster on child legs and
arms, bandages on heads and thin bodies were fresh and
clean. The children have learned not to move, because moving hurts them more, but their eyes, large and dark, follow
you. We have not had to see, in our own children's eyes,
this tragic resignation.

Apparently children are classified as adults nowadays
if they are over 12 years old. During a short, appalled
visit to the big My Tho provincial hospital, among hundreds

of wounded peasants, men and women, I noted a 13-year-old
girl who had lost her left foot (bomb), sharing a bed with
an old woman whose knee was shattered; a 14-year-old girl
with a head wound (mortar shell); a 15-year-old girl with
bandages over a chest wound (machine-gun bullet.) If you
stop to ask questions, you discover frequently that someone
nearby and loved was killed at the same time, and here is
the survivor, mourning a mother or a little brother; loneliness added to pain. All these people suffer in silence.
When the hurt is unbearable, they groan very softly, as if
ashamed to disturb others. But their eyes talk for them.
I take the anguish, grief, bewilderment in their eyes, rightly,
as accusation.

The Red Cross Amputee Center in Saigon is a corrugated
tin shed, crowded to capacity and as comfortable in that
heavy, airless heat as an oven. Two hundred amputees, in
relays, have lived here. Now 40 Vietnamese peasants, male
and female, ranging in age from six to 60, sit on chromium
wheelchairs or their board beds or hobble about on crutches
and though you might not guess it, they are lucky. They
did not die from their wounds, they are past the phase of
physical agony, and in due course they will get artificial
arms or legs.

The demand for artificial arms and legs in South Vietnam may be the greatest in the world, but the supply is
limited; for civilians it had run out completely when I was
there. These maimed people are content to wait; Saigon is
safe from bombs, and they are fed by the Red Cross. To
be certain of food is wonderful good luck in a country where
hunger haunts most of the people.

A girl of six had received a new arm, ending in a small
hook to replace her hand. Bomb fragments took off the lower
half of her arm and also wounded her face. She has a lovely
smile, and a sweet little body, and she is pitifully ugly, with
that dented, twisted skin and a lopsided eye. She was too
young to be distressed about her face, though she cannot
have felt easy with her strange arm; she only wore it to have
her picture taken.

An older girl, also a bomb victim, perhaps aged 12,
had lost an eye, a leg and still had a raw wound on her
shoulder. She understood what had happened to her. Since

the Vietnamese are a beautiful people, it is natural that they should understand beauty. She hid her damaged face with her hand.

A cocky, merry small boy hopped around on miniature crutches, but could not move so easily when he strapped on his false, pink-tinted leg. Hopefully he will learn to walk with it, and meanwhile he is the luckiest person in that stifling shed, because the American soldiers who found him have not forgotten him. With their gifts of money he buys food from street vendors and is becoming a butterball. I remember no other plump child in South Vietnam.

A young Red Cross orderly spoke some French and served as interpreter while I asked these people how they were hurt. Six had been wounded by Viet Cong mines. One had been caught in machine-gun crossfire between Viet Cong and American soldiers, while working in the fields. One, a sad reminder of the endless misery and futility of war, had lost a leg from Japanese bombing in World War II. One, the most completely ruined of them all, with both legs cut off just below the hip, an arm gone, and two fingers lopped from the remaining hand, had been struck down by a hit-and-run U.S. military car. Thirty-one were crippled for life by bombs or artillery shells or bullets. I discussed these figures with the doctors who operate on wounded civilians all day, and day after day. The percentage seems above average. "Most of the bits and pieces I take out of people," a doctor said, "are identified as American."

In part, it is almost impossible to keep up with the facts in this escalating war. In part, the facts about this war are buried under propaganda. I report statistics I have heard or read, but I regard them as indications of truth rather than absolute accuracy. So: there are 77 orphanages in South Vietnam and 80,000 registered orphans. (Another figure is 110,000.) No one can guess how many orphaned children have been adopted by relatives. They will need to build new orphanages or enlarge the old ones, because the estimated increase in orphans is 2,000 a month. This consequence of war is seldom mentioned. A child, orphaned by war, is a war victim, wounded forever.

The Govap orphanage, in the miserable rickety outskirts of Saigon, is splendid by local standards. Foreign

charities have helped the gentle Vietnamese nuns to construct
an extra wing and to provide medical care such as intravenous
feeding for shriveled babies, nearly dead from starvation.
They also are war victims.   "All the little ones come to us
sick from hunger," a nun said, in another orphanage.   "What
can you expect? The people are too poor."   The children
sit on the floor of two big, open rooms.   Here they are again,
the tiny war wounded, hobbling on crutches, hiding the stump
of an arm (because they know they are odd): doubly wounded,
crippled, and alone.   Some babble with awful merriment.
Their bodies seem sound, but the shock of war was too much
for their minds; they are the infant insane.

Each of the 43 provinces in South Vietnam has a free
hospital for civilians, built long ago by the French when they
ruled the country.   The hospitals might have been adequate
in peacetime; now they are all desperately overcrowded.   The
wounded lie on bare board beds, frequently two to a bed, on
stretchers, in the corridors, anywhere.   Three hundred major
operations a month were the regular quota in the hospitals I
saw; they were typical hospitals.   Sometimes food is supplied
for the patients; sometimes one meal; sometimes none.   Their
relatives, often by now homeless, must provide everything
from the little cushion that eases pain to a change of tattered
clothing.   They nurse and cook and do the laundry and at
night sleep on the floor beside their own wounded.   The
hospitals are littered with rubbish; there is no money to
spend on keeping civilian hospitals clean.   Yet the people
who reach these dreadful places are fortunate; they did not
die on the way.

In the children's ward of the Qhi Nhon provincial hospital I saw for the first time what napalm does.   A child of
seven, the size of our four-year-olds, lay in the cot by the
door.   Napalm had burned his face and back and one hand.
The burned skin looked like swollen, raw meat; the fingers
of his hand were stretched out, burned rigid.   A scrap of
cheesecloth covered him, for weight is intolerable, but so
is air.   A week ago, napalm bombs were dropped on their
hamlet.   The old man carried his grandson to the nearest
town; from there were flown by helicopter to the hospital.
All week the little boy cried with pain, but now he was better.   He had stopped crying.   He was only twisting his body,
as if trying to dodge his incomprehensible torture.

Farther down the ward, another child, also seven years old, moaned like a mourning dove; he was still crying. He had been burned by napalm, too, in the same village. His mother stood over his cot, fanning the little body, in a helpless effort to cool that wet, red skin. Whatever she said, in Vietnamese, I did not understand, but her eyes and her voice revealed how gladly she would have taken for herself the child's suffering.

My interpreter questioned the old man, who said that many had been killed by the fire and many more burned, as well as their houses and orchards and livestock and the few possessions they had worked all their lives to collect. Destitute, homeless, sick with weariness and despair, he watched every move of the small, racked body of his grandson. Viet Cong guerrillas had passed through their hamlet in April the old man said, but were long since gone. Late in August, napalm bombs fell from the sky.

Napalm is jellied gasoline, contained in bombs about six feet long. The bomb, exploding on contact, hurls out gobs of this flaming stuff, and fierce fire consumes everything in its path. We alone possess and freely use this weapon in South Vietnam. Burns are deadly in relation to their depth and extent. If upwards of 30 percent of the entire thickness of the skin is burned, the victim will die within 24 to 48 hours, unless he received skilled constant care. Tetanus and other infections are a longtime danger, until the big, open-wound surface has healed. Since transport for civilian wounded is pure chance and since the hospitals have neither staff nor facilities for special burn treatment, we can assume that the children who survive napalm and live to show the scars are those who were least burned and lucky enough to reach a hospital in time.

Children are killed or wounded by napalm because of the nature of the bombings. Close air support for infantry in combat zones is one thing. The day and night bombing of hamlets, filled with women, children, and the old, is another. Bombs are mass destroyers. The military targets among the peasants--the Viet Cong--are small, fast-moving individuals. Bombs cannot identify them. Impartially, they mangle children, who are numerous, and guerrilla fighters, who are few. The use of fire and steel on South Vietnamese hamlets, because Viet Cong are reported to be in them (and

often are not), can sometimes be like destroying your friend's
home because you have heard there is a snake in the cellar.

South Vietnam is somewhat smaller than the state of
Missouri. The disaster now sweeping over its people is so
enormous that no single person has seen it all. But everyone in South Vietnam, native and foreign, including American
soldiers, knows something of the harm done to Vietnamese
peasants who never harmed us. We cannot all cross the
Pacific to judge for ourselves what most affects our present
and future, and America's honor in the world; but we can
listen to eyewitnesses. Here is testimony from a few private
citizens like you and me.

An American surgeon, who worked in the provincial
hospital at Danang, a northern town now swollen with refugees and the personnel of an American port-base: "The
children over there are undernourished, poorly clothed, poorly
housed and being hit every day by weapons that should have
been aimed at somebody else.... Many children died from
war injuries because there was nobody around to take care
of them. Many died of terrible burns. Many of shell fragments." Since the young men are all drafted in the Vietnam
Army or are part of the Viet Cong, "when a village is bombed,
you get an abnormal picture of civilian casualities. If you
were to bomb New York, you'd hit a lot of men, women, and
children, but in Vietnam you hit women and children almost
exclusively, and a few old men.... The United States is
grossly careless. It bombs villages, shoots up civilians for
no recognizable military objective, and it's terrible."

An American photographer flew on a night mission in
a "dragon ship"--an armed DC-3 plane--when Viet Cong were
attacking a fortified government post in the southern Delta.
The post was right next to a hamlet; 1,400 is the usual number of peasants in a hamlet. The dragon ship's three guns
poured out 18,000 bullets a minute. This photographer said:
"When you shoot so many thousand rounds of ammo, you
know you're gonna hit somebody with that stuff ... you're
hitting anybody when you shoot that way ... a one-second
burst puts down enough lead to cover a football field.... I
was there in the hospital for many days and nights.... One
night there were so many wounded I couldn't even walk across
the room because they were so thick on the floor.... The
main wounds came from bombs and bullets and indiscriminate
machine-gunning."

A housewife from New Jersey, the mother of six, had adopted three Vietnamese children under the Foster Parents Plan, and visited South Vietnam to learn how Vietnamese children were living. Why? "I am a Christian.... These kids don't ask to come into the world--and what a world we give them.... Before I went to Saigon, I had heard and read that napalm melts the flesh, and I thought that's nonsense, because I can put a roast in the oven and the fat will melt but the meat stays there. Well, I went and saw these children burned by napalm, and it is absolutely true. The chemical reaction of this napalm does melt the flesh, and the flesh runs right down their faces onto their chests and it sits there and it grows there.... These children can't turn their heads, they were so thick with flesh.... And when gangrene sets in, they cut off their hands or fingers or their feet; the only thing they cannot cut off is their head."

An American physician, now serving as a health adviser to the Vietnamese government: "The great problem in Vietnam is the shortage of doctors and the lack of minimum medical facilities.... We figure that there is about one Vietnamese doctor per 100,000 population, and in the Delta this figure goes up to one per 140,000. In the U.S., we think we have a doctor shortage with a ratio of one doctor to 685 persons."

The Vietnamese director of a southern provincial hospital: "We have had staffing problems because of the draft. We have a military hospital next door with 50 beds and 12 doctors. Some of them have nothing to do right now, while we in the civilian hospital need all the doctors we can get." (Compared to civilian hospitals, the military hospitals in Vietnam are havens of order and comfort. Those I saw in central Vietnam were nearly empty, wasting the invaluable time of frustrated doctors.) "We need better facilities to get people to the hospital. American wounded are treated within a matter of minutes or hours. With civilian casualties it is sometimes a matter of days--if at all. Patients came here by cart, bus, taxi, cycle, sampan, or perhaps on their relatives' backs The longer it takes to get here, the more danger the patient will die."

There is no shortage of bureaucrats in South Vietnam, both Vietnamese and American. The U.S. Agency for International Development (A.I.D.) alone accounts for 922 of them.

In the last 10 years, around a billion dollars have been al-
lotted as direct aid to the people of South Vietnam. The results of all this bureaucracy and all this money are not impressive, though one is grateful that part of the money has
brought modern surgical equipment for the civilian hospitals.
But South Vietnam is gripped in a lunatic nightmare: the
same official hand (white) that seeks to heal wounds inflicts
more wounds. Civilian casualties far outweigh military casualties.

Foreign doctors and nurses who work as surgical teams
in some provincial hospitals merit warm praise and admiration.
So does anyone who serves these tormented people with compassion. Many foreign charitable organizations try to lighten
misery; I mention only two because they concentrate on children. Both are volunteer organizations.

Terre des Hommes, a respected Swiss group, uses
three different approaches to rescue Vietnamese children
from the cruelties of this war: by sending sick and wounded
children to Holland, Britain, France and Italy for long-term
surgical and medical treatment; by arranging for the adop-
tion of orphans; and by helping to support a children's hospital in Vietnam--220 beds for 660 children. This hospital
might better be called an emergency medical center, since
its sole purpose is to save children immediately from shock,
infection and other traumas.

In England, the Oxford Committee for Famine Relief
(OXFAM) has merged all its previous first-aid efforts into
one: an OXFAM representative, a trained English nurse, is
in Vietnam with the sole mission of channeling money, medi-
cine, food, clothing and eventually toys (an unknown luxury)
to the thousands of children in 10 Saigon orphanages.

Everything is needed for the wounded children of Vietnam, but everything cannot possibly be provided there.   I
believe that the least we can do--as citizens of Western
Europe have done before us--is to bring badly burned children here. These children require months, perhaps years,
of superior medical and surgical care in clean hospitals.

Here in America there are hopeful signs of alliance
between various groups who feel a grave responsibility for
wounded Vietnamese children. The U.S. branch of Terre

des Hommes and a physicians' group called The Committee of
Responsibility for Treatment in the U.S. of War-Burned Vietnamese Children are planning ways and means of caring for
some of these hurt children in the United States. Three
hundred doctors have offered their skills to repair what
napalm and high explosives have ruined. American hospitals
have promised free beds, American families are eager to share
their homes during the children's convalescence, money has
been pledged. U.S. military planes, which daily transport
our young men to South Vietnam, could carry wounded Vietnamese children back to America--and a chance of recovery.

The American Government is curiously unresponsive to
such proposals. A State Department spokesman explains the
official U.S. position this way: "Let's say we evacuate 50
children to Europe or the United States. We do not question
that they would receive a higher degree of medical care, but
it would really not make that much difference. On the other
hand, the money spent getting those 50 children out could
be better used to help 1,500 similarly wounded children in
Vietnam. It seems more practical to put our energies and
wherewithal into treating them on the scene in Vietnam."
The spokesman did not explain why we have not made more
"energies and wherewithal" available to treat the wounded
children, whether here or in Vietnam. Officially, it is said
that children can best be cured in their familiar home environment. True; except when the home environment has
been destroyed and there is no place or personnel to do
the curing.

We cannot give back life to the dead Vietnamese children. But we cannot fail to help the wounded children as
we would help our own. More and more dead and wounded
children will cry out to the conscience of the world unless
we heal the children who survive the wounds. Someday our
children, whom we love, may blame us for dishonoring America because we did not care enough about children 10,000
miles away.

CHAPTER IV

1967

By 1967 there were nearly 500 accredited correspondents in Vietnam, but this number included wives of newsmen, journalists on brief visits, television crew members, secretaries, managers, and interpreters.

One of the newsmen's wives who was a successful war correspondent on her own was Linda Grant Martin; she was married to Everett Martin, Newsweek's Saigon bureau chief. Linda Martin, herself a former researcher-reporter for Newsweek, tended to write human interest stories, chronicling the effect of the war upon villages and families. In a 1967 article, "When Crisis is a Way of Life," which appeared in Mademoiselle magazine, Martin wrote about the women of South Vietnam. Although Vietnamese women appear fragile and delicate, she wrote, they are in fact strong and determined, with a history of heroism going back to the famed Trung sisters, who led the first Vietnamese rebellion against the Chinese in 39 A.D.

In mid-1967 Martin wrote about the more than one hundred U.S. military nurses, five-sixths of whom were women, who staffed the hospitals and dispensaries in South Vietnam. Martin, who was twenty-seven years old at the time, easily identified with the brave young nurses who were treating horrible wounds and living, in some cases, in remote field hospitals which were choked with dust in the dry season and seas of mud during the monsoon. Of the war itself, Martin wrote:

> "The Viet Nam war is a grimy, dirty war. It's a war where nothing is ever quite certain and nowhere is ever quite safe."[1]

While Martin concentrated on human interest stories,

other women correspondents were battlefield reporters such
as Jurate Kazickas. Kazickas, a free-lance writer and photographer, had arrived in Saigon in February 1967. It was
her second trip to Vietnam, but her first as a correspondent.
In 1965 she had stopped in Saigon for three days on her way
home from a year spent in Africa. She had become almost
obsessed with the idea of returning as a war correspondent,
for several reasons. One was because, like many Americans,
she was becoming obsessed with the war itself. Another
reason was that she had read the Time article on women war
correspondents, and had realized that it was possible for her
to cover the war. As a reporter, she felt that she should
go to Vietnam. Kazickas also had a more personal reason for
wanting to go to Vietnam. She had fled with her family from
Communist-occupied Lithuania after World War II. As a refugee from Communism herself, she felt that she should do
something to "save the world from Communism."

Over the objections of her parents, who pointed out
to her that they had gone to a great deal of trouble to remove
her from the dangers of war, Kazickas set about finding a
way to get to Vietnam. She first asked Look magazine, where
she was then working, to send her as a correspondent. Look
refused, citing the dangers of the assignment. Finally, Kazickas received letters from the North American Newspaper
Alliance, the Lithuanian Daily Worker, Maryknoll Magazine--
on the premise that she would write about Vietnamese Ca-
tholics--and Insider's Newsletter. Still she had no money,
so she went on the television program "Password," won $500,
and bought a one-way ticket to Saigon.

Kazickas' first story from Vietnam, on "Dear John"
letters and their demoralizing effect on soldiers, was published in Mademoiselle magazine in March 1967. At first
she had difficulty in obtaining permission to go on a mission;
permission would first be granted, then withdrawn. Beautiful
and statuesque, Kazickas often found herself hampered by the
paternalistic attitude of the officers, who persisted in treating her like a Las Vegas showgirl. One officer explained to
her that a lady shouldn't be out where she would get hurt.
Kazickas wondered what she was supposed to say. Was she
supposed to assure the officer that she wasn't a lady?

Ultimately Kazickas was allowed to go along on a five-
day patrol tromping through the jungle searching for a North

Vietnamese regiment. The regiment proved elusive, but the patrol introduced Kazickas to the rigors of military life, as she struggled under the weight of a 30-pound rucksack. In June 1967 she was at last under fire near Pleiku. She was surprised to find that she was not afraid, but she later said that she had a feeling of invulnerability when she was first in South Vietnam. She felt herself to be a spectator, and not really part of the war. By August she had been under fire so many times that the Marines were beginning to think she was a jinx. As soon as she arrived at a forward base, there would be an artillery attack.

Although she found the officers hostile to her as a woman correspondent, Kazickas had exactly the opposite experience with the ordinary G.I.'s, or "grunts." They liked the idea of a woman sharing their troubles and hazards, and they also enjoyed the fact that her presence distressed the officers. To find material, Kazickas would pick out a likely-looking grunt and interview him. Since his hometown newspaper would always buy the story, her income was assured. Kazickas was fascinated by the fact that some of the grunts actually seemed to enjoy the war. "Make no mistake of it," she said, "some of them really got high on killing."[2]

In November Kazickas found herself involved in the brutal battles at Dak To. She was horrified and sickened by the battle. Italian correspondent Oriana Fallaci, who was also at Dak To, wrote:

> The attack lasted sixty minutes and it seems that the first person to get to the top of the hill was Eurate (sic) Kazickas, a girl photographer ... when the Americans got there all they found was Eurate and stones and burnt tree trunks and pieces of bodies.[3]

Commenting on Fallaci's description of the battle of Dak To, Kazickas said only, "Don't believe everything Oriana writes."[4]

Fallaci herself had arrived in South Vietnam in November 1967, just in time for the battle of Dak To. She was already a renowned journalist, known for her sharp-tongued and sharp-witted interviews with the famous. When she arrived in Saigon she was impressed with the illusion of a normal

society. In the hotel everything was working. In the re-
staurant the table was filled with fresh fruit and the waiters
were dancing attendance. War and death seemed very remote. Fallaci has been accused of going to Vietnam prejudiced against the American cause, which she denies, but
she does admit to being prejudiced against war in general.
Born in Italy in 1930, she had grown up surrounded by war.
Her father was a partisan, often imprisoned for his anti-
Fascist activities. As a child Fallaci acted as a courier for
the partisans and guided downed British and American fliers
and escaped prisoners of war along the underground escape
routes. She wrote that the war in Vietnam was a tragedy
for everyone, for the Americans as well as for the Vietnamese.
Still, she was openly contemptuous of Americans like the U.S.
embassy employee who told her that the United States had a
duty to civilize people in the world who did not live in a
democracy, and she scoffed when Barry Zorthian of JUSPAO
told her that if Vietnam were to fall to Communism it would
be followed by Laos, Cambodia, Thailand, and Indonesia.
She had been hearing that song since before Dien Bien Phu,
she wrote.

If war seemed remote in Saigon, Fallaci found it almost
immediately, when she and a photographer named Moroldo
went to Dak To. Fallaci wrote that she was frightened, but
calm and alert, during the battle. Three days later she
went on a bombing mission. After seeing a napalm strike,
she admitted ruefully that she had been too preoccupied with
the pilot's ability to keep them both from being killed to feel
any pangs of conscience for the victims on the ground.

On December 19, 1967 Fallaci left Vietnam. Once outside the country she felt as if she had awakened from a bad
dream. "This must be why people accept war," she wrote.
"From a distance they don't believe it; they don't realize it
exists."[5]

One of the people Fallaci met in Saigon was Catherine
Leroy. She wrote of Leroy:

> She is a small blonde girl of twenty-three, with the
> body of a child and the face of an old woman. Her
> right arm, her right leg, her cheek, are covered
> with scars and she walks with a limp because the
> wound in her foot won't heal. I've asked, "Why

don't you go home, Catherine?"   She has shrugged,
as if I'd said something stupid.[6]

Leroy's wounds were the result of being hit by some
twenty pieces of shrapnel on May 19, 1967, while with the
U.S. Marines near the DMZ.   She spent a month in the hospital, which she described as her first holiday in many months.
She was hit while walking behind the advancing Marines, keeping three or four of them in her camera viewfinder.   She was
trying to get a shot of a Marine being hit when she herself
was wounded.

By this time Leroy had become one of the four or five
best free-lance photographers in South Vietnam, according
to Horst Faas of Associated Press.   She was still determinedly
in the front lines as much as possible.   On February 23, 1967,
she made a combat jump with the 173rd Airborne during a
battle called "Operation Junction City."   The following day
Brigadier General John R. Dean gave her the paratroop wings
with the gold star signifying a combat jump.   She wrote that
the wings would always be her best souvenir of Vietnam.

In May Leroy was with the second wave of Marines who
stormed Hill 881 near Khe Sanh.   At the summit she dove
into a bomb crater, but her camera never stopped clicking.
Life published six pages of Leroy's photographs of Hill 881,
including one particularly poignant series of a corpsman's
anguish as his friend died in his arms.   Leroy later wrote
of the experience

> I was with the Marines on Hill 881 and from now on
> the leathernecks will always remind me of what we
> call the Foreign Legion, 'des grandes queules au
> coeur d'or' (bigmouths with hearts of gold).   The
> pictures I took of a Navy corpsman leaning over his
> dead buddy summed up for me my fifteen months of
> war--I understood then what I was in Vietnam for.[7]

Two weeks later she was wounded.   She was still fran-
tically trying to get the film out of her damaged camera as
she was being loaded onto the evacuation helicopter.

Meanwhile Leroy's countrywoman Michele Ray had achieved
a measure of fame in quite a different way.   Deciding that what
she really wanted to do was to meet the people of Vietnam, Ray

concluded that the best way to meet them would be to drive from Camau in the south to the DMZ at the 17th parallel in the north. She brushed aside the fears of people who pointed out to her that many of the roads were controlled by the Viet Cong, and she convinced the Renault company to give her a car by assuring them that if she did meet Viet Cong, they would be sure to show her all the respect due a woman and a journalist. On December 8, 1966 Ray began her trip.

Tall and good-looking, Ray had no trouble in meeting the people of Vietnam. Children crowded around her; women wanted to touch her and talk to her, although she spoke no Vietnamese. American military personnel were understandably flabbergasted when she drove up. "Would you believe it," gasped one American sergeant, "a female reporter here in Camau, driving alone and with no grenade or pistol.... My God, I must be dreaming.!"[8]

At Blau, north of Saigon, Ray met a European family who were running a plantation, trying to remain neutral and conduct business as usual. Farther north she visited a leper hospital run by an American woman who had been there since 1959. She was Dr. Patricia Smith, called by the Montagnards "Ya Payang Ti," which means "the grandmother of all medicines." At another leper hospital at Banmethuot, Ray spent New Year's eve with the European Benedictine sisters. When she left them she traveled briefly with a Montagnard interpreter named Louis and a six-year-old Montagnard boy called Popol, who had become attached to her.

Viet Cong stopped Ray on the road to pay a toll, yet when she arrived at the MACV headquarters only a few hours down the road she was told confidently by the American senior officer that the Americans were winning the war and that the Viet Cong in the area were starving. In contrast, a Vietnamese lieutenant told her a few days later that he believed that, one way or another, the Viet Cong would win the war.

On January 17, 1967 Ray's Renault had a flat tire near Bongson on the central coast. Two Vietnamese students stopped to help her and were changing the tire when a Viet Cong patrol appeared. The students were released but Ray, feeling like "Gulliver among the Lilliputians,"[9] was taken prisoner. The group that marched away from the hidden and booby-trapped Renault included the Viet Cong leader, a young

man who told Ray that he was a Communist professor, and two
porters.   The captors sang revolutionary-sounding songs as
they marched, and commanded Ray to sing as well.   She sang
every song she knew, ending up with the "Marseillaise."

Ray was held prisoner for three weeks in a village,
listening to lectures about Communism given by the young
professor and, in turn, teaching him the words of the "Marseillaise."   During a bombardment of the village, she huddled
in a shelter with the professor for twelve terrifying hours.
Crying from rage and fear, and clutching the professor's
hand, Ray imagined the American pilots laughing and joking
as they pushed the buttons to release the bombs.

Finding her height quite a joke, the Viet Cong made
Ray a pair of their well-known black "pajamas."   She also
wore "Ho Chi Minh" sandals made of old tires.   She was
treated politely and solicitously by her captors, who told her
that she would be held for a "certain time."   Ray was strongly
attracted to the intense nationalism of the guerrillas, and concluded that she would be a NLF partisan if she were Vietnamese.   She noted that they hated the term "viet cong,"
preferring to be called the National Liberation Front.   She
wrote of one of them:

> Like every other soldier I had met, the head of the
> province soon brought out his wallet and showed me
> photos of his family, his children, and Ho Chi Minh.
> The same thing had happened on the other side, but
> with one difference.   What G.I. would carry a photo
> of President Johnson?[10]

In spite of her admiration for the guerrillas and their
cause, however, when given paper and pen and asked to
write a declaration that American Imperialists were killing
women and children, Ray refused.

On the morning of February 6 Ray was taken to Route
1 to a site within a few hundred yards of a South Vietnamese
Army outpost.   Her captors told her that she was to be set
free, and that any journalist would be welcome to come to
see how they suffered under the bombardments.   The leader
wished her "Au revoir" and invited her and her son to visit
his family after the war.   Ray was deeply moved.   She was
driven to the village of Tan Quan and released.   Crying

and confused, Ray nevertheless told the Americans who greeted her, "I'm feeling great!"[11]

Ray's good health, exuberant spirits, and high praise for the treatment she had received from the Viet Cong led to accusations that she had staged her capture. At the very least, grumbled American officials, she had been used by the Viet Cong to make propaganda. Ray countered that all she was doing was pointing out that the enemy was human. In principle, she insisted, she was neutral, but she admitted that she had found out that it was impossible to remain neutral in such a war. Her sympathies, she said, were not Communistic but nationalistic, but she was quite sure that she did not approve of the Americans dropping tons of napalm and bombs on the Vietnamese in order to save them from Communism. Ray left Vietnam amidst a storm of criticism, unperturbed by her critics, one of whom had pointed out that she had said before leaving France that she wanted to see the Viet Cong side of the war as well as the American.

Ray admitted nothing. But later she wrote:

> I may know nothing about politics ... but on the human side I have always thought of the G.I.s as my friends. But never have I identified with them as I did with the Viet Cong during those three weeks. Perhaps because the Americans are not overly enthusiastic about this war, they did not succeed in making me share a faith they do not have.[12]

Even as Michele Ray was making her rather unlikely assertion that she knew nothing about politics, two women correspondents who knew a great deal about politics came to South Vietnam. Politics was, in fact, the focus of their journalism. One, Elizabeth Pond of the Christian Science Monitor, came to South Vietnam on assignment; the other, Georgie Anne Geyer of the Chicago Daily News, came because she was in love.

Georgie Annie Geyer was already a well-known foreign correspondent when she came to Vietnam, but her area of specialization was Latin America. She wrote that Vietnam was one area she never mastered. "But, then," she added philosophically, "nobody else really did."[13]

Born in Chicago in 1935, Geyer was expected by her traditional German family to marry and settle down when she finished college. Instead, driven by a desire to be intellectually free and to see and investigate the world, she chose a career in journalism. In 1960 she joined the Chicago Daily News and in 1965 was sent on her first foreign assignment, to cover the revolution in the Dominican Republic. It was such a dangerous assignment that her editor offered to send her to Vietnam instead, telling her she could stay safely in Saigon. Geyer opted for the Dominican assignment. Thinking that "first revolutions are like first loves"[14] in that one has to work out one's own approach, Geyer was determined not to be a clone of the male journalists and to remain very much a woman. Nevertheless she was equally determined to ask for no favors because of her sex. The Dominican assignment was a success; there followed assignments in Chile, Cuba, and Boliva. Geyer became known for her sensitive and accurate coverage of Latin American politics. But she was unknown in Vietnam, and the country was unknown to her.

Geyer went to Vietnam because she had fallen in love with Keyes Beech, who was the Saigon correspondent for the Chicago Daily News. Their bemused editor accepted the inevitability of two of his best correspondents being in the same place at the same time, and agreed that Geyer could go to Vietnam in June of 1967. The trip was unsuccessful romantically, as Geyer and Beech struggled to come to terms with their relationship, but professionally Geyer scored a major coup when she was able to visit Cambodia at a time when Prince Sihanouk had expelled all foreign correspondents, and was able to obtain an exclusive interview with the Prince.

When Geyer arrived as a tourist in Cambodia, she learned that Prince Sihanouk was at Angkor Wat making a movie with his wife Princess Monica. Sihanouk, who was not overly burdened with modesty, directed, produced, and starred in his own movies. He liked American tourists, Geyer was told, and he might speak to her if he did not know she was a journalist. At Angkor Wat Geyer was able to meet Sihanouk, who theoretically did not know her profession. They talked for twenty-five minutes, during which he revealed to her that he was aware that Viet Cong guerrillas were in Cambodia, but felt that he could do nothing to stop them, since Cambodia was a small country with a small army. Geyer did not

believe that her tourist masquerade had fooled Sihanouk.
And, in fact, when the interview was published Sihanouk,
instead of being angry, sent her a cable congratulating her
on her objectivity.

Geyer found that covering the war in Vietnam was unlike any assignment she had had in Latin America. Fighting
was going on all over the country. As an accredited correspondent she could travel anywhere by American planes
and helicopters, but she found that often she would arrive
where a story was supposed to be happening only to discover
that the story was elsewhere. She, like many Americans,
was bewildered by the apparent passivity of the majority of
the Vietnamese people. She was distressed to discover that
the press corps, which was a close-knit and supportive group
in other areas, was bitterly divided in Vietnam. There was
conflict between the older correspondents, like Beech, who
tended to still be hawkish about the war, and the younger
generation who were idealistic and generally opposed to American intervention in Vietnam. There was outsider-insider
conflict between the "old hands" who had good friends among
the officials, and the newcomers who were suspicious of official statements. Geyer left Saigon in early 1968 disturbed
not only by the fact that personality conflicts and her own
overwhelming need for independence were undermining her
relationship with Beech, but also disturbed by the fact that
in Vietnam she had encountered for the first time journalists
who felt that they had the duty and the right to make judg-
ments and change society through their writing. She found
this attitude towards journalism dangerous.

Like Geyer, Elizabeth Pond also found a disturbing
kind of journalism in Vietnam. Pond, who, like Geyer, concentrated on the political aspects of the war, found that most
reporters covering the war had come to Vietnam with preconceived ideas about the war, and had then concentrated on
finding evidence to support their ideas. There was so much
evidence to support whatever theory the journalist preferred,
she discovered, that it was easy to practice this kind of journalism. "It wasn't dishonest in the sense of manufacturing
false material," she later wrote, "But it was at least evasive
in omitting the abundant material that contradicted one's pre-
conceptions."[15]

Pond, a Harvard graduate in international relations,

decided to go to Vietnam because she felt that the stories she
was reading in the media were not giving an accurate picture
of the situation.   She would have gone on her own, but was
sent by the Christian Science Monitor in August 1967 to cover
the South Vietnamese elections.   Her articles in the Monitor
about the elections stressed the bewildering aspects of South
Vietnamese politics.   In the 1967 election there were forty-
eight slates of ten candidates each vying for only six open-
ings in the Senate.   The tickets were trying to be all things
to all people by pulling together various regional, religious,
and racial factions.   In the presidential race two strong civilian candidates, Phan Khac Suu and Tran Van Huong, were
opposing the military leaders Nguyen Van Thieu and Nguyen
Cao Ky.   Suu was said to have the support of Thich Tri
Quang, the powerful Buddhist leader who had been instrumental in the downfall of Ngo Dinh Diem.   Pond covered a
provincial political rally which neither Thieu nor Ky attended,
to the annoyance of the populace.   Nevertheless, after out-
manuevering Ky for the top position on the military ticket,
Thieu was elected to the presidency of South Vietnam on
September 3, 1967.   After the election, Pond remained in
South Vietnam as a special correspondent to the Monitor to
observe the political situation.

A journalist who would certainly have fitted Pond's
description of having pre-formed opinions, Philippa Schuyler
returned to South Vietnam in early 1967.   This time there
was no official reception to welcome her.   She arrived quietly,
stayed with Asian friends, and rarely stopped more than one
night in the same place.   Once again she wore Vietnamese
clothing and once again she encountered official hostility.
In the months since her last visit, some of the activities of
JUSPAO had been taken over by OCO, the Office of Civilian
Operations, whose officials were no more helpful to Schuyler
than those of JUSPAO had been.   Angered by her Vietnamese
costume, an American official told her pompously, "It is the
consensus of opinion of PFC's up to generals that an American girl must wear American clothes."[16]   Schuyler concluded
that what he really meant was that it would be easier to follow her if she wore conspicuous American clothes.   Dressed
in her conical hat, ao dai, sandals, and black satin trousers,
she looked enough like a Vietnamese to convince most of the
people she met.   This made it difficult for the officials to
keep an eye on her, a fact she did not regret.

Unhappy incidents plagued her as soon as she arrived
in South Vietnam. In Saigon a bicycle swooped out of an
alley, knocking her down and injuring her leg. In Danang
her suitcase mysteriously disappeared and was returned hours
later with clothes and valuables gone and private documents
torn and disarrayed. And in Hue, as she sat writing, her
hotel room was invaded by three soldiers who broke in the
door. The soldiers, two Vietnamese and an American, told
her that they thought she was harboring Viet Cong in her
room. Outraged, Schuyler wrote:

> Is this an example of the quality of intelligence work
> here? There were no Viet Cong in my room--there
> was nothing but a typewriter and some mosquitoes.
> Yet at that moment real Viet Cong agents were busily
> mining the roads around Hue and real plots of "strug-
> gle movements" were being fomented within the an-
> cient imperial city itself. [17]

Schuyler wrote a series of articles for the Manchester
Union-Leader called "Vietnam--A Sea of Futility." In the
articles she fumed at the transparent attempts of American
officialdom in Vietnam to hamper her movements and influence
her writing. She raged over America's failure to take the
initiative in the war and win decisively over Communism. "We
cannot spend money and lives at this rate for years," she
wrote angrily, "If we are capable of winning, we ought to
do it now."[18]

Schuyler cited American racism and lack of understanding of the Vietnamese as a major flaw in American policy.
She admired what she considered American generosity in Vietnam, but did not believe that it was matched by American
intelligence. She was aware of the fact that she angered officials and intelligence agents by her ability to establish rapport with the Vietnamese, to live among them and be friends
with them. In Hue she had, despite OCO opposition, persuaded Air Force officials to airlift some Vietnamese students
to Danang to take their exams. One American official told
her that he couldn't see any reason why a Vietnamese should
go to school at all.

In Hue a fortune teller looked at Schuyler's palm, read
the cards, and told her that she was in danger of assassination. He warned her to beware of accidents and crowds. She

was astonished, recalling the bicycle accident of only a few
weeks before. But Schuyler was fearless, and remained in
Hue in spite of the fact that the city was virtually under
siege at that time. The roads around the city were heavily
mined, and the sounds of gunfire and shelling could be heard
at night. One night Schuyler was visiting the MACV enlisted men's club when word came that Viet Cong were only
a block away, planning to attack. Schuyler huddled in the
darkened club all night, waiting for the attack which never
came. She could not understand how it could be that the
Americans were on the defensive, waiting for the Viet Cong
to overrun Hue. Why were the Americans not attacking,
driving the Communists back into North Vietnam? Amidst
rumors that seven Viet Cong regiments were around the city,
poised to attack, Schuyler helped with the evacuation of Hue.
She was particularly concerned with students at the Catholic
school and orphans at the Catholic orphanage. Her unpopu-
larity with the American officials did not extend to the military, which provided transport for the children.

Her assignment for the Union-Leader completed, Schuyler
notified her parents that she would stay in Vietnam for a
few days longer to help the nuns evacuate the children from
the Hue orphanage to Danang. On May 9, 1967 Schuyler left
Hue in a helicopter with nine children. Ten minutes from its
destination, the helicopter crashed into Danang Bay. Rescue
helicopters rushed to the scene and pulled the crew and eight
children to safety. Philippa Schuyler and one of the children
were instantly killed.

Schuyler's requiem mass at St. Patrick's Cathedral in
New York City was celebrated by Francis Cardinal Spellman
and attended by 2,000 mourners. Honor guards provided
by the Third Naval District and Haryou-Act, a Harlem anti-
poverty agency, escorted the coffin into the cathedral. Schuyler's career as a war correspondent had been short, but her
abilities had impressed Union Leader publisher Loeb to the
point where he wrote, "had Philippa lived, she would have
probably been the outstanding foreign correspondent of our
day."[19] Loeb took up Schuyler's cause in the pages of the
Union Leader, stressing not that Americans should pull out
of Vietnam, but that they should increase their efforts and
win.

The death of Philippa Schuyler left Patches Musgrove

as the only woman correspondent in Vietnam at the time who
spoke out in favor of American involvement in the war. In
Vietnam, Musgrove had settled in and had become a virtual
member of the military. She traveled about the country, not
with the rest of the correspondents, but by hitching rides
with pilots who were friends, and riding in the cockpit. To
her collection of patches from various units she added a collection of hundreds of engraved cigarette lighters given to
her by the "boys." She campaigned against corruption in
the USO and for legalized prostitution on the grounds that
fewer Amerasian children would be born if servicemen visited
prostitutes rather than set up housekeeping with Vietnamese
women. Like Philippa Schuyler she complained against high-
level incompetence which she believed was prolonging the
war, and railed against anti-war activities back in the United
States.

But with the exception of Musgrove the women reporters
in Vietnam were now either vociferously opposed to the war
or were neutral in their reporting. A neutral stance was
insisted upon by the wire services so her own personal opinions never intruded upon the writing of Kate Webb, who came
to South Vietnam in 1967 from Australia. Webb came as a
free-lancer, and stayed to work for UPI. Born in New Zea-
land, Webb had been working in Australia, covering stories
of ANZAC troops who were being sent to Vietnam for the
Sydney Daily Mirror. Listening to "Vietnam talk" in bars,
Webb was struck by the fact that no Australian or New Zea-
land correspondents were covering the war, although ANZAC
commitment was considerable. One day she overheard a journalist say that anyone who could get to Saigon could get work
as a stringer, so she saved her money, took a five-week vacation, and went to Vietnam. She arrived in Saigon in March
1967 and "hung around" the UPI office doing odd jobs until
she was hired as a stringer. After a few months she began
to get stories on the political beat because of her knowledge
of French. It was also because she spoke French that she
was sent to Cambodia to cover Jackie Kennedy's visit to Prince
Sihanouk in November 1967. Webb soon impressed UPI with
her abilities as a hard-working, dedicated reporter. She
once spent ten days with South Vietnamese troops in the field
when she was supposed to be on vacation. Of her first experience under fire, she told an interviewer:

The first time I went out, there was a bit of a fire

fight, and I was so scared that I wet my pants. I
hoped the GI's would think that it was sweat and that
no one would notice. Then I saw that some of the
GI's had wet pants, too, and it didn't matter anymore.[20]

Neutrality such as was demanded by the wire services
was, by this time, rare. Many American voices were being
raised against the war. One such voice was that of novelist
Mary McCarthy, who was already an anti-war activist when
she went to Saigon in 1967. McCarthy admitted that she was
looking for material damaging to the American interest. As
Elizabeth Pond would have predicted, McCarthy found what
she was looking for.

McCarthy was shocked by the overpowering American
presence in Saigon, which reminded her of a western city
in the United States with a large Asian population, rather
than a city in Asia. When she went to Sunday Mass, she
was annoyed to encounter an American priest and a service
in English, although she found out later that there were
later services conducted in Vietnamese. She resented the
American products for sale everywhere, the smog, the children plucking at the sleeves of servicemen offering an intro-
duction to their "sisters."

Traveling throughout South Vietnam, McCarthy found
little of which she could approve. She visited refugee camps,
hospitals, and schools, but where Philippa Schuyler might
have seen evidence of Americans helping Vietnamese, Mc-
Carthy saw interference. And, although the two women would
have agreed that American policy in Vietnam was filled with
blunders, their solutions to the situation were antithetical.
Whereas Schuyler had insisted that the Americans must use
all of their power to win the war, McCarthy insisted that
the Americans must get out of Vietnam immediately. Not
surprisingly, McCarthy's assertions met with some criticism.
She was accused of simplistic thinking and of seeing only
what she wanted to see. But McCarthy was far from alone
in her critical attitude towards the war. In April 1967 massive demonstrations were held in both New York and San
Francisco. Approximately 100,000 Americans from every walk
of life demanded that the American forces pull out of Vietnam. Even so, citing the Tonkin Gulf Resolution, President
Lyndon Johnson announced that American troop strength in

Vietnam would be increased to over 500,000 and that bombing would continue in North Vietnam. At almost the same time, the U.S. President announced that he would be willing to cease the bombing if the North Vietnamese would negotiate for peace. The North Vietnamese, planning a massive offensive for 1968, understandably declined to negotiate. And the war went on.

VIETNAM VIGNETTES _____ Jurate Kazickas

<u>April 1967</u>. <u>Pleiku</u>: They tell me I can go on a bombing mission but at the last minute, the colonel decides he doesn't like the idea of a woman flying where it might be dangerous.

So we go, instead, on a parachute drop of supplies to a Special Forces camp in the Delta.

Back at the officer's club, I listen to their war stories, then some pilot comes in and tells us Bud has been shot down over North Vietnam. I remember seeing pictures of Bud's children. I think he was supposed to go home soon. All of a sudden, I feel depressed and lonely. Go to sleep in a big ugly tent and wake up in the middle of the night with the rain.

<u>May</u>. <u>Bong Son Plain</u>: They promised me lots of enemy action but everytime things looked as if they'd start to happen, the colonel's helicopter arrived to take me to another company.

They wouldn't even let me put my foot on a landing zone named after me--LZ Kazickas! A lady shouldn't be out there where she might get hurt, the colonel explains. What was I supposed to say, "I'm no lady?"

Managed to get into another battalion and spent five days tromping through the jungles in search of some North Vietnamese regiment. We didn't find a thing.

The heavy rucksack was killing my back and I told the captain it was starting to wear me down. He pointed to the loads the GI's have to carry.

When I got back to my bunker and my gear, there were three black mortar rounds strapped neatly to my pack.

So, I picked up the 30-pound pack and started to walk away.
"Yup, she's hard-core," someone said.

June. The Oasis, near Pleiku: It has to happen. My
first bad firefight. Strange to explain ... I wasn't afraid.
Guess I'm too stupid or there is just too much happening ...
Noise of guns, explosions, shouting, the cries of the wounded.
It seemed as if the fighting lasted all afternoon, but when the
shooting stopped only an hour had gone by. Felt so helpless
with the wounded.

One blond, smooth-faced boy--a bloody bandage across
his chest--keeps squeezing my hand and tried to smile. Just
don't know what to say. "Does it hurt very much?"

He probably thought, what a dumb dame, but instead
said "Oh, no, ma'am, only when I breathe."

June. Dragon Mountains: La-de-da. Dinner with the
general. He is magnificent. Tall, with gleaming boots and
starched uniform. Me: Blood stains on my fatigues.

Great roast beef, cucumbers in oil, even red wine.
Candles that keep flickering with the wind coming through
the tent.

Must remember what he said. "Real proud of my men.
Why they were just boys from the streets and here in Vietnam, they become men." Talks about kill ratios, miles of
opened roads, pacified villages.

He doesn't like the ice cream and orders it taken away.
Keeps dropping bits of spam into his dog's mouth.

July. Que Son Valley: Quiet times of war. Out on
patrol we come to a grove of coconut palms, pineapples, and
oranges. I discover that by mixing Kool-Aid with coconut
milk and pouring it into a pineapple shell we get a super
drink. Someone calls it Airborne Ambrosia.

We dig in for the night. Two husky, handsome GI's
share my trench. They are from New York. In the dark we

smoke and talk about their girls, nightspots they used to visit, the future.

Sitting on a bunker watching the sun go down. The sky over the village is swirl of pastels while off in the distance a jet plane drops its bombs and the horizon becomes a white tree-shaped cloud. I'm tired but not unhappy. The men are kind and friendly and the war seems to have stopped for a few days. Cool evening wind. Sound of children singing somewhere.

August. The DMZ: The Marines think I'm a jinx. I arrive at a forward base and minutes later there is incoming artillery.

"It's that broad's fault," I hear someone say. I chopper to another base. A quiet few days. An hour after I leave, ten rocket rounds struck inside the perimeter.

August. Hills near Khe Sanh: Am assigned a Marine escort for the long, tough patrol near the DMZ. Never did I walk so much or get so hot, dirty and tired.

I want to admit that maybe I am too weak for all that climbing, but am determined to stick it out because the captain can't stand me. I'm told later that my big, burly sergeant escort has collapsed at the base of the hill and is to be evacuated. He was nervous, apologetic, embarrassed.

"Can you imagine, she's tougher than a Marine," someone whispers--loud. I don't feel particularly proud.

September. Saigon: How good to look like a woman again! There is a package from home--some frilly slips, more ribbons, even mascara. I go to the press briefings and discover to my dismay that I am taller than General Westmoreland.

My Vietnamese family tells me that I shouldn't go into the jungles alone. "Why don't you look for a husband maybe," the lady of the house says.

November. Dak To: Bad, brutal battles for nameless hills. Two dead GI's, like young, tired boys sleeping against a tree. Can't write of the horror. Don't want to take pictures anymore.

December. Bu Dop: I've got to leave. I need a morale boost. My fatigues are sweat-stained and I itch. Sneak behind a tree to put on some lipstick and a ribbon in my hair. A GI walks by and shakes his head. "Where do you think you are lady? Fifth Avenue?"

March, 1968. Khe Sanh: Never, never will I forget this day. Interviewed a young lieutenant from New York. There was a shrill whistle and then a loud crash. We started running for a bunker but a rocket got in the way. When I touch my face there are pieces of shrapnel in my cheek. Blood on my fingers.

Why did it happen to me? I'm not a soldier.

Four Marines are wounded too and we are taken to Charley Med. No one is quite sure what to do with me.

There is a piece of shrapnel in that place where I sit and the doctors wonder how to be proper about it all. I am lying on my stomach. Have to say something. "Will the scar be below my bikini mark, doctor?" I asked.

He glances down and smiles. "Most affirmative, ma'am."

May. The Delta: I'm afraid of combat now. Thought I was so tough but now I can't fall asleep on the hard ground knowing that there might be a rocket attack.

There is only one course ... go home.

Reprinted by permission of Associated Press from the Eugene (Oregon) Register Guard, May 1, 1969.

What is really happening in Vietnam? Official statistics released to the American people make it seem that we are winning. Statistics released by the North Vietnamese government to their people "prove" the Viet Cong are winning.
One independent observer told me the Viet Cong control
about seventy per cent of the land in South Vietnam. We
and the South Vietnamese government control or "protect"
eighty per cent of the people.

So, who is winning? Hue, the third largest city, is
now so dangerous that most American women there have been
forcibly evacuated. The roads around Hue are heavily mined.
One takes a fantastic risk in going by road from Hue to Quang
Tri or down to Da Nang. The last time I went by road from
here to Da Nang, a vehicle was blown up near Hue, killing
four passengers and injuring two others.

I have received strict warnings from many American
officials in Hue to "get out of this hell-hole before you're
shot to bits." Curfew is eight p.m. for most American soldiers
in Hue. They are granted no liberty, and they are tense with
frustration.

Sixty-five miles north, the "peace bridge" called Hien
Luong, spans the Ben Hai river at the DMZ. North Vietnamese troops recently grabbed the permanent police post just
south of the bridge. I have met members of the International Control Commission team who had to flee south to Hue
because they had lost all control of the situation at the border. Quang Tri city, the capital of Quang Tri province,
was recently overrun by a massive Viet Cong attack. Thua
Thien and Quang Tri are the farthest north of the forty-odd
provinces in South Vietnam. Thua Thien adjoins Hue.

One observer told me that thirty-four district headquarters

in Thua Thien were under Viet Cong control, and only four
were not.   The Viet Cong want to cut off Quang Tri and
Thua Thien province just south of Hue.   They want to iso-
late Hue, and have the glory of capturing the ancestral im-
perial capital.   But also, they want to establish a new frontier south of Hue that will go from the sea to the Laos border.   The Viet Cong are flooding Hue with leaflets announcing
their intent.   Behind this is a strategic aim: the Viet Cong
want to chew off the top of South Vietnam so they will have
something to bargain with if there is a peace conference table.

Some analysts thought the Viet Cong would not really
try to capture Hue because it was a rest and recuperation
center for Viet Cong in need of a vacation.   At any specific
moment, Hue may be thickly infiltrated with Viet Cong soldiers recuperating their strength before they renew the
struggle against our soldiers in the countryside.

There are constant violent incidents in and around Hue.
Ten young Vietnamese girls were killed while en route to work
at the nearby Phu Bai American base.   A province chief and
many Vietnamese soldiers have been recently assassinated in
Hue.

Last night, I was in the enlisted men's club at the
MACV American military advisors compound in Hue.   One
hundred forty men live here, in the former Thua-Hoa hotel.
The E-M Club is bleak, with no entertainment but slot machines and a juke box which is now out of order.   At eight
p.m. the alarm rang in the club.   It was announced that a
company of Viet Cong troops were just down the street, preparing to attack.   A Viet Cong company frequently has more
strength than an American company, and may have as many
as forty men.   These are tough fighters and have aroused
a near-legendary respect.   There was a recent case of a
whole battalion of Vietnamese Army troops fleeing when a
Viet Cong company was sighted, and leaving four American
"advisers" alone to be attacked.

I was worried, because the Convent of the Sacred
Heart was just around the block from the military compound,
and a priest's residence was nearby.   These innocent people
might be injured by gunfire from either side if there were
a battle.

A great deal of machine-gun fire could be heard.   The
explosion of plastic bombs and grenades made a jungle rhythm
around the area.   The lights of the compound were suddenly
blacked out.   We rushed downstairs from the club and the
soldiers dashed to various posts.   Soon, they stood with
rifles poised at every window.   No one knew exactly from
which direction the Viet Cong would come.   I recalled the
horror pictures I had seen of Vietnamese villages half-destroyed
by the Viet Cong, and of the mutilated corpses they left in
their wake.

I was told to hide in the latrine if the Viet Cong should
break into the compound, or if bullets should start coming
through the windows.

I remembered with relief that I had been instrumental
in arranging the evacuation of twenty-four Vietnamese students
from Hue the day before.   Transportation had been hard to
find, but at least these young people were now safely in Da
Nang.   And I recalled a young nun whom I had been able to
help evacuate the week before.   While I was not personally
afraid, the noise of repeated gunfire from the dark shadows
of Hue made one tense and nervous.

The harsh, ugly rhythm of repeated gunfire went on
nearly all night.   But, miraculously, the compound was not
attacked.   About midnight, I walked alone out of the compound
and walked through grim, ominous Hue.   Sometimes I passed
groups of Vietnamese soldiers, half of whom were asleep.
The other half were chattering amiably.   They did not seem
greatly disturbed by the fact that war was taking place a
few blocks away.   Thinking I was Vietnamese, they greeted
me cheerfully.   They seemed to feel a bit of conversation
with me would break up the monotony of the night.

After twenty-seven years of military friction, war has
become monotonous in Vietnam.   The Vietnamese soldier, who
has never known a state of peace, has become very casual
about the whole affair.

Can one blame them for their terrific desertion rate?
Or for their frequently lazy approach to combat?   Vietnamese
are affectionate, sensitive men, who love their families.   They
are very sentimental about their wives and children.   Seeing

little purpose or progress in the war, they want to preserve
their lives for their families.   The Viet Cong are intense and
ferocious fighters, because they have an ideology.   Our va-
cillating strategies have kept those Vietnamese who are on
our side from having a sense of direct commitment to the war.

     The next morning, I asked many people what had really
happened in Hue the night before.   As is typical in the Orient,
everyone had a different story.   Some said the incident had
started near the sports stadium of Hue.   Others said the Viet
Cong had run into an ambush near the Providence high school.
In a park which was usually crowded with people, there was
a strange emptiness.   The astrologers and fortune-tellers who
usually congregated there had vanished, except for one, who
was being harassed by the police.   Pedicabs were hard to
find, and taxis, as usual, were nonexistent.   Later in the
day, I went out, for the first time in days, in Western clothes.
The pedicab driver insisted in covering me completely with a
canvas tarpulin so that only my eyes were visible.

     It is hard, under these circumstances, to feel sure that
"we are winning the war."   And even when you live in a city
like Hue, it is difficult to know what is really going on, or
to foresee what tomorrow will bring.

Reprinted by permission from the Union Leader, Manchester,
New Hampshire, April 21, 1967.

Dickey Chapelle (courtesy of the State Historical Society of Wisconsin)

Helen Gibson (courtesy of Helen Gibson)

[Opposite:] Georgie Anne Geyer (left) and Ernie Banks (center) of the Chicago Cubs with troops in Vietnam, 1969 (courtesy of Georgie Anne Geyer; photo by A. Fleishman)

Marguerite Higgins (courtesy of George Arents Research
Library, Syracuse University)

Marlene Sanders, Pleiku, Vietnam, 1966 (courtesy of Marlene Sanders)

Patches Musgrove (courtesy of Patches Musgrove)

Philippa Schuyler (courtesy of the Manchester [New Hampshire] Union Leader)

Marina Warner (courtesy of Marina Warner)

Elaine Shepard (U.S. Air Force Photo)

CHAPTER V

1968

t was Tet, the Vietnamese New Year. The Year of the Monkey was about to begin. At approximately 2:30 in the morning of January 31, 1968, nineteen Viet Cong commandos blasted through the wall of the United States Embassy in Saigon, killing two military policemen inside. Held off by the Embassy's Marine Guard, the attack lasted until dawn. By the time U.S. troops had regained control of the building at nine in the morning, the Embassy garden was strewn with the bodies of dead commandos. The attack had failed, but the shock of the assault on the Embassy was felt all over South Vietnam, and in the United States.

At the same time, other commando groups had attacked Tan Son Nhut airport, the Presidential Palace, and the military headquarters of ARVN. Some 4,000 guerrillas had infiltrated Saigon and were barricaded in the central city. And in Hue, 5000 guerrillas had been joined by 7,000 regular North Vietnamese soldiers, and had captured the city. Since January 21, the U.S. Marine outpost at Khe Sanh, near the North Vietnamese border, had been under siege. Dramatic headlines and stories such as Newsweek's on the Khe Sanh siege, and pictures of corpses in the U.S. Embassy garden, contradicted the official United States line that the war was going very well, indeed. Walter Cronkite of CBS, when he read the news agency tapes of the Tet offensive in the newsroom in New York, is said to have demanded, "What the hell is going on? I thought we were winning the war!" Although Hue was recaptured on February 25, and the Khe Sanh siege was lifted by April 1968, the damage done to American credibility was extensive, and probably fatal. Tet has been called "of decisive importance ... to the final outcome of the war."[1]

The importance of the Tet offsensive was not military, for by all military indices it was a defeat for the North

Vietnamese and Viet Cong. The Viet Cong never fully recovered its strength after the offensive nor could it now
justify its claim of being an army of liberation, since the
people of Saigon and Hue did not rise up against the foreigners and support the guerrillas. But the headlines and
the televised reports of fighting in the cities of South Vietnam strengthened the anti-war movement that was growing
in the United States. When President Lyndon Johnson announced on March 21, 1968 that he was not going to seek re-
election to the Presidency, it was seen as a victory for the
anti-war movement.

The Tet offensive was covered by several women correspondents. Still living in her "hootch" near the hospital,
Patches Musgrove was cut off from communication with the
Jacksonville Journal for thirteen days. When her editors
called the U.S. Embassy in Saigon they were told that the
Embassy had never heard of her. According to Musgrove,
the American military must have known that the Tet offensive
was about to happen. As early as Christmas 1967 there had
been fighting in the streets of Saigon which she saw as indications of a major offensive to come.

Also in Saigon during the offensive were Henny Schout
and Kate Webb. Fighting took place all around Schoute's
villa and she remained, at some risk to her life, to describe
the battle into her tape recorder microphone. Schoute's tape
of the battle of Saigon were a sensation in Europe. Webb
was among the first reporters to arrive at the Embassy on
the morning of January 31. She described the Embassy compound as "like a butcher shop in Eden, beautiful but ghastly
The green lawns and white ornamental fountains were strewn
with bodies."[2] Shortly after, she left for Pleiku, one of the
first cities to be attacked during the offensive. In the next
two weeks she filed stories on American bombers taking advantage of a break in the monsoon weather to bomb every
major North Vietnamese airfield, on a captured Viet Cong report of months of training prior to the Tet offensive, and on
members of the diplomatic corps sending their dependents to
other countries for safety in anticipation of a renewed enemy
attack.

Meanwhile Jurate Kazickas was in Khe Sanh. In March
while the outpost was still under siege, Kazickas was interviewing a young lieutenant from New York when they were

caught in a rocket attack. Kazickas was painfully, but not seriously, wounded with shrapnel in her cheek, forearm, leg, and buttocks. Although earlier she had seen a man's head blown off, Kazickas had felt herself to be somehow protected from danger. During her two week's convalescence from her painful wounds, she found herself considering the possibility that the head that had been blown off might have been her own. Although she lingered in Vietnam, mostly because of a romantic attachment, she was now afraid. She felt that her work was deteriorating. In May 1968, Kazickas went home.

When the Tet offensive began, Catherine Leroy was in Danang. Along with correspondent François Mazure of Agence France Presse, Leroy left immediately for the U.S. Marine base at Phu Bai, where the two hitched a ride with an American convoy to Hue. When the convoy stopped a few miles from the city, they rented a bicycle from a man on the road, and proceeded riding tandem into the city. They shouted "Bonjour, bonjour!" at the few people they passed, so that it would be clear that they were French and not American.

About a mile from Hue, they found themselves under fire as South Vietnamese bombers attacked the city. Leroy and Mazure realized that they were in an area of the city controlled by the Communists, and as bullets flew around them, they began to realize how much trouble they were in. They sought refuge in a cathedral already crowded with 4,000 refugees, but were told that they would have to leave the following day because the refugees feared that the presence of two foreigners in their midst might enrage the North Vietnamese.

Leroy and Mazure left the cathedral waving a white flag made out of one of the priest's robes and wearing big signs which said "Phap bao chi bale." (French press from Paris.) Leroy had stuffed her American and Vietnamese military identity cards and several cans of exposed film into her bra as the two correspondents tried to reach the military compound in Hue where the Americans were holding out. Distressed by her altered figure, the diminutive Leroy asked Mazure, "Look at my bosom. Does it look strange?"[3]

Almost immediately the two correspondents were stopped by the North Vietnamese soldiers. At first their cameras

were confiscated, but eventually were returned by a cordial
young officer who told them that Hue had fallen to the North
Vietnamese, who were now "liberating all of Vietnam." The
young officer seemed pleased when Leroy asked if pictures
could be taken. He acted as if he would be happy for the
publicity, and reminded her of American information officers
she had met. Most of the North Vietnamese soldiers insisted
on striking heroic poses holding grenades or leaning on a
captured American tank. Leroy and Mazure attempted to act
nonchalant as if hanging around with the North Vietnamese
army was something they did every day. Picture-taking
completed, Mazure said casually, "Well, we have to get back
to Paris with our story, so we'll be running along now."[4]
To their immense surprise, no one objected, and the two correspondents strolled away.

Leroy and Mazure made their way back to the cathedral,
where they were welcomed back by the refugees as returning
heroes. But their troubles were not yet over. They were
still in the midst of territory occupied by the North Vietnamese
When they again left the cathedral, Leroy told Mazure that
she would kiss the first two Americans she met. Cautiously
making their way through the streets of Hue, they came at
last to an ARNV compound and found two wounded Americans
there. Leroy promptly kissed them. After sitting out a firefight with the ARVN and the wounded Americans, Leroy and
Mazure finally reached the safety of the U.S. military compound the following morning.

Unlike Michele Ray, Leroy was not accused of having
staged her capture. She blamed her frightening adventure
on the fact that the U.S. Marines had told her the road to
Hue was secure, and it obviously was not. Nevertheless, the
story Mazure and Leroy told was deemed harmful to the war
effort by the South Vietnamese government, and Mazure was
expelled from South Vietnam. No action was taken against
Leroy, whose photographs of the youthful "liberators" of Hue
were published in Life magazine, but she remained in South
Vietnam only a few months longer.

When the stories of the Tet offensive reached Oriana
Fallaci, she was not in South Vietnam. She immediately
grabbed her knapsack, her tape recorder, and a bottle of
Chianti wine for her friend François Pelou of Agence France
Presse, and hurried back to Saigon. She found the city de-

serted. Refused a room at the Hotel Continental, she took
the bottle of Chianti and walked across the city to Agence
France Presse to a reunion with her friends. She was sympathetic to the plight of François Mazure, whom she felt had
been made a scapegoat because the South Vietnamese government could not expel the entire Agence France Presse staff,
although they disliked the tone of the French reporting. She
believed that Leroy was not expelled only because she was
working for an American news agency.

On February 25 Fallaci spent the entire day on the run-
way at Tan Son Nhut, cursing, waiting for a plane to take
her to Danang. The following day she was back at the airport, where she continued cursing until that afternoon, when
she finally learned of a cargo plane leaving for Danang. It
was the same plane in which Catherine Leroy, tired and dirty,
had just returned from Hue. In a brief meeting at the airport, Leroy warned Fallaci to be careful. But by the time
Fallaci reached Danang she learned that the final battle of
Hue had taken place, and the city recaptured by the Americans and South Vietnamese. "War is made up of this as well,"
she wrote, "wasted time, disappointments, anger."[5]

Fallaci left South Vietnam again, but returned in May
1968. She had learned of a new attack in which General
Loan, chief of the Saigon police, had been wounded. Loan
had gained worldwide notoriety during the Tet offensive when
he was photographed shooting a bound prisoner. Fallaci had
disliked Loan during a previous interview, but she was anxious to ask him about the incident of shooting the prisoner.
Interviewed by Fallaci in the hospital, a weeping Loan told
her he had shot the man because of rage over the fact that
the man had not worn a uniform and taken the risks of a
military man.

On May 9 Fallaci escaped death when a bridge was
attacked as she stood on it, and ten days later she was again
under mortar attack at Dak To. But she wrote: "In Vietnam I had been, like many journalists, very lucky ... you
have the impression to be invulnerable; that nothing can
happen to you, just because you are a spectator."[6] Fallaci
left South Vietnam disillusioned, unsure of what she felt
about the war there, or about war in general. Shortly after
she left, Pelou wrote her that Saigon was under constant bombardment and that Khe Sanh and Dak To, which had cost so

many lives to secure, had been abandoned. War seemed futile.
But less than a year later, Fallaci's invulnerability failed, and
an incident occurred which changed her attitude.

On October 18, 1968 Fallaci was in Mexico City, covering the story of Mexican students protesting the Olympic
Games. The students, and Fallaci with them, were fired
upon by Mexican soldiers. Shot and seriously wounded, Fallaci lay for hours on a balcony until she was taken to the
hospital. From this experience, and from her admiration of
the students who were willing to die for their beliefs, she
came to the conclusion that, in spite of all the horror of war,
it was sometimes necessary to fight and even to die for what
you believed in.

Even as Fallaci came and went from South Vietnam as
a visiting reporter, women members of the Saigon permanent
press corps continued their day-to-day coverage of the war.
Both Elizabeth Pond and Beverly Deepe were reporting for
the Christian Science Monitor. On January 3, 1968, shortly
before the Tet offensive, Pond interviewed a Viet Cong cadreman in an area within a few hundred kilometers of Saigon.
The cadreman told her that the Viet Cong considered itself
the only true representative of the fourteen million people of
South Vietnam. He assured her that the Viet Cong would
continue to fight for "five, fifteen, twenty years"[7] until
Vietnam was a unified country. If the Americans were to
withdraw their support, he continued, the government of
Thieu and Ky would simply evaporate.

The Thieu/Ky government had survived the shock of
Tet, with Thieu then solidifying his position by appointing
the respected civilian Tran Van Huong as Prime Minister.
Writing some years later, however, Pond pointed out that
Thieu's emerging dominance had in fact been underwritten
by the United States, which had made it eminently clear to
the military in South Vietnam that it would not tolerate another coup. By July 1968 Pond wrote, the corruption of the
Thieu government was viewed by Saigon's intellectuals as being as bad as that of the Diem government of 1963.

Lest one assume that the situation in South Vietnam
was in any way clearer than it had been before Tet, it shoul
be noted that in the same week that Pond was writing pes-
simistically in the Monitor about the corruption in the South

Vietnamese government, Beverly Deepe was writing optimis-
tically in the same newspaper about a decline in the quality
of both the Viet Cong and regular North Vietnamese fighting
man.   Furthermore, Deepe wrote, there was dissention between the North Vietnamese regular army and the southerners
in the Viet Cong.   But Deepe admitted that there had been
successful reconnaissance missions within Saigon, and that
North Vietnam's plan was to end the war during 1968 with
conclusive victory on the "many-faceted battlefield of South
Vietnam."[8]

Beverly Deepe had been in Saigon during the Tet offensive, and had written a three-part series in The Christian
Science Monitor about the impact of the offensive on the American position.   One Vietnamese observer told her that the
Communist offensive had precluded any American military
victory in South Vietnam.   In the kinds of terms which were
later to be condemned by General Westmoreland and others
who believed that the media had overreacted at Tet, Deepe
wrote that the Communist offensive had "dropped the political administration and military of the Vietnamese Government
control to its all-time low."[9]   Deepe correctly analyzed the
Communist offensive, concluding that it was not so much a
military victory as a propaganda victory.   The final impact
of Tet, she wrote, "would seem to be an increase and strength-
ening of previously dormant or unexpressed antiwar sentiment...."[10]

In May 1968 the United States, South Vietnam, and
North Vietnam began formal peace talks in Paris.   Georgie
Ann Geyer, who had returned to South Vietnam, wrote that
a mood of acceptance for a coalition government was beginning
to spread in South Vietnam.   On the other hand, she wrote,
the North Vietnamese, who were not interested in a coalition
with the Thieu government, were prepared for the war to
continue for two or three years longer in order to achieve
their goals.

In November Geyer went to Cambodia to attend a daylong "extravaganza" for foreign press and diplomats in the
provincial town of Battambang.   Prince Sihanouk astonished
the press by admitting that it would be to his benefit for
the United States to remain in South Vietnam.   Sihanouk
feared Communism within his own country, and he feared
Vietnamese invasion.   He seemed aware that his regime

was doomed. Showing Geyer and other journalists through
a western-style motel in Battambang, he told them without
emotion, "But soon we will all die."[11]

Geyer wrote of the dissent between the Saigon govern-
ment and the United States. The South Vietnamese sought
reassurance from the United States that there would be no
coalition government and no recognition of the Viet Cong.
At the same time that he was publicly denouncing the Paris
Peace Talks, however, Thieu was privately organizing a South
Vietnamese delegation to attend them, Geyer wrote. By December, when an agreement was finally reached to send a
South Vietnamese delegation to Paris, Geyer likened the
South Vietnamese and American governments to "squabbling
lovers." As with many couples, Geyer wrote, "the main point
of contention was who should be the boss and who might ap-
pear to be."[12]

Just as the American military commitment in South Vietnam peaked at 536,000 troops in 1968, the number of correspondents covering the war also reached its highest point of
more than 450 just before the Tet offensive. A list of accredited correspondents at the time includes the names of a
number of women. Working for American media were Anne
Allen and Ann Bryan of Overseas Weekly, Joyce Bolo and
Flora Lewis of the Washington Post, Louise Stone and Kate
Webb of UPI, Frances Tate of Scripps-Howard Newspapers,
and Johanna Tuohy of the Los Angeles Times. Free-lancers
included Virginia Anderson, Eloise Henkel, Rebecca Lescaze,
Helen (Patches) Musgrove, Gloria Needham, and Elizabeth
Resler. In addition, there were Kristina Bohman of Sweden's
Dagens Nyheter, Suzanne Strauss of the Canadian Broadcasting Corporation, Isabell Van Geen of the French publication
Vietnam Nouveau, Marie Helene Lylap, a French woman working for CBS news, and Shirley Pelou, an American working
for Agence France Presse. Some of these women were wives
of newsmen and may have had accreditation in order to be
with their husbands.

Some of the newsmen's wives were journalists in their
own right, however. Helen Gibson came to Saigon because
her husband, Nat Gibson, was sent there by UPI. After
she arrived in March 1968, however, she worked for UPI herself, covering both political and military stories. Gibson's
experiences included going along on bombing missions in both
American and Vietnamese bombers, going on a defoliating mis

sion, and interviewing pilots on American aircraft carriers.
She learned to parachute with the Vietnamese airborne and
was in one of their camps while it was under siege. Gibson
spent some time with the Special Forces, "drank rice wine
as an initiation rite with the Montagnards, rode elephants."[13]
On a patrol with the Vietnamese paramilitary police in the
Delta, the American sergeant assigned as Gibson's escort was
blown up by a mine. She herself was caught in a rocket
attack on the Marine press center in Danang.

Another newsman's wife who was herself a journalist
was Susie Kirk, a 1965 graduate of the Columbia School of
Journalism. Upon graduation she married Donald Kirk of
the Washington Star, and a few days later they went to Asia
as free-lance reporters. Going first to Hong Kong and Indonesia, they arrived in South Vietnam in December 1967.
Kirk worked in South Vietnam for DPA, the German Press
Agency. She admitted that she was pretty new at war correspondence, but in her opinion none of the correspondents
was doing a good job of covering the war. The war was so
complex, she said, that the correspondents "just haven't been
able really to keep up with what's going on here."[14]

Liz Trotta of NBC agreed with Kirk. "This war has
been covered by people who have come here with assumptions
already formed," she said. "Valid opinions about this war
are not easy to come by."[15] Trotta arrived in South Vietnam
on six months assignment in August 1968. She was 31 years
old, a veteran of eight years' experience in news work with
Newsday, the Associated Press, the Chicago Tribune, and
NBC.

Spending about three-quarters of her time in South
Vietnam in the field, Trotta covered any and every available story. She was impressed with the quality of the troops,
both Vietnamese and American. "They are such gentlemen and
so brave,"[16] she wrote. Traveling with her cameraman Yuni-
chi Yasuda, Trotta saw action at Tay Ninh, Trang Dang, and
in the Delta. She wrote of wading through leech-filled water,
and hitting the dirt under sniper fire. Crouched in the mud
with the soldiers, Trotta looked up to see Yasuda still standing, calmly filming the action.

Trotta found some of her experiences in South Vietnam
bizarre, as when she was in a helicopter going to cover an

operation in the Mekong Delta, and an army major hitched a
ride part of the way. The happy major was due to go home
in a few days. When the helicopter stopped to refuel at Long
Binh, the major got off and returned with martinis for everyone except the flight crew. Trotta found it decidedly weird
to be drinking martinis in midair while below her people were
dying.

Trotta was aware of the dangers in her assignment.
"Every now and then I'd ask myself what I was doing here,"
she wrote. "And then the answer was the same, you're covering a story."[17]

Trotta's observation that many reporters were covering the Vietnam war with assumptions already formed was
nowhere more evident than in the writing of Mary McCarthy
and Susan Sontag, women who were vehemently opposed to
American intervention in the war. McCarthy's call for immediate withdrawal from South Vietnam (in her essay reporting on her 1967 visit to Saigon) was met with criticism both
from those who advocated staying in the war until we won
and those who urged eventual withdrawal but thought that
McCarthy's recommendations ignored America's commitment
to democracy and anti-Communism, not to mention our commitment to the South Vietnamese. Unperturbed, McCarthy
returned to the war, only this time she went to North Vietnam

Arriving in Hanoi in March 1968, McCarthy was somewhat taken aback by the anti-American rhetoric and the
portraits of Josef Stalin she saw. Nevertheless, she was
pleased with Hanoi, with the clean hot water at the hotel,
with the lack of mosquitoes. She noted that Hanoi was re-
markably clean, in spite of the bombing, and noted that
there were no prostitutes or ragged children with sores, and
that wherever she went she was met with smiles, cheers, and
applause.

McCarthy has been accused of purposely suppressing
what she did not want to see and hear in Hanoi. When she
inquired about dissenters in North Vietnam she was told that
the license to criticize was a capitalist luxury. McCarthy,
a critic by profession, let this statement pass without com-
ment. When she interviewed two American prisoners-of-war,
she was baffled by their apparent naiveté and stiff phraseolog
which she finally attributed to "mental malnutrition" brought

on by their inferior American schooling and Army training.
One of the men later wrote a book in which he explained that
he and the other man had seemed constrained because they
had been playing the parts of "grateful prisoners" in order
to avoid torture, a possibility which seemingly never occurred
to McCarthy. At any rate, McCarthy did not deny that she
was biased in favor of North Vietnam, so strong was her
belief that America had no right to be in Vietnam at all.

McCarthy visited the Hanoi War Crimes Museum, where
she was presented with a ring made from a downed American
plane. She wrote that she was horrified, but did not have
the courage to refuse the ring. She visited the Hanoi zoo,
and noted that the lions and tigers had been turned loose in
the forests lest they be accidentally freed in the city by a
bombing attack. Oddly, McCarthy equated this with the dis-
persal to other hospitals of leprosy patients after a leper
hospital was bombed. McCarthy visited schools and hospitals
in Hanoi, and scrambled for the safety of air raid shelters
with the North Vietnamese citizens. She saw nothing in North
Vietnam that she could not admire, or at least justify. Mc-
Carthy's report on North Vietnam was criticized for "lack of
objectivity so profound as to make even sympathizers wary,"[18]
but she had never pretended to be objective.

Similarly, critic Susan Sontag, arriving in Hanoi in
May 1968, was biased in favor of North Vietnam before she
arrived. Nevertheless, her essay on her trip to North Vietnam is more even in tone than McCarthy's highly emotional
one. Sontag suffered some misgivings when she first arrived
in Hanoi, and was at first unable to identify with the North
Vietnamese. Furthermore, she was aware that her praise
for North Vietnam evoked the "cliché of the Western left-
wing intellectual idealizing an agrarian revolution."[19]

Gradually, however, Sontag found her attitude changing. As she found it easier to communicate with the North
Vietnamese people, she came to the opinion that their's was
a remarkable society, and that the North Vietnamese were
a remarkable people. Like McCarthy, Sontag was impressed
that the North Vietnamese seemed to bear no grudge towards
Americans. McCarthy had noted, in fact, that she had encountered more hostility against Americans in South Vietnam
than in North Vietnam.

Having been won over by the North Vietnamese society, Sontag did not hesitate to idealize it. She wrote that the North Vietnamese government was one which believed that nothing was more precious than independence and liberty. The pictures of Stalin hanging on nearly every wall bothered her as they had McCarthy, but, whereas McCarthy had offered no explanation for pictures of Stalin appearing in such a peace and love-oriented society, Sontag rationalized that they had not been removed because the North Vietnamese hated to waste anything. Or perhaps, she suggested, the pictures were a way of paying a polite tribute to the "idea" of unity and solidarity between Communist societies. It did not seem possible to her that the North Vietnamese could actually admire a totalitarian dictator.

Sontag remained in North Vietnam for two weeks. She traveled in the countryside, talked to people at every level of society, and viewed the ruins left by American bombs. Unlike McCarthy, she did not talk to captured Americans, but had no trouble believing the information given her by a North Vietnamese Army officer, who told her that the prisoners were well treated and were given bigger portions of food than the North Vietnamese people, because they were bigger people. Also unlike McCarthy, Sontag did write that she suspected at times that she was succumbing to what she wanted to believe. But finally she concluded that her abstract suspicions must be overruled by her actual experiences. She left North Vietnam convinced that the North Vietnamese genuinely loved and admired their leaders, and what was even more astonishing, that the government loved the people in return.

Another woman correspondent who traveled in North Vietnam in 1968 was Gemma Araneta from the Philippines. Araneta arrived in Hanoi in May 1968, and may have been there at the same time as Sontag, although there is no record that they met. Araneta favored the North Vietnamese cause, and was impressed with the North Vietnamese people and their determination to win the war. However, she wrote that by the end of her tour she was growing weary of North Vietnamese propaganda, which she decided was every bit as ludicrous as American propaganda.

Araneta visited the Women's Association of Vietnam, where she was told that the three responsibilities of women of North Vietnam were to guarantee production in order to free men for fighting at the front, to encourage husbands and sons to fight, and when necessary, to fight themselves. She was told that the "Three Responsibilities" movement was very popular and that two-and-a-half million women belonged. Araneta thought the women of North Vietnam feminine and flirtatious in spite of the shapeless army fatigues and factory smocks they wore. But, when she asked them what kind of man they would like to marry, unromantic pragmatism took over, and they told her that the ideal man was one with progressive ideas, compatible with the socialist regime. Staggered, Araneta wondered if the lovers she had seen strolling in Hanoi had been whispering romantically or simply discussing the struggle against American Imperialism. Her fascination with the women of North Vietnam was returned, as the women told her they had never seen an Asian woman as tall as the 5'10" Araneta.

Araneta traveled in the provinces, interviewing peasants and military people. She was particularly impressed with meeting Nguyen Thi Hanh, the young woman commander of a provincial defense unit, who was a national heroine because she had personally captured a downed American pilot. Such courage was typical of the North Vietnamese, according to Araneta. "Determination is evident all over the Democratic Republic of Vietnam, she wrote. "Political slogans, graffiti on the mud walls of humble peasant huts, rallying mottoes carved on mountain peaks--all echo the indomitable Vietnamese spirit."[20]

Such descriptions of the North Vietnamese, being written by Americans like McCarthy and Sontag as well as writers from other countries, represented what was by now a serious problem in the United States. The Tet offensive, while not a military victory for the North Vietnamese, had severely damaged American credibility, and many people were beginning to ask just what we were doing in Vietnam. As had been foreseen by Marguerite Higgins four years earlier, the American people were turning against the war.

The Communists' aim for the last half of 1968 is to end the Vietnam war--on their terms of victory.

For the North Vietnamese and the Viet Cong, the eight year-old Vietnam war has entered its most decisive phase.

Again, as during Tet, the Communists appear to be attempting to amalgamate their general (countrywide) military offensive with fresh moves at sparking a general political uprising.

The final phase of their 1968 short-range plan calls for the "liberation" of Saigon--the military occupation of the capital city and the political seizure of power from the constitutional government of President Nguyen Van Thieu.

Allied intelligence sources predict that a minimum of three and a maximum of five Communist offensives into Saigon can be expected through the remainder of 1968, with perhaps the final wave coinciding with the American presidential elections in November.

The short-range Communist objective: victory, although not a victory of the classical, conventional-war mold.

Unless the American delegation in Paris concedes to the Communists their demands, the Communist plan for victory is to be secured on the many-faceted battlefield of South Vietnam, and then formally ratified at the conference table.

The Communist plan does not call for "total victory," which would mean militarily defeating the one-million-plus allied troop force. It speaks of "decisive victory," involving intermeshing political, economic, and military actions during pivotal time phases.

Informed sources have reached these conclusions after
studying secret Communist documents from the Viet Cong high
command to its subordinate units and interrogation of high-
ranking Communist prisoners of war and defectors by the
Vietnamese government.

One captured document issued to the "command committee of all subordinate units," and recently released to
the Western press here by the American mission, urged:

"Particularly emphasize the fact that whether the war
ends or not depends on the military might of our armed forces
and not on discussions at the conference table. This
(conference) is but a minor part of our diplomatic activity,
which itself is but one aspect of our political struggle. Therefore we do not view this conference as being of basic or
principal importance...."

The two pivotal questions on which the Vietnam war
here hinges through the remainder of 1968 are:

Will the Communists actually be militarily or politically
able to implement their ambitious plan?

If so, will they succeed or fail either on the military
battlefields or in the psychological-political arena?

If they succeed, the Vietnam war will end in something
close to defeat for the allies. If the Communists fail in their
"victory" plan, they maintain the option of remaining flexible
enough to carry on an "expanded and prolonged war" into
the beginning of 1969 and into Cambodia, Laos, and possibly
Thailand.

In one captured document, the Viet Cong high command
has ordered its troop commanders "to consolidate and develop
armed and political forces in the rear to gain more continuous
and solid victories...." with a spirit of urgency, while, at
the same time being "prepared flexibly to face the expanded
and prolonged war."

The captured document states:

"According to the instructions of the military and political headquarters of COSVN, (the Viet Cong high command),

we must mobilize the whole (Communist) party and the whole country will be determined to consolidate what has been won and to develop it and to urgently repair shortcomings in order to continuously attack the enemy and to motivate the people to uprise to take over the government."

Clearly the captured document unveils Saigon as the eye of the turbulent storm.

"We should be determined to hang on and fight very violently and continuously in all directions of the compass around Saigon," the document continues, "inside and outside the city, while being closely knitted with the people's uprising to create the revolt among the puppet troops, to carry the economic struggle in order to first wear out and then exterminate or disintegrate one part after another of the puppet troops and the puppet government infrastructure, their defense system, and to annihilate the biggest enemy leaders and central nerve headquarters in order to make the enemy more paralyzed every day."

The plan in the captured document clearly maintains that the final period of the Vietnam war is to be written in Saigon.

VIETNAMESE OBSERVER PESSIMISTIC
ON WAR _____ Elizabeth Pond

"It's the same atmosphere as it was in '63 (before former President Diem's assasination)," the Vietnamese intellectual commented while describing the present mood of Saigon.

"There are the same confusion, criticism of the government, repression of the press, jailings, corruption. There are more funny stories about Thieu and Ky than there were about Mrs. Nhu, Ngo Dinh Nhu, and Ngo Dinh Can."

"But there's one difference." Mr. Thuc continued. "In 1963 people had the feeling Diem would be overthrown and things would improve. There would be more freedom, better government, no more arrests, their aspirations would be satisfied. They didn't worry about the Communists because the Communists were weak, and they knew the Americans wouldn't abandon them."

"Now people have the same belief that this government won't stand, but they think it can only accelerate to a worse situation."

Mr. Thuc is not a congenitally alienated Saigon intellectual, but a man with close associations over a broad spectrum of upper-middle-level officials. He leans to the pessimistic side personally, as might be expected, given the death and tragedy his own family has suffered from the war.

He cited as typical a friend--reasonably high in official circles--who went to a fortune teller periodically because of his misgivings. But he discreetly chose a fortune teller who would deserve his 100 or 200 piastres by not painting too black a picture of the future. "Fortune tellers," Mr. Thuc added wryly, "are our psychiatrists."

He continued, "Those who were strongly against Diem now regret his overthrow very much, including those who plotted the coup."

He did not agree that lack of confidence had deteriorated to the extent implied in the recently banned issue of Newsweek, however.

This article described South Vietnamese jitters over the Paris peace negotiations and a general exodus by monied Vietnamese to Europe.

Mr. Thuc saw the purchase of gold and the flow of Vietnamese money to Europe as a result of economic rather than a political uncertainty, Many fear an upsurge of inflation and possibly another devaluation.

Moreover, these people don't want their children to be drafted. Quite a few who can afford the necessary bribes-- especially wealthy Chinese, who feel little urge to fight for any Vietnamese--do take children out of the country as they approach draft age.

There are well-to-do Vietnamese leaving the country as well, but this is chronic and far from undermining the ability of the government.

Of more concern to Mr. Thuc than a potential flight of wealthy Vietnamese are corruption, the prevalence of "yes men" in high places, and the failure of the Thieu government to rally any wide strata of Vietnamese citizens to its cause. The Vietnamese people dislike both the National Liberation Front (NLF) and the government, in Mr. Thuc's analysis, and the NLF is ominously better organized.

The difference between corruption in President Diem's time and today, he pointed out, is that under President Diem it was controlled and disciplined. It was all run by Mr. Diem's brother Nhu. Now it is rampant and uncontrolled--every policeman takes his cut.

The untroubled tenure of several notoriously corrupt generals in positions of authority under President Thieu, Mr. Thuc indicated, alienates the Vietnamese man-in-the-street from the government. So does the ease with which the wealthy

can buy exemption from the draft--i.e. go on the rolls as a
phantom troop--for a hundred thousand piastres ($1,833).

As an aside on the corruption issue, Mr. Thuc said
with a grin that the under-table-cost of exit visas has gone
up as a result of the famous Newsweek article.   Some of the
intermediaries are now keeping the banned magazine on their
desks.

When they are offered the more usual bribe of 100,000
or 200,000 piastres, they solemnly claim inflation and show
the Newsweek figure of one million piastres as proof that they
are giving a bargain by only charging 300,000 piastres.

On the issue of "yes men," Mr. Thuc said that very
few of Mr. Thieu's subordinates dare to speak up to him.
In a number of cases President Thieu seems to prefer keeping
weak men around him so he can control them.

This tendency extends right down the chain of command,
both civilian and military.   Mr. Thuc related instances where
good intelligence officers refrained from giving their real
analyses of enemy capabilities and intentions to their superiors.
Through experience they have learned that if they do not tell
their bosses what they want to hear, they may be accused of
succumbing to NLF propaganda--or may be deliberately assigned impossible tasks to discredit them.

As to the failure to involve citizens at large in the
government, students provide a prime example.   Young people
pitched in on the rebuilding, after the Communist Tet offensive of 1968.   They were ready to bury past complaints against
the government in the common emergency.

However, the government remained suspicious of them,
and never cooperated fully in student efforts.   Then on top
of this disillusionment for the students, the government dropped
a widely popular Youth Minister and replaced him with a mar-
tinet whose primary interest is military training in the schools.

When asked if the NLF had not been weakened critically
in the past six months to a year, Mr. Thuc replied that according to his information it had not.   It has suffered considerable losses of supplies and logistical capability, but it
has not yet lost cadres to the point of breakdown.   Corrup-

tion has begun to appear in NLF ranks, indicating loss of
discipline. But it is nothing on the order of corruption on
the government side, he said.

Nor have North-South conflicts become serious on the
NLF side, Mr. Thuc says. North Vietnamese are clearly as-
cendant in the Communist Party proper, but village cadres
tend to be Southerners.

Mr. Thuc's gloomy conclusion was that it would be
very difficult for the Americans to buy enough time for the
Saigon government to shape up and engage the Vietnamese
public on its side.

"Thieu really wants to do something, but how can he?
We have so many top-priority problems to be solved: the
war, inflation, the Chinese problem, political organization,
corruption, red tape, land reform."

"With the pressure of one and a half million armed troops
we still haven't defeated the Viet Cong. I don't think the
United States wants to buy any more time for us to stand
still."

"Attachez vos ceintures, s'il vous plait." "Fasten your seat belts." The hostess, plump, blonde, French, brown-eyed, in a light-blue smock, passed through, checking. It was funny to find a hostess on a military plane. Like the plane itself, loaded with mail, canned goods, cases of beer, she was a sort of last beep from the "other" world behind the mountains in Vientiane. Born in Hanoi, she had been making the run from Saigon with the I.C.C.--Poles, Indians, Canadians, of the inspection team--six times a month, weather permitting, for thirteen years, practically since the Geneva Accords.

As the I.C.C. plane, an obsolete non-pressurized Convair, circled in the dark above Hanoi, waiting to get the OK to land, out the window, by stretching against our seat belts, we could see tiny headlights of cars moving on the highways below and then the city all lit up like a big glowworm. In Phnom Penh, at the North Vietnamese Delegation, where they issued our visas, they had prepared us for this surprise, but it remained a surprise nonetheless. I thought of the Atlantic coast during World War II and the blackout curtains we had had to buy on the Cape--a Coast Guard order designed to foil enemy submarines. When the Convair taxied to a stop, it instantly doused its lights, though, and the hostess held a flashlight for the boarding officials to examine our papers. But then the airport, brilliant white and blazing with electricity. "You really don't have a blackout!" I exclaimed to the delegation from the Vietnamese Peace Committee who had come to meet us, with bouquets of snapdragons, pink sweet peas, pale-pink roses, larkspur, and little African daisies. A Japanese author and a journalist from a Tokyo paper were receiving bouquets, too. The Vietnamese did not know the word "blackout," and I tried couvre-feu. They dismissed the term "curfew" with laughter. "Passive defense!" In fact, there was no curfew of any sort in Hanoi--except the bell that

rang at eleven o'clock nightly, closing the hotel bar--though
there was one in Saigon. It was only when the sirens blew
that the lights of the city went out and the cars and trucks
halted and waited for the All Clear.

On the way from Gia Lam Airport into the city, we had
our first alert--a pre-alert, really, given by loud-speakers;
the pre-alert usually means the planes are sixty kilometers
away; it is not till they are within thirty kilometers of the
center that the sirens scream. Suddenly, still deep in the
countryside, the driver braked the car; he had heard the
pre-alert on his radio. He turned off the engine. I sat in
the back seat, holding my bouquet in my lap and feeling
quite apprehensive. On March 17, two days before, the
much-feared swing-wing F-111A's had appeared in Thailand;
there had been pictures of them in the Bangkok papers. The
driver got out of the car. "He is looking for the shelter,"
one of my companions explained. "He has found the shelter,"
they announced a few minutes later, and we all climbed out
of the car. In the moonlight, we could see the remains of
a brick house, with its roof torn off; up the lane, there had
been a hamlet, but now there were only indistinct masses of
debris and, somewhere in the dark, the shelter, which I never
actually saw. It was enough to know that it was there.

Outside Hanoi, the driver's first job, I discovered, was
to look for a shelter for the passengers whenever the alert
or the pre-alert sounded. Every hamlet, sometimes every
house, is equipped with a loud-speaker, and the alarm is
rung out by the hamlet bell--the same bell that calls the
peasants to work in the fields. When there is no hamlet
nearby, a band of young soldiers, tramping along with a
transistor radio, may warn you that the planes are coming.
Once, in Hoa Binh Province, out in the west, I sat huddled
in the car with the thin, large-eyed young woman interpreter
while the driver conducted the search; he came back, and
there was a quick conference in Vietnamese. "Here there is
no shelter," she whispered, gravely touching my arm, as we
listened to the bombs, fortunately some miles off. Though
the shelter may be only a hole in the ground, the assurance
that there is such a burrow handy gives a sort of animal
comfort--possibly not unlike the ostrich's. Or maybe it is
a grateful sense that somebody, an unknown friend, has
thought about your safety; even if the uncovered earth shelter cannot protect you from a direct hit, the thought, as they
say of small presents, is what counts.

In the city, there are individual cement cylinders, re-
sembling manholes, every few feet, with round fitted covers
of cement or of plaited reeds--good against fragmentation
bombs.   In a pinch, they will accommodate two small Vietnamese.   But what happened, I wondered, if there were more
people on a given street when the alarm sounded than there
were shelters to hold them?   As in a game of going to Jeru-
salem or musical chairs, who would be left outside?   It is a
schoolmen's problem, that of the outsider, which is posed in
the scramble of extreme situations, and I was curious--anxious,
even--about the socialist solution.   But I never was able to
observe for myself what did in fact occur; in my two and a
half weeks in North Vietnam, it chanced that only once was
I in the city streets during an alert and then only long enough
to see the people scattering as our driver raced toward the
hotel and its communal shelter.   And I felt that it would be
somehow impolite to express my curiosity in the form of a
point-blank question; there are many questions one does not
want to ask in Hanoi.

In any case, the target of the Hanoi government is one
shelter per person within the city limits--I am not sure whether
this ratio takes into account the communal shelters attached to
the institutions.   During my stay, hundreds of brand-new
cylinders were lying along the sidewalks, waiting for the pavement to be dug up and holes sunk to contain them, and every
day trucks kept dumping more.   Production and delivery were
ahead of the picks and shovels.   "Manufacturing shelters is
one of our principal industries now," people remark, rather
ruefully, watching the gray cylinders being put into place.
What can be done with these grim manholes, war memorials,
when and if peace comes?   The only answer I could think of
was to plant flowers in them.

Johnson's speech of March 31--and the subsequent
eerie absence of alerts--did not cause even a momentary flag-
ging in the shelter program.   Yet, so far as I could tell,
the shelters were more a symbol of determination than places
to settle to when the planes approached.   The city popula-
lation had a certain disdain for using them.   "there are toads
in them," a pretty girl said, making a face.   Like the white-
gowned surgeon I met, a Hero of Labor, who had calculated
the statistical probabilities of being killed by a bomb in the
night and decided that he preferred to stay in bed, to be
fresh for operating the next morning, many people in Hanoi

decline to leave their beds or their offices when the peremp-
tory siren shrills; it is a matter of individual decision. Only
foreign visitors are hustled to safety by their guides and interpreters and told to put on their steel helmets or their
pellet-absorbent hats of woven reeds or straw. A pellet in
the brain is the thing most dreaded by the Vietnamese--a
dread that as a brain-worker I more than shared; unfortunately the hat they gave me was too small for my large Western
head, and I had to trust to my helmet, hurriedly strapping
it on as I trotted down the hotel stairs to the communal shelter and glad of the excuse of social duty to do what private
fear was urging.

Your guides are held responsible by the authorities if
anything happens to you while you are in their care. This
applies particularly to guests invited by North Vietnamese
organizations (which we were); accredited journalists are allowed more rein. I was asked not to go out into the street
alone, even for a short walk, though the rule was relaxed
when the bombing of Hanoi stopped on April1--Hanoi time.
This of course limited one's bodily freedom, but I accepted
it, being a law-abiding person. Our hosts of the Peace Committee told us that they had been severely reprimanded because some frisky young South Americans had eluded their
control last summer and roved unsupervised about the country; one got a pellet in the brain and had to be sent to Moscow to be operated on; he lived. Whenever we traveled, one
of the comrades of the Peace Committee made sure I had my
helmet by personally carrying it for me. I was never alone,
except in bed or writing in my room. In the provinces, when
we stayed at a guesthouse or came to inspect a village, each
time I went to the outlying toilet, the young woman interpreter went with me as far as the door, bearing my helmet,
some sheets of tan toilet paper she had brought from Hanoi,
and, at night, the trusty flashlight. She waited outside till
I was through and then softly led me back.

That first night, driving in from the airport, everything was novel. The driver had left the radio turned on in
the car when he switched off the lights. We could hear it
talking, as if to itself, as we paced up and down, and I had
the foolish notion that the planes, wherever they were, might
hear it, too. Other shadowy sedans and passengers were
grouped by the roadside; there had been a great influx at
the airport that night because for over three weeks, four

times running, the I.C.C. flight had not been able to make
it down the narrow air corridor from Vientiane to Hanoi.
On the road we had passed several cars with diplomatic
license plates, one, surely, containing the Indonesian ambassador, who had boarded the plane with his golf clubs; he
used them to exercise on his lawn. Now abruptly all the
headlights went on again; motors started. "They are going
away. They are going away," the radio voice had said in
Vietnamese; the pre-alert was over.

Activity resumed. A chattering stream of people, mostly
young, was flowing along the highway toward us from the
city, walking or riding bicycles and motor bikes: boys in
work clothes or uniforms, with camouflage leaves in their
helmets, girls and women, some riding pillion, carrying bas-
kets of salad greens; now and then a wrinkled old peasant,
in black, with balance-pole on his shoulder or pushing a cart.
A cow raised its head from a field. All that nocturnal movement and chatter gave an impression of revelry, as if a night
ball game or a theater had just let out; probably a work shift
had ended in the factories. Along the road's edge cases of
supplies were stashed, covered with jute or tarpaulin. Jeeps
and military trucks, some heavily camouflaged, were moving
steadily in the opposite direction.

We were passing pretty rows of small, compact trees
--perhaps pruned fruit trees; it was too dark to tell--a pre-
alert to the fact that Hanoi is a shady, leafy city, like Minneapolis or Warsaw; like Minneapolis, too, it has lakes, treated
as a municipal feature, with parks and promenades. The
people are proud of the trees, particularly of the giant camp-
hor, wreathed in a strange parasite with dangling coinlike
leaves. Near the bombed brick house where we waited during the alert, there was a big bare blasted trunk, maybe an
oak, which was putting out a few new leaves; my companions
eagerly pointed them out, making sure I did not miss the
symbol of resistance and rebirth. To the North Vietnamese,
I soon became aware, everything is now a symbol, an ideogram,
expressing the national resolve to overcome. All of Nature
is with them, not just the "brother socialist countries." Nod-
ding their heads in time with a vast patriotic orchestra, they
are hearing tongues in trees, terrible sermons in stones and
the twisted metal of downed aircraft. In Hung Yen Province,
you eat a fresh-caught carp under a red-and-white nylon
canopy, like a billowing circus tent enclosing the whole room;

it is the giant parachute of the pilotless reconnaissance plane
they have shot down. Near Hanoi, in a village co-operative,
raising model pigs and making handicrafts, they show you a
small mute cluster bomb, olive drab, and, beside it, the mute
rusty primitive soil-scratching implement the young peasant
was using in the co-operative fields when pellets from the
cluster bomb killed him. Visual education, they feel, for
the people, and they are not afraid of hammering the lesson
in. But it is Johnson, finally, they wish to give food for
thought.

Growth statistics, offered everywhere, on bicycle owner-
ship, irrigation, rice harvests, maternity clinics, literacy are
the answer to "the war of destruction," which began February 7, 1965; a bombed oak putting out new leaves is a "reply"
to the air pirates of the Air Force and the Seventh Fleet.
All Communist countries are bent on furnishing growth statistics (it is their form of advertising), but with Hanoi this
is something special, carrying a secondary meaning--defiance.
On a big billboard in the city center, the number of U.S.
planes shot down is revised forward almost daily in red paint--
2,818, they claimed when I left, and the number keeps growing. In villages, the score is kept on a blackboard. Everything they build is dated, down to the family wells in a ham-
let--a means of visibly recording progress, like penciling the
heights of children, with the dates opposite, on a door. And
each date has a clear significance in the story of resistance:
1965 or 1966, stamped on a well, proclaims that it was built
in spite of the air pirates.

Hanoi, it is whispered, is going underground, digging
shelters, factories, offices, operating theaters, preparing for
"the worst," i.e., for saturation bombing by the B-52's or
even--draw a deep breath--for atom bombs, although if you
mention those to one of the leaders, he tersely answers that
Johnson is not crazy. The feverish digging, while dictated
no doubt by a very practical mistrust of the Pentagon, seems
to have a secondary meaning, too--mythic, as though the city
were an allegorical character. Hanoi appears to be telling
its people that it is ready to go underground, harrow hell,
to rise again like the rice plants from the buried seed. To
a Westerner, this sounds fantastic, so much so that I hesitate
to bring it up, after all, you can tell me, Hanoi's leaders
are Marxists, and Marxists do not believe in resurrection
stories.

Yet the Vietnamese folk beliefs are highly animistic;
they venerate (or did) the souls of their ancestors, resting
in the rice fields, and the souls of rocks and trees. Their
classic relief sculpture surprises you with delicate, natural-
istic representations of plants, birds, animals, and flowers--
much more typical of Vietnamese art than grotesque images
of gods and the Buddha. The love of Nature is strong in
their literature, too, and is found even in the "captured
enemy documents" the U.S. is fond of distributing for publication. This helps explain their root-attachment to the fatherland, as every observer has noticed, going deeper than politics, into some sphere of immanence the foreigner is almost
embarrassed to name--"spiritual," "religious?" Much is made
in the North of the fatherland's sacred, indivisible unity,
and, despite or because of a history of partitions like Poland's,
the sentiment of being one country seems to be authentic and
shared, incidentally, by the South Vietnamese firebrands who
would like to "march on Hanoi." As a symbol of that unity,
the North has planted the coconut palm; the visitor may be
slow the grasp the significance of this. "Coconut trees."
"Yes, I see them." "Before, here in the North, we did not
have the coconut tree. It is a native of Saigon."

In Hanoi you find cabbages and tomato plants growing
in the ornamental garden of a museum, in parks, around an
anti-aircraft unit; the anti-aircraft battery has planted a
large flower garden as well and it has chickens running
around the gun-replacements. Today the abundant use of
camouflage--exuberant springs of plants, fronds, braches,
leaves of coconut and banana on helmets, anti-aircraft, military vehicles, even tied to the backs of school children--
cannot be meant entirely to fool the enemy overhead. For
one thing, the foliage on the anti-aircraft artillery does not
begin to conceal the guns' muzzles. This camouflage, snatched
from Nature, must be partly a ritual decoration, a "palm" or
"laurel" of prowess and connected with ancient notions of
metamorphosis--pursued by a powerful enemy, you could
"survive" in the verdant form of a tree. In Hanoi, the innocent protective mimicry of coconut leaves "disguising" military hardware always made me think of Palm Sunday in a
Catholic country and the devout coming out of church with
palm leaves or olive branches--a pre-Easter mood. In the
country, a column of army trucks and half-tracks proceeding
under its thatch of greenery made me feel that Birnam Wood
was rolling on to Dunsinane: "Your leavy screens throw
down,./And show like those you are."

The determination of Hanoi appears at first incredible--
legendary and bizarre; also disturbing. We came eventually
to the pontoon bridge, floating on bamboo, the replacement,
for automobiles, of the Paul Doumer Bridge that still hangs,
half bombed, like a groping tentacle, over the Red River.
On the bridge, the traffic goes single file, and you wait for
the oncoming cars to finish their turn before a policeman
gives you the signal to advance. This waiting in line by the
river's edge is scary--there has been a lot of bombing in
the area, as you can see by looking around--and it is even
scarier when you start across the frail, wavy bridge; traffic
moves very slowly, with many halts, and if the bombers should
come while you are there, suspended over the water, there
would be no escape; useless to look for shelters on the in-
substantial bridge, obviously, and you could not jump into
the dark, quite swift river. You just have to put your mind
on something else, make conversation; I always dreaded this
crossing, the sense of being imprisoned in a metal box, a
helpless, all-but-motionless target, and I had the impression
that the Vietnamese did not care for it either; each time,
there was a general easing of tension when the bridge was
finally negotiated.

In the hotel, to my stupefaction, there was hot water,
plenty of it. During nearly a month spent in South Vietnam
the year before, I had had one hot bath--on the U.S.S. En-
terprise. In my room at the Continental in Saigon, there
was only cold water, and when I was once offered a bath in
the room of a New York Times correspondent,* the water ran
dark red, too rusty to get into. In theory, they had hot
water in the Marine Press Base at Da Nang, but in practice
they didn't. Other luxuries I found at the Thong Nhat Hotel
were sheets of toilet paper laid out on a box in a fan pattern
(keys at the desk were laid out in a fan pattern, too), a
thermos of hot water for making tea, a package of tea, a tea-
pot, cups and saucers, candies, cigarettes, and a mosquito
net draped over the bed and tucked in; in Saigon, I had
been tortured by mosquitoes.

It was obvious that the foreigners at the Thong Nhat
lived better than the general population, but this could be
said, too, of the foreigners at the Continental, who moreover

---

*Jonathan Randal, now of the Washington Post.

had to pay for what they got, whereas in Hanoi a guest of
a Vietnamese organization was not allowed to pay for anything--
I never had to change so much as a dollar bill into dongs.
The knowledge of living much better than others (the meals
were very good) and at the expense of an impecunious government whose food-production areas were being pounded every
day by my government produced a certain amount of uneasiness,
which, however, wore off. There was nothing to be done
about it anyway, and I soon was able to verify that outside
no families were sleeping in the streets, as they had been
in Saigon, nobody was begging or in rags, and the people
appeared healthy, though tired in some cases, particularly
those who were old and had doubtless been hungry a good
part of their lives.

On opening the window, I found that there was an
extraordinary amount of traffic, extremely noisy traffic, though
nobody in Hanoi owns a private car--only bicycles and motor
bikes. The honking of horns and screeching of brakes went
on all night. To someone who lives in a European city where
it is against the law to honk your horn, the constant deafen-
ing noise seems very old-fashioned. My ears had forgotten
those sounds, as they had forgotten the clanging of streetcars and the crowing of cocks at 4:00 a.m. Hanoi still has
both cocks and streetcars, and you can hear the whistle of
trains, as well as the more up-to-date noise of MIGs overhead
and the almost continuous voice of the loudspeakers, invariably
feminine and soothing, sugared, in tone. Unless you know
Vietnamese, you cannot guess whether they are announcing
an air raid or telling you the planes have left or simply giving
a news broadcast or a political diatribe.

There is a good deal in North Vietnam that unexpectedly
recalls the past. Waiting to cross the Red River recalled my
first trip to Italy, just after world War II, when most of the
bridges were down ("Bombed by the Liberators," in Italian,
was scrawled all over the devastated cities and towns) and
our bus crossed the Po or the Adda on a tremulous pontoon
bridge; the loud-speaker outside the hotel window ("Attention, citizens, attention") recalled the loud-speakers in Flor-
ence during a spring election campaign ("attenzione, cittadini,
attenzione"). Jouncing along a highway deeply pitted by pellets from cluster bombs made me think of my childhood:
bumpy trips in northern Minnesota; Grandma in a motoring
hat and duster; and how each time we struck a pothole her

immense white head, preceded by the hat, would bounce up
and hit the car's canvas top. North Vietnam is still pioneer
country, where streams have to be forded; the ethnic minori-
ties, Meos, Muongs, and Thais, in the mountains of the wild
west, though they do not wear feathers, recall American Indians. The old-fshioned school desks and the geometry lesson on the blackboard in an evacuated school, the kerosene
lamps in the villages, the basins of water filled from a well
to use to wash up before meals on an open porch, the one-
or two-seater toilets with a cow ruminating outside brought
back buried fragments of my personal history. I was aware
of a psychic upheaval, a sort of identity crisis, as when a
bomb lays bare the medieval foundations of a house thought
to be modern.

The daytime alerts in the hotel reminded me very much
of fire drill in school. During my stay there was no bombing
near the hotel, though the siren sometimes sent us to the
shelter as often as six times in twenty-four hours. After a
while you estimate the distance of the explosions you hear--
six kilometers, ten, fifteen--and you think you can tell the
full, resounding noise a bomb makes from the crackle of ack-
ack. In the hotel, I began to have a feeling of security,
like the veteran correspondents who usually did not bother
to get up during night raids or who, if they were up already,
wandered out into the street to watch the anti-aircraft activity. In the daytime, it became a slightly tiresome routine
to walk, not run, to the shelter, where a delegation of Chinese
in gray uniforms--who never spoke to anyone--were always
the first arrivals, and wait for the All Clear. And as in
the case of fire drill, I began to half wish for some real excitement, for the bombs to come a bit nearer and make a
louder bang. It got to be a disappointment if the alert was
a false alarm, i.e., when you simply sat in the shelter and
heard no action at all. The other foreigners must have felt
the same way, for when the explosions were noisy and the
guns replied, the conversation in the shelter became much
livelier, and there were giggles.

An alert was also a social event; you saw new faces
and welcomed back old friends--that is, people you had known
a few days-reappearing from a trip to Haiphong or Nam Dinh.
One day in the shelter I met the Danish ambassador to Peking
and another time a whole diplomatic dinner party, men in dark
suits, large, freshly waved ladies from the bloc countries in

low-cut silks and satins, an Indian lady in a truly beautiful
blue sari, joined us drab "regulars" on the underground
benches, having left their double rows of wine glasses and
their napkins on the table of the hotel's private dining room,
reserved for parties--this euption, as of a flight of butter-
flies, was a momentary wonder in our somewhat mothy, closet-
like existence.

The late-night alerts were different. Though I had
concluded that there was no real danger of bombing in the
immediate neighborhood of the hotel--unless Johnson escalated
again, with B-52's or "nukes," in which case my personal
survival was not of any interest; I would not care to survive--
at night, when the shrilling of the siren waked me, I forgot
and would jerk up from the pillow with my heart pounding,
grope my way out of the mosquite neeting, find the flashlight in the dark, slippers, dressing gown, et cetera, and
stumble, still unnerved, down the stairs and out through the
hotel garden, pointing my flashlight down, searching for the
entrance to the shelter. Those late-March night raids made
everybody angry. According to the Vietnamese, who were
experts on such matters, they consisted of one or two planes
only, whereas before they had come in large purposeful waves;
their object now must be psychological--without any military
pretext--to harass the population at random, deprive it of
sleep, while at the same time lessening the risk to themselves
of being shot down, for it is harder to hit a single plane in
the sky than to pick off one or two out of a serried dozen
or twenty.

No planes, so far as I know, were shot down over
Hanoi during my stay, though one, they said, an Intruder,
had been shot down the day of our arrival. The foreign correspondents agreed that the bombing was slowing down, at
least in the region of Hanoi, and they wondered whether the
Americans could be short of planes, on account of the number
destroyed or damaged in the late-January Tet offensive.
The date of manufacture stamped on a shot-down plane was
always of great interest; if a plane manufactured in July was
shot down in August, this suggested that stocks were low.

In fact, though we did not know this in Hanoi, the
"return" of the bombing, in dollars terms, had been added
up early in the year by the accountants in Washington. The
April number of Foreign Affairs was revealing that it had

cost the U.S. six billion dollars to destroy an estimated 340 million dollars' worth of facilities: clearly a low-yield investment.   The cost in lives of U.S. pilots in comparison with estimated North Vietnamese losses seems not to have been computed--where, on the balance sheet, would the lone target, working in a rice field, of an anti-personnel bomb figure? Left out of the calculations also--surely an oversight?--was the cost to the North Vietnamese government of the shelter program, not to mention the cost of the loud-speakers and the personnel to man them.

Only once in the city while I was there did a bomber "sneak through" the warning system. It happened in the country, but there it was less spectacular to hear the thud of bombs before, so to speak, listening to the overture of the sirens; in the country, as I said, there are no sirens anyway and surprises were to be expected. In Hanoi, it happened one evening at the Museum of War Crimes, when we were sitting down to little cups of tea at a long table following a tour of the exhibits. Suddenly, there was a long-drawn-out, shrill, banshee-like, shrieking noise, succeeded by a shattering explosion. At the same time, out the window, we could see a plane streak across the sky. The museum director, an officer in uniform, rushed us out into the garden; guiding me by the arm, he was propelling me toward the shelter. Big red stars looking like skyrockets were bursting in the dark overhead. Then the siren must have blown, though I have no memory of hearing it. In the museum's shelter, we heard more bombs exploding. "The museum is near the bridge," the interpreter murmured, as if to excuse the fact that a raid had come so close. When the All Clear sounded, we went in and found the tea cold in our cups. Back at the hotel, during the next alert, one of the guests told us that there had been three bombs and a Shrike.

To return from a shelter to a disarrayed table where the tea has grown cold in the cups and resume a conversation at the precise point it had left off ("You were saying ... ?") is a daily, sometimes an hourly, occurrence in the North--inevitably so, since tea is served visitors on every ceremonious occasion, and all occasions, however sickening or painful, are ceremonious. Hospitality requires that tea should be served at the beginning and end of any visit: tea, cigarettes, candies, and long slender little cakes that

taste of bananas.   The exceptions were the Journalists' Union
and the War Crimes Commission, both of which served beer,
and the prison where the captured pilots were held, which
offered a choice of beer or a soft drink, plus bananas.   I
could never make out the reason behind these slight variations of an otherwise inflexible precept.   It was easy to guess
why beer was served to journalists (newsmen drink), while
the Writers' and Artists' Union served tea, but why beer at
the War Crimes Commission and tea at the War Crimes Museum?
Maybe beer is more expensive, and Mr. Luu Quy Ky of the
Journalists' Union and Colonel Ha Van Lau of the War Crimes
Commission had bigger budgets than the others.   In some
instances, tea was followed by coffee.

Perhaps I should have asked, but the Vietnamese are
sensitive, and to wonder aloud why beer was served instead
of the customary tea might have been taken, I thought, as
a criticism of the hospitality: "Why did they not serve tea?"
In the same way, I was reluctant to ask why in some coopera-
tives, factories, and associations there were portraits of
Marx, Engels, Lenin, Stalin, and Ho, while in others there
was only Ho.   Was it a matter of personal preference on the
part of the administrator?   That did not appear likely.   Once,
in a village co-operative I thought I saw Marx, Engels, Lenin,
and Ho, and no Stalin--which made a joyful impression on
me--but when I got up from my chair, I found that Stalin
had been behind me all along, chuckling.   The explanation
may be that if the center you are visiting is a branch headquarters of the Lao Dong (Workers') Party, you get the whole
pantheon; otherwise, only Ho.   The absence of portraits of
Mao and of the current Soviet leaders seemed self-explanatory
("Vietnam asserts it independence"), but it could not be remarked on, any more than you can remark to a host on the
absence of certain persons who you might have thought would
be invited to a party.

In the War Crimes Museum, that evening, among the
exhibits they had showed us a Shrike, so that the sudden
advent of the live missile had the air, to us, of a coincidence
("Speak of the devil ... "), but of course, to the North
Vietnamese, nearly all the exhibits in the museum "matched"
what was befalling them regularly.   The museum, unlike that
at Auschwitz, is strictly contemporary.   There were cluster
bombs--guavas and pineapples--some of the delayed-action
type, regarded as the most fiendish, ordinary placid TNT

bombs of varying weights, ranging from babies of 200 to big
daddies of 3,000 pounds, rockets, an assortment of missiles,
crop-spraying powders (with the results in a bottle), tear
gases, front and rear views of patients hit by a spray of
pellets from the "mother" bomb, X-rays of pellets in human
skulls, photos of napalm and phosphorous victims (napalm
has not been used in the vicinity of Hanoi and Haiphong, or,
as the Vietnamese say, "not yet"), quite a collection of exhibits.   And shuffling about among the displays was a small
middle-aged Vietnamese woman in a bunched sweater, wide
trousers, and sandals, who was staring, as if drawn by some
morbid, fascinated curiosity, at the weapons and devices in
the glass cases, at the big bombs arranged, like modern
metal sculptures, on the floor; she bent to read the labels,
sometimes furtively touched.   They told us, lowering their
voices, that she had been haunting the museum ever since
she had lost her twenty-year-old son early in the year.

     An American apologist might claim that she was an ex-
hibit, too, a "plant" to invoke the sympathy of soft-headed
pacifists and other bleeding hearts, but in fact the museum
personnel seemed somewhat put out by her presence and by
the occasional snuffling, sobbing noises she made, interrupt-
ing the scholarly presentation of the material.   In short, they
reacted like museum officials anywhere who were not lacking
in heart but had their professional duties, which included
discouraging nuts and people with "troubles" from intruding
on official visits.   It was true, she was causing our attention
to stray.   Then, as if guiltily conscious of being a disturb-
ance, she would hastily quiet down and regain her composure,
peering into the glass cases with an air of timid wonder, like
a peasant viewing the tools of modern civilization and wondering what they were for.   She seemed to be trying to put her
lost son and these efficient implements together in some sa-
tisfactory manner, as though to make a connection and localize
the source of her pain.   Sometimes, appearing to find it for
a moment, she actually smiled and nodded to herself.

     She had gone, I guess, when the Shrike came.   Perhaps
one of the museum employees had persuaded her to go home
finally or given her some tea in the kitchen.   To tell the
truth, when the Shrike came, I forgot about her; I had got
used to the fact that during an alert the ordinary Vietnamese
chambermaids, cooks, waiters, desk clerks, tea servers--
vanished from sight, only to reappear when the alert was

over. Either they proceeded to their own shelters, separate
from those for foreign guests, or, like the chambermaids in
the hotel who doubled as militia, they shouldered guns and
went up to the roof, or they continued quietly with their
jobs, like the cook I once glimpsed in the hotel sitting in
his white apron and hat at the kitchen table when the All
Clear blew. The siren was a Last Trump separating the
sheep--us--from the nimble goats. At the National Liberation
Front Delegation, the distinction was marked by a heavy
dark-brown curtain dividing the communal shelter between
personnel, on one side, and, on the other, the Chief of Mission, his immediate staff, and his guests. In an American,
such a frank distinction appears ipso facto undemocratic.

At the museum, in a parting ceremony, they presented
us with rings made from downed U.S. aircraft. Like a wedding
ring, mine is engraved August 1, 1966--they day the plane
was shot down--and has the initials H. Y., which must stand
for Hung Yen Province. They also gave me a woman's comb
of the same material. Such souvenirs seem to be popular in
Hanoi, but though, as they watched, I murmured "Merci
beaucoup" and hurriedly, like one rapidly swallowing medi-
cine, tried the blunt ring on my finger, I instantly slid it
off and dropped it into my handbag; luckily, I had the excuse that it was a man's ring; too big. Back in the hotel,
I shut it up in a drawer out of sight, but it kept troubling
my mind, making me toss at night, like an unsettled score.
For some reason, the comb, scalloped in the Vietnamese style,
did not bother me.

Perhaps, if I had had the courage, I might have declined to take the ring, handed it back to the Vietnamese
as soon as I realized what it was. As my grandmother tried
to teach me, one need never be afraid to say no. But from
their point of view, it was a symbol of friendship, a medal
pinned on my chest. They were proud to bestow it. What
was it that, deeper than politeness, which was urging me to
do so, made it impossible for me to keep it on my finger,
even for a few minutes--just not to give offense? Maybe
the premonition that if I once put it on, I could never take
it off; I could not sport it for the rest of my stay and then
get rid of it as soon as I left the country--that would be
base. Yet equally repugnant to my nature to my identity,
whatever that is, to the souls of my ancestors, would be to
be wedded for life or at least for the duration of this detestable

war to a piece of aluminum wreckage from a shot-down U.S.
war plane. Or was it just the fact that it did not "go" with
my other jewelry?

    Nor could I drop it in the wastebasket of my hotel
room. The chambermaids would find it and return it to me:
"Votre bague, madame." Or, worse, they would feel that,
to me, their friendship band was rubbish. But if respect
for the feelings of others forbade my junking it in a waste-
basket of the Thong Nhat Hotel, then there was no sea anywhere deep enough for me to drop it into. I had to keep
it. The comb, presenting no problem, a simple keepsake and
rather pretty, remained openly on my bureau in the Thong
Nhat with my other toilet articles. Yet I now slowly realize
that I never passed it through my hair. Mysterious. I cannot explain the physical aversion, evidently subliminal, to
being touched by this metal. Quite a few of the questions
one does not, as an American liberal, want to put in Hanoi
are addressed to oneself.

CHAPTER VI

1969–1970

During 1969 and 1970 the number of American forces in South Vietnam continued to decline, from 475,000 in 1969 to only 156,800 by the end of 1970. As the number of American forces in South Vietnam decreased, so did the number of correspondents covering the war. It became difficult to get stories on Vietnam published, as the war became "old news." During this time the war expanded into Laos and Cambodia, with Americans once again accompanying South Vietnamese troops as advisers. Although the Americans were talking about "de-escalation," the war in fact grew bloodier. Fifteen thousand Americans were killed between 1968 and 1971, and there were more South Vietnamese civilian casualties than ever before. These years were also deadly for the correspondents who remained. Between 1969 and 1971 thirty-one correspondents were either killed, or were missing and presumed dead, in the Vietnam War. Nine other correspondents, including two women, were captured and later released.

As the Americans announced that their goal in South Vietnam was now "Vietnamization," a slow withdrawal of American troops and the build-up of South Vietnamese troops to replace them, President Nguyen Van Thieu continued his rise to pre-eminence in the South Vietnamese government. Among the correspondents chronicling this rise to power was the Christian Science Monitor's Elizabeth Pond.

In October 1969 Pond wrote that Thieu was organizing a new political party with its nucleus in the army, a move which she compared to Ngo Dinh Diem's strategy when he was president. In the optimistic view, Pond wrote, this would strengthen Thieu's position to allow South Vietnam to muddle through while the Americans disentangled themselves. In the pessimistic view, however, it could mean that Thieu was apt to run afoul of the same religious and political complications that had defeated Diem. In his rise to power Thieu

had been aided by an American fiat against more coups, and
also by some stray American rockets that had killed several
officers who were supporters of Nguyen Cao Ky.

Earlier in 1969, as the U.S. government announced its
intention to pull American ground troops out of South Vietnam, Pond's articles in the Monitor had a decidedly upbeat
tone. She wrote about the people who lived in sampans on
the River of Perfumes, and stressed that life for these people
was continuing in a "normal" manner and even improving with
the improvement in the South Vietnamese economy. In another article she quoted an American lieutenant who had spent
a year as adviser to the new South Vietnamese National Defense College, and who believed that the allies were "winning
big" in South Vietnam. The lieutenant pointed out that the
Viet Cong had not seized the advantage after Tet, and cited
the new plan of "Accelerated Pacification," which simply meant
that villages which had been lost to the Viet Cong during
Tet were being re-occupied by the South Vietnamese. Wrote
Pond cautiously, "it is impossible in the fog of war to know
just how badly the Viet Cong have been hurt."[1]

In September 1969, having been awarded a fellowship
by the Alicia Patterson Fund, Pond took a leave of absence
from the Christian Science Monitor. With few exceptions the
articles she wrote for the Fund over the next year were analyses of the political situation in South Vietnam. Discussing President Thieu's decision to re-establish close ties between the military and the government, she wrote:

> It will be argued by doves that the history of U.S.
> involvement in Vietnam has decreed this outcome
> from the start ... perhaps the doves are right. But
> politically, until September 1969 there was a chance
> of salvaging something from the deaths of 90,000
> South Vietnamese, 40,000 Americans, and over half
> a million North Vietnamese ... after September this
> chance seemed remote.[2]

In March 1970 Pond began a series of articles on the
trial of South Vietnamese dissident Tran Ngoc Chau. Chau
was a minor political figure, a passionate nationalist who had
been a member of the Viet Minh fighting the French until
the resistance had been taken over by the Communists. His
brother, Tran Ngoc Hien, a high-ranking officer in North

Vietnam, had returned to the South as a spy. When Tran
Ngoc Hien was captured in 1969, and it became known that
he had met with his brother several times, Chau was tried,
not for treason, but on the lesser charge of not informing
on his brother. After being convicted Chau took refuge in
the legally inviolate Chamber of Deputies. When police stormed
the Chamber of Deputies, roughing up a few journalists for
good measure, and arrested Chau, the Thieu government was
criticized for its handling of the situation. Discouraged poli-
ticians told Pond that Thieu had played right into the hands
of the Communists by acting in such a dictatorial fashion.
"What Chau did is bad, but not so dangerous for the country," one person told her. "What Thieu did is very dangerous."[3]

     In March 1970 Prince Norodom Sihanouk of Cambodia
was overthrown, and his successor Marshal Lon Nol, moved
to destroy North Vietnamese and Viet Cong sanctuaries in
Cambodia. In support of Lon Nol, South Vietnamese and
American troops entered Cambodia on April 30, setting off
student demonstrations across the United States, including
the tragic encounter at Kent State University in Ohio on
May 4, which resulted in the deaths of four students. An
estimated 60,000 to 100,000 Americans demonstrated against
the war in Washington, D.C. Clearly anti-war sentiment in
the United States was no longer limited to a disgruntled few
leftist students, but had become a popular movement.

     Like many other Americans, Elizabeth Pond had not
approved of the American decision to send troops into Cambodia, but she was a journalist, so she went to Cambodia
too. On May 7, 1970 Pond was driving on Highway 1, about
three kilometers west of Svay Rieng, Cambodia, with Richard
Dudman of the St. Louis Post Dispatch and Michael Morrow
of Dispatch News Service International. The three journalists
had driven from Saigon that morning to report on the effects
the invasion was having on the civilian population in the region, and to observe the American and South Vietnamese
forces that were attempting to clear the main highway from
Saigon to Phnom Penh, Cambodia.

     Suddenly two men with rifles stepped out from behind
a tree and motioned for the automobile to stop. Morrow told
the armed men that the three were Canadians, which in his
case was true. The journalists were taken prisoner. At

first they were treated roughly by their captors, blindfolded
and paraded as American captives before hostile Cambodians.
Pond wrote later that she hoped to convince the villagers
who crowded angrily around the truck in which the prisoners
were being held that she was not an enemy. She wrote:

> As I looked at the people I tried to convey to them
> that I bore them no ill will, that I loathe war and
> the passions of war, destruction and hatred and en-
> mity between men--and that if any of them had lost
> loved ones my heart went out to them.[4]

Separated from her two companions, and feeling that
they were all very close to being killed, Pond was placed
blindfolded in a room. Crowds of people came in to stare
at her, but she was touched only once, when a man grabbed
her sandals and threw them against the wall. A short time
later her guard took her rings, but when she talked to him,
calling him "brother," he decided to return them. At this
point a high-ranking officer learned of the capture of the
three journalists, and intervened to assure that they would
not be harmed.

Reunited with Dudman and Morrow, Pond learned that
they too had been roughly treated until they were rescued
by the officer. The three were told that if they really were
journalists, they had nothing to fear. Although they continued to be interrogated, their treatment grew more civil,
and the prisoners settled into a routine of village life. They
were never formally guarded, but were kept in a house all
day and allowed outside in the evening to go to a well and
wash. They were moved from village to village, traveling at
night, and quartered with Cambodian families, some of whom
became quite friendly. One old man taught Morrow some
words in the Khmer language. When Dudman began to pass
the time by whittling chessmen, another villager chalked lines
on the floor of his house so they could play chess. Thereafter the nightly chess game became popular with prisoners
and guards alike.

Pond, Dudman, and Morrow were held prisoners for
five-and-a-half weeks, an experience Pond later described
in a five-part series in the Christian Science Monitor. They
were guarded by five men, only one of whom was Cambodian.
The others were Vietnamese, from both North and South Vietnam

Eventually the guards initiated ideological discussions with the prisoners.   The guards were men with the single-minded persistence of true revolutionaries.   Everything was subordinated to the "cause."   Pond noted that there was no softening of this attitude in the female nurse who was with the captives for a week.   She carried a pink and white polka dot purse in her pack, but her every thought was for the revolution.   "Women are part of the revolution," she told Pond, "and there is no stopping the revolution."[5]

One evening a high commander in the region visited the captives and told them that they were to be released. There was a brief recording session at which Morrow read a statement about their treatment and impressions, and Pond thanked the commander for the good treatment they had received.   There was a gala farewell dinner attended by nearly every official they had met during their weeks of captivity. Pond thanked the people in whose homes she had been kept as a prisoner, and the five guards were given the chess set as a good-bye present.   On June 14 the captives were driven to a village schoolyard where a celebration was beginning. Under banners which thanked the American people who opposed the Cambodian invasion, Pond, Dudman, and Morrow listened to speeches in Cambodian, which were not translated into English.   Speaking in French, Pond again thanked the people in whose homes she had stayed.   The next day the three journalists were taken back to Highway 1 and given white flags and money to get them back to Saigon.

Pond wondered why she and the others were released when twenty-nine other newspaper correspondents captured in Cambodia were still missing.   She concluded that the attitude she and the others had displayed--one of non-confrontation--may have favorably impressed their captors.   It so happened that all three honestly opposed the Cambodian invasion, and had freely expressed this view in informal conversation with their captors.   They were not asked to condemn the invasion formally, and the formal statements they did make concerned the fact that they had been well-treated and that their captors had high morale, both of which were true statements. Considering whether they should have been silent regarding their personal opinions of the Cambodian invasion since their beliefs were in opposition to the official policy of the American government, Pond wrote: "There is no ethical code for journalists in situations of this sort, and I am not sure that any could be established."[6]

Pond returned to the United States where she continued to write articles for the Alicia Patterson Fund, including two which analyzed the politics of one of her captors, and one on the aftermath of the trial of Tran Ngoc Chau. She wrote that Chau's trial was "the delicate point in the balance"[7] where President Thieu's power would begin to decline. Pond predicted that the United States would continue its policy of withdrawal and de-escalation in South Vietnam; that the South Vietnamese government would continue to fragment and deteriorate under Thieu, but that American intervention would prevent another coup; and that the North Vietnamese and Viet Cong would be able to take advantage of the deterioration of the Thieu government.

By the time Pond returned to the United States the other woman correspondent for the Christian Science Monitor, Beverly Deepe, had also left South Vietnam. Deepe, who had covered the war since 1961, left Saigon for what she said was the only reason she would leave while the war was still going on--love. In 1965 she had met a Marine named Charles Keever when he was assigned as her escort officer at Danang. Several years later she married him and by early 1970 she had returned with him to Washington, D.C. where he was assigned to the Pentagon. Deepe announced that she was giving up her career in journalism, except for occasional pieces she could write at home. "You can't be a wife and a journalist and do a good job at both," she said.[8]

At about the same time Georgia Anne Geyer came to the same conclusion, but chose the opposite solution to the dilemma. Faced with the choice between the independence of her career and traditional marriage to a man she loved, Geyer chose her career. You can't have everything, she told herself sadly. But before she left South Vietnam in early 1969, Geyer wrote a series of articles which she considers to be the best she did on the Vietnam War.

In the articles Geyer wrote about a new attitude she had observed in American soldiers. For the first time, Geyer wrote, the GI was asking why he was being sent to die in a war. To the young men, the unquestioning patriotism of the older traditional officers was simply tiresome. Geyer compared the "revolution" within the armed forces to the changes which were going on within the United States, on campuses, in ghettoes, and in the total social structure of the country.

Acknowledgment of this attitude had led to a new kind of
training, with the emphasis on the building up of a spirit
of teamwork and cooperation rather than on simple obedience
to superior officers.

At the same time, Geyer noted, the particular circumstances of the Vietnam War were leading to a growing disillusionment among some American servicemen. They were
appalled by the graft and corruption of the Saigon government. They realized that many of the South Vietnamese civilians hated them. They found themselves admiring the
unity and dedication of the Viet Cong and questioning whether
America really had the right to impose its governmental
system on other nations. One young officer asked Geyer,
"What right do we have to tell these people how to live their
lives? What right do we have to be here?"[9]

Like the young officers, some war correspondents were
open in their opposition to the war. Gloria Emerson of the
New York Times, who arrived in Saigon in February 1970,
was to become one of the war's most outspoken opponents.
Emerson had visited South Vietnam before. In 1956 she had
left her job as reporter for the women's section of the New
York Journal American and traveled to Vietnam with "no
money, a one-way ticket, and only an American beau in the
Marines in Saigon."[10] She later described this decision to
leave a good job and go to Vietnam in 1956 as the most sig-
nificant choice of her lifetime. When she returned to the
United States the following year, she went to work for the
New York Times, where she was assigned to "women's news."
In 1960 she went abroad with her husband, and rejoined the
Times at the Paris news bureau. By 1970 she was divorced, and
had been a correspondent in the Middle East, Eastern Europe,
Africa, and London.

On her second arrival in Saigon in 1970, Emerson found
that the correspondents were living comfortably, along with
the more than 2,000 other Americans working for the embassy,
consulate, and other U.S. governmental agencies. Emerson
found that she chould get a room at the Hotel Continental
and an American meal at one of the many pleasant western-
style restaurants. It was all very pleasant, and Emerson
was angry.

In May Emerson flew on medical evacuation missions and

was told that eventually she would get used to the blood and
death. Medical personnel told her it would all become normal
to her in time. "They lied," she said.[11]

Emerson was able to concentrate on the war's effect on
the Vietnamese people because her newspaper was "rich
enough" to have several correspondents covering the war.
Unlike many other newspapers, the New York Times had not
decreased the number of its correspondents in South Vietnam
as the number of American troops declined. By 1972 the
Times had more people covering the Vietnam War than it had
on any war story since World War II.

Typical of Emerson's articles on the Vietnamese people
was one in May 1970 which told of a thirteen-year-old boy,
a Vietnamese who was raised in Cambodia, and who was one
of the more than 16,000 refugees who had crowded into Saigon. The boy and his family were living on the crowded
veranda of a Saigon orphanage. They had been forced to
sell many family possessions, including the boy's bicycle,
when they fled Cambodia. "It is the loss of his green bicycle that hurts him the most," Emerson wrote, "but, like
most children of Asia, 13-year-old Than Minh Hoang does
not complain."[12] Emerson's series of articles on refugees
were to win the George Polk Memorial Award in 1971.

Other articles written by Emerson in 1970 were not so
well received in some quarters. Writing in National Review
in early 1971, Gerry Kirk complained that Emerson was "break-
ing Tokyo Rose's record for the transmission of unadulterated
bad news from a war in which the U.S. was engaged."[13]
Among the articles cited by Kirk were stories about the rarity
of rehabilitation for wounded civilians, on the red tape which
confronted a war widow in Saigon, and on the hatred Vietnamese felt for Americans. Another story which annoyed
Kirk was one about new recruits arriving in South Vietnam.
Although American troop withdrawals had been accelerated,
Emerson pointed out that new recruits were still arriving in
South Vietnam, and that each man had to serve one year.
Furthermore, reported Emerson, soldiers were arriving for
second tours, not out of patriotism, but because they would
receive extra money for them. Even more frightening, one
young soldier told Emerson he had put in for a second tour
because "If you have to kill you might as well do it here instead of in the United States."[14]

Kirk particularly objected to Emerson's article in the
Times on October 21, 1970 which revealed that the Army had
awarded a Silver Star for valor to a brigadier general, based
on acts of heroism which were invented by the enlisted men
who wrote the citation.   Kirk bewailed the fact that Emerson
seemed to concentrate on bad news in her reporting, but he
did not deny that the stories she was writing were true.
Kirk criticized Emerson for not having anything good to say
about the war in Vietnam and, of course, he was right.   To
Emerson there wasn't anything good to be said about the war.

Furthermore, Emerson's stories on what was wrong
about the war in Vietnam were raching an American public
which was quite prepared to believe the worst.   Every night
on television Americans watched horror and death.   They
saw Marines burning villages while women and children wept.
On November 13, 1969 several American newspapers, including the New York Times, ran the story of an incident which
had occurred over a year earlier, on March 16, 1968, at a
little village called My Lai.   To its shock, the American public learned that American servicemen had gathered the villagers into groups and murdered them.   Photographs printed
in the Cleveland Plain Dealer showed the bodies of tiny children killed in the massacre.   The public was outraged.   It
was no use for the military to protest that these things happened in wars; that thousands of civilians, including children,
had been murdered by the North Vietnamese in Hue during
the Tet offensive.   It was no use to offer the "explanation"
that My Lai had been a Viet Cong stronghold.   The public
was not ready to accept six-month-old babies as "the enemy."
The reality of a dirty, racist war became evident to the American people.

Still reeling from the impact of My Lai, Americans then
learned that the South Vietnamese were torturing prisoners
and holding them in tiny stone compartments called "tiger
cages."   To make matters worse, it was apparent that the
American advisers to the South Vietnamese police had known
all along about these tactics.   When conditions at the Con
Son prison, South Vietnam's largest civilian prison, became
public after the investigation of a team of visiting U.S. Con-
gressmen, there was another indignant public outcry.   One
of the articles which had exposed the conditions at Con Son
had been written by Gloria Emerson, who interviewed a South
Vietnamese tailor who had been imprisoned there.   The tailor

told her of the deplorable conditions in the prisons, and of
being kept in a "tiger cage" for many months. He insisted
that he had been innocent of any crime, and that he risked
reprisals for talking to an American correspondent. Emerson's angry articles were a far cry from those of Marguerite
Higgins and Dickey Chapelle only a few years earlier; or
even from those of Philippa Schuyler, who had complained of
American racism and stupidity, but had basically still believed
in the war. To Emerson there was nothing to approve of in
the war.

In comparison, UPI's Margaret Kilgore, who arrived
in South Vietnam in January 1970, had no preconceived notions about the war, and also had an immense respect for
the military. Like Elizabeth Pond, Kilgore's major emphasis
in her writing was on politics. A graduate of Syracuse University, Kilgore had nearly fifteen years of experience with
UPI, including seven years of covering Congress and the
White House. She also had a low tolerance for boredom and
was not finding her current assignment of covering the Department of Agriculture very exciting when she was asked if
she would like to go to Vietnam. She had no trouble making
up her mind to go.

Because she arrived at the time when the Americans
were withdrawing personnel from South Vietnam, Kilgore
found that she had some difficulty in getting around the
country. The cutback in American troops had resulted in
the loss of some of the handy American air transport which
correspondents had used. In Cambodia, the correspondents
had no access to air transport, and sometimes rode to war
in an air-conditioned Mercedes limousine, but would have to
go to Phnom Penh to find a telephone to transmit the story.
In Laos, strict military or enemy control kept reporters from
getting anywhere near the war at all.

Kilgore also found that the American withdrawal had
created some problems which were specific to women correspondents. The military PX, at which correspondents had
privileges to purchase up to $25.00 worth of materials, had
stopped stocking "women's products," as the majority of the
female personnel had returned to the United States. Kilgore made a deal with Kate Webb, her UPI counterpart in
Phnom Penh, Cambodia. Whichever of them went to Hong Kon
for a rest trip would bring back enough tampons for both,
and tampons were sent back and forth over Highway 1.

The one-room apartment Kilgore rented in Saigon featured "robust" rats in the stairwell. Nevertheless, she
settled in happily, and soon developed a local reputation
for making spaghetti dinners. She was supposed to stay in
South Vietnam for eighteen months, but stretched her tour
to twenty-one months in order to cover the South Vietnamese
elections in late 1971.

"Nothing in my previous background really prepared
me for South Vietnam," Kilgore wrote. She found that she
was expected to cover all facets of the war, from politics to
battle. She found that a correspondent in South Vietnam
must be a "political reporter, an expert on tactics, more
familiar than many soldiers with a vast assortment of weaponry,
a linguist, diplomat, administrator, daredevil, and one of
the most suspicious, cautious people on earth."[15]

Kilgore wrote sympathetically of the effect the war had
had on Vietnamese people of the educated class. She wrote
of a woman law professor at the University of Saigon whose
family had lost all of its possessions when they fled Hue during the Tet offensive. Although she did not feel that the
Americans and South Vietnamese were going to win the war,
Kilgore did not believe that it was the place of a reporter to
criticize the military. She was in South Vietnam as an observer, doing a job. Still, she admitted that she was biased
against war in general, and that she was unprepared for her
first midnight rocket attack, her first near-hit in a helicopter
skirmish, and her first dead body.

At that time there were "about a half-dozen" women
correspondents in South Vietnam and Cambodia, according to
Kilgore. One was Patches Musgrove, still in her little hootch
in Saigon. In August 1969 she had her name legally changed
to Patches from Helen. She was the only correspondent who
flew on a combat mission in an AC 119 gunship on a "Shadow
Operation" out of Phang Rang Air Base. In May 1970 she
was selected as an "Honorary Shadow" for "outstanding service to Shadow combat operations in the Republics of Viet
Nam and Cambodia." In August she was selected as the "Un-
sung Heroine of the Year" by the Women's Auxiliary of the
Veterans of Foreign Wars. Now over fifty years old, she
still slogged through the rice paddies with the G.I.s, who
admired and loved her. They gave her hundreds of patches
for her collection, and told her that she reminded them of
their mothers back home.

Musgrove wrote human-interest stories, such as a 1970
series on an American father who had journeyed to South
Vietnam to visit his wounded son, but she also liked to stir
up trouble. A skirmish when she tried to store USO popcorn
in her hootch to keep it from being stolen led to her near
explusion from Vietnam in 1968. To Musgrove, the "popcorn
war" was ridiculous, and her beloved GI's joined in the fight
to prevent her expulsion. She was reaccredited in a few
months, but found herself in trouble again two years later
when she wrote a series on the Black Market, and implicated
Americans in the corruption. It would be two years more
before she was proved correct when charges were filed against
the Americans.

Another woman correspondent in South Vietnam in 1970
was a woman known to Margaret Kilgore only as "the Greek
woman." Most probably this was Mary Joannidis of Agence
France Presse. Joannidis was awarded the Cross of Gallantry
for her assistance in helping wounded South Vietnamese soldiers during fighting in Cambodia. Another woman correspondent was Patricia Penn, who wrote in New Statesman of
a hospital at Quang Ngai, which was under virtual siege.
The hospital was run by the American Friends Service Committee. The Friends, or Quakers, were pacifists and openly
opposed to American intervention in Vietnam, which earned
them the animosity of most of the Americans in Quang Ngai
and also of the Vietnamese who had lost relatives at the hands
of the Viet Cong. Like Martha Gellhorn in 1967, Penn pointed
out that most of the injuries at the hospital were caused by
"friendly" fire.

Back in the United States, but still very much involved
in the Vietnam War, Elaine Shepard had written her book
The Doom Pussy, and had been traveling to promote the book
and to drum up support for the men who were fighting the
war. Early in 1970 she published an article in Twin Circle
magazine about a Green Beret who had escaped in 1969 after
five years of captivity with the Viet Cong. In December
1970 she followed up this article with a second one about this
man, and wrote that he and other returned prisoners of war
were jubilant about the November 1970 unsuccessful attempt
to liberate American prisoners from North Vietnam's Son Tay
prison, even though the rescue attempt had failed, because
even an aborted rescue would let the prisoners know that
they had not been forgotten. Shepard had not wavered in

her support for the war and the men fighting it, and was
bitter about the writing of the anti-war journalists.   She
wrote:

> Leaders of the pack of New Journalism are determined
> that there be no heroes in this war ... no warriors
> of the Vietnam conflict are to be glorified ... they've
> decided war in Asia is unromantic, bad taste, unac-
> ceptable ... free press should mean true press. [16]

Although the controversy about press coverage of the
war continued, actual coverage of the war declined.   Journalists hoping to establish reputations no longer sought a Vietnam assignment.   As Margaret Kilgore put it, "The war is
so far along now that it is difficult to sell it as a way for
a young reporter to become another Ernie Pyle."[17]   Television correspondents were told that the peace negotiations
in Paris and the withdrawal of American forces were now the
major Vietnam stories.   In short, the war was no longer a
hot story.

OUR NEW GI: HE ASKS WHY _____ Georgie Anne Geyer

<u>January 13, 1969</u>

The Vietnam war has witnessed the birth of a new American
soldier, bred for professionalism and honed by skepticism.
If once American fighting men went out with flags flying to
save their country and the world, today they--the career
servicemen particularly--go out primarily to prove themselves
as professional soldiers. If once American soldiers obeyed
automatically, with no thought whatsoever of questioning,
today they have become the soldiers who ask why.

As one colonel says, "The American GI today wants to
know why he's being sent in to die. It's not enough any
more to simply tell him to do it."

In many ways, the new army they fight in is far more
democratic internally than the army their fathers fought for
in World War II. There are still sadistic sergeants who physi-
cally mistreat their men, but they are out of style. There
are still officers who believe that they command, period,
without any thought of persuasion, but they are considered
out of step.

As Marine General Raymond Davis remarked, "You get
more done by leading men than by driving them."

It is still an army that combines draftees with one eye
on the calendar and mustering-out day, with career men who
take their service seriously. It is an army that draws on a
broader and more representative social base than every before in history. Yet, paradoxically, that does not necessarily
assure its attitudes towards issues such as civilian control
of the military. For it is becoming a professional force that
may lead, many speculate, to an all-volunteer army, and to
the time when not all Americans will feel it is necessary to
fight for their country.

Side by side with this highly professional group, which
tends to view warfare as a technical endeavor, is a large and
vociferous group that frankly does not believe in the war it
is fighting and says so with amazing candor.   In between
these two groups is a group that seems to be smaller--those
men who feel they are fighting for patriotism and to protect
their own country's shores.

For anyone who has been regularly and closely in contact with the American army in Vietnam, it is perhaps the
most amazing--certainly the most bewilderingly complex--
fighting force the world has yet put forth.   It is going
through a revolution of its own--the military's companion
piece revolution to the much more heralded revolutions on
the campus, in the ghetto and in American social structures.
It has an Old Right, a New Left, a large middle ground,
some aimless existentialists and a number of confused officers.

The new situation begins with the primary fact that so
many men and officers today are so well educated.   In the
Air Force, for example, of 118,000 line officers, 11,864 have
master's degrees and 508 have doctorates.   In the Marines,
99.9 per cent of the officers are high school graduates, 56.02
per cent have college degrees, and 3.22 per cent have master's
degrees.   Among Navy officers, only 448 did not finish high
school.   There are 19,216 high school graduates, 45,588 with
college degrees, and 14,882 with advanced degrees.   Even
among the Navy enlisted men, there are 9,630 with bachelor's
degrees and 610 with advanced degrees.   In the Army itself,
67 per cent of the officers hold college degrees today; of
these 17 per cent are advanced degrees.   This is revolutionary in terms of the educational makeup of 10 and 20 years
ago, and it has led directly to more democratic relations between officers and men.

As one young officer said, "The troop-sergeant relationship has changed totally.   A sergeant who's been in 20
years can't tell a college graduate what to do.   He'll talk
back to his officer.   It's become very free and open among
people in the system."

This sort of thing has led to imbalances, however, and
sometimes to older officers leaving in bitterness over what
they consider to be failures in discipline.   Take the case of
General Charles Stone, who left the service in December.
Frustrated by the casualness and lack of discipline in his

camp near Pleiku, he put through an order by which soldiers
who did not salute would be sent to forward areas. Roundly
criticized and not upheld by the Department of Defense,
General Stone, a generally respected officer, retired, an
embittered man.

For the impatient young officers, on the other hand,
things are not changing fast enough. The number of young
officers, particularly from the West Point classes of 1964 and
1965, who are leaving the service, has become a major problem. Part of the reason cited is the long tours of duty in
Vietnam. But part of it is a military generation gap--they
say they feel the older officers are trying to inspire them
with an "outdated" style of patriotism that they find simply
tiresome. But to many, these problems of permissiveness
versus discipline are being resolved in a happy manner.
There are fewer commands, more self-generated actions.

Morris Janowitz, who has written the two classic books,
The Professional Soldier and The New Military, about the
changes in the American military, cites these basic points:

1. There has been a change in the basis of authority
and discipline in the military establishment, a shift from authoritarian domination to greater reliance on manipulation,
persuasion and group consensus.

2. The technical character of modern warfare demands
that the military develop more and more of the skills and
orientations common to civilian administrators and leaders.

3. The military elite has been undergoing a basic
social transformation since the turn of the century, shifting
its recruitment to a broader base. But this does not necessarily mean a "democratization" of outlook and behavior, one
aspect of which is accountability to civilian authority.

4. The military man is less and less prepared to think
of himself as merely a military technician. He is becoming
a far more politically alert man.

To some, these changes are exhilarating; to some,
frightening. To others, they raise interesting questions.

Are we, indeed, headed toward a totally professional--

a volunteer--army, as President-elect Nixon has urged?   Are
we training men who ask "why" but then go ahead and kill
in a war they don't believe in?   What will the new political
awareness of the military lead to?   What will it mean to American democracy if the time comes when all Americans are not
expected to defend their country?

No one yet knows the answers.   But they are some of
the most fascinating questions boiling in American life today.
Their cauldron is Vietnam.

January 14, 1969

Captain Stephen Berti sat at the end of the dinner table in
the remote Vietnamese village of Binh Hung, gritting his
teeth while his men squabbled about the important matter of
whether they should engage a new laundress.

Some thought it was a good idea.   Others were shouting
angrily because it would cost an extra $1 a month.   Finally
Berti, a handsome, able young officer, brought his fist down
on the table.

"That's enough," he shouted, drowning out their shouts.
"We're going to get the new laundress and that's it.   Because
that's what I say."

"I'm not gonna pay it," his sergeant pouted angrily.

Berti pointed his finger at him.   "You're exempted,"
he said.   "Get your laundry done the way you want."   Then
his voice rose even higher.   "And I don't want to hear ...
one ... more ... word about it."

It was a usual enough domestic hassle in any Army
billet in Vietnam, particularly down in the quiet rice fields.
But noteworthy about this scene was the aftermath.   Berti,
considered by his commanders to be one of the best of the
young new-style officers, sat momentarily and brooded.

"I really don't like to have to do that," he said, sitting
in the quiet delta night, deep in enemy territory.   "But
sometimes you just have to."

"And now," he said, looking broodingly at a visitor,
"you won't believe any of what I've been telling you all afternoon." Berti had been explaining what it is, in effect, that
makes the New American soldier in Vietnam--in particular,
what it is that typifies the new officer-soldier relationship.

"I really believe that anyone commanding a company
today should take a course in psychology," he had said.
"You just can't go in and expect men to do something if you
don't know something about it. It's not like before, when
you treated him like a dog. Today, there's too much individualism."

"Leadership is the most important subject in officer
training. Leadership ability means the ability to get Joe
Blow to do what you want willingly, not to hold a court mar-
tial over him. Everything has changed. We've got rid of
the old theory that because you're in the Army you're an
animal."

The change in leadership is only one part of the "revolution" in the U.S. armed forces today. Although some of
the strict, blood-and-guts old military still exists, a new
military is emerging.

Not only has the officer-troop relation become more
democratic, despite Berti's momentary and bemourned aberra-
tion, but the entire formation of the American fighting man
today has changed.

He is a fighting man who asks "why"--and his entire
training is aimed at making him ask "why." He is not only
commanded, he is persuaded. With exceptions, he is likely
to be treated as an individual. Officers say such things as
"Men must be challenged and feel they're doing worthwhile
things" and "The new relationship between officer and men
is more teacher than commander."

"His motivation comes down to what he does well,"
says one general in Saigon. "Anything they learn to do
well they are proud of. I think professionalism has become
a substitute for patriotism. Many guys do not know why
they're here, but they take pride in doing a professional
job."

You hear this all over Vietnam. To be sure, there
are soldiers who believe--and believe fervently--that they
are here for a "cause." But the primary motivation of most
troops is professional pride. Most are like Specialist 5 James
Kelly.

"I love it here," he says, "because I love helping other
guys out. I love the action."

Or they're like the young Mexican-American in the
delta who asked to be returned to combat because "that's
what I do well--and I like to do it."

The new American soldier is, in general, so well educated and so well trained and comes out of such a dramatically changing society that his relations with his officers have
been transformed in a revolutionary manner.

"It is no longer enough to be a leader," said Colonel
Carl Merck, who until recently was in charge of the American contingent in the Mekong Delta's Bac Lieu Province.
"You have to be a manager. You can't just give an order
and if it's wrong, ignore it."

"Now you draw in your gut and admit you were wrong.
They're such sophisticated soldiers, you have to tell them
exactly why they must do things."

Or as one American general said, with a wry smile,
"we have got to a point where, if an officer doesn't get along
with his men, we transfer the officer."

The younger officers such as Berti have devised new
and effective ways--which arose spontaneously out of their
society--to deal with their men. When he was commander
of a company in the states, Berti always had an "open door"
for his men. They could come in to discuss personal problems at any time.

His method was: "I'd call the guy in and seat him in
front of me. He'd just sit there and wouldn't say a word.
Suddenly, his whole life story would burst out. The guy
had gone AWOL because his sister was getting married and
he was afraid to tell his sarge. I explained it to the sarge
and said, 'Let me know if you let this man go for the wedding.'

I'd leave the decision to him. I knew he'd recommend he
could go."

Another young officer with the same ideas, Captain
Leslie Raschko of Fort Polk, Louisiana, now in Tay Ninh,
kept interview cards on every man in his basic training company. He saw each man every week, dealt with his personal
problems, often called a man's mother or wife long-distance
when something was wrong.

"It's the evolution of American society," Raschko says.
"There's more concern for the individual. And in this war,
it still takes the individual doing his own job. A computer
can indicate directions but it can't execute a mission."

To motivate each man to fulfill his potential, Raschko
also would take college graduates aside and explain that he
knew basic training was even harder for them than the other
guys. He told them he knew the repetition was boring but
that they should help the slower guys.

"And, you know, it worked," Raschko says. "Of
course, the old sergeants couldn't understand this. They'd
say, 'You're trying to baby them.'"

"No. If you treat them like men, they'll act like men."

January 15, 1969

A revolution in training that began in the 1950s and has
reached its zenith in the Vietnam war is largely what has
led to the new American soldier. It used to be--and still
is to some extent, of course--that officers gave orders, period, and chewed a guy out for anything he did wrong. Today this is no longer the ideal.

Captain Stephen Berti, serving in the Mekong delta,
tells of his admiration for his former commanding officer,
Colonel Roswell Round, also now in Vietnam.

"He never got mad, he never panicked," Berti explained
of Round. "When our companies failed inspection, I thought
he was going to storm. All he said was, 'Well, Steve, it looks
like you'll have to do a hell of a lot better. I wouldn't feel

too bad about it.   I know you'll be superior next time.'   If
you ever saw five company commanders work their tails off...."

"The next time we all passed with flying colors.   He
didn't harass you or chew you out.   He let you do it--and
so we would have done anything for him."

What, the traditional disciplinarians might well ask, has
happened to the Army?

To see the startling contrast between yesterday and
today, go back to World Wars I and II, when American soldiers went off to fight and die backed by great patriotic
groundswells.

In World War II, there were large numbers of draftees,
and yet we had what was probably the best army we ever
put in the field.   We emphasized training and discipline.   For
the first time in history we had a really professional army.

Then General Harold Johnson became chief of staff of
the Army and the "revolution in training" began.   He changed
the fundamental idea of training, believing you had to do more
than command, you had to challenge men.

The vehicle for the revolution in training was the drill
sergeant.

"I told my drill sergeants to treat each of their men as
individuals, to know their problems and their individual psychology and to deal with it."

"Some of the old-style sergeants would take the men
out the first day and run them up and down in 104-degree
heat.   I told them that's not the way.   You work slowly--it
takes a little more time."

"And I told them, 'You're not only an instructor, you
have to be a good teacher.   You have to look in a man's eyes
and see if he understands.'"

A Marine officer, Captain Rob Robinson, who serves
at Dong Ha near the DMZ, carries it still further.   "Before,
if a man taught class and you went to sleep, he'd throw his
helmet at you."

"Now the instructor is so good he won't want to go to
sleep. The technique of military instruction--that's what
we learn."

And in every aspect of training the "whys" were stressed,
largely in response to the sophisticated equipment used. "Before we just used to tell them to do it," one officer explained.
"Now we tell them why the strategy is this way."

Before this revolution in training, for an officer to be
sent into training was like being relegated to the garbage
heap. Today a command in a training center is ranked equal
to combat command.

One group of American troops is totally professional in
orientation. They are not essentially patriotically inspired.
They are the ones who take pride in a job well done, just as
a plumber or an executive takes pride in his work.

Their "whys" are totally technical--related only to techniques, to strategies. They are as cool and as professionally
disinterested in moral or patriotic questions as a Turkish janis-
sary or a French foreign legionnaire.

But there is another group, also large and including
many of the best-educated of the young officers, whose "whys"
extend to moral and metaphysical questions--in particular the
rights and wrongs of the Vietnam war and American involvement in it.

And so you find in this richly complex American military in Vietnam another great dichotomy--the technocratic
professional soldier and the dissident New Left in uniform,
with the majority somewhere in between.

January 16, 1969

A dissident young officer, one of the brightest American
military men in Vietnam, was speaking of how the men and
officers here rationalize their way out of their original in-
stinctive belief that the Vietnam war is wrong.

"It's like this," he said. "You suddenly go out on a
whim and you buy a new car and you spend more than you

should. So it has to become the best car on the market.
You begin passing over the ads for the other cars to back
up your choice."

"Applying it to Vietnam is very simple," he summed
up. "You're sent to Vietnam, or you volunteer. Once you
arrive and see the conditions, you have to regain your mental
balance by justifying why you're here."

And so, he explained, after hours of "subconscious
self-argument," a soldier is forced back on the feeling that
there must be a reason why he's here. So he simply ration-
alizes it. His higher-ups know why he's here and they must
be right.

"Any time there is an imbalance, the human mind will
bring a balance back. And so most argue themselves eventually into supporting why they're here."

But because of this strange teeter-tottering back and
forth, he argued, you can talk to a man one week and his
position will be anti-war. The next week he may have gone
through this metamorphosis and made peace with his doubts.

But the amazing thing about the military here is that
there are so many who do not. A correspondent who has
roamed the country for six months and talked with hundreds
of troops found that fully half of the men encountered were
against the war to some extent.

Some of their reasons were moral. Others simply saw
no sense to it. Many despised their Vietnamese colleagues
so much for their corruption and languor that they came to
hate the entire scene.

Often, strangely enough, those who thought we never
should have come and that it made no sense, later felt that,
being here, we should go all the way and win fast regardless
of the means.

A Marine pilot in Chu Lai, standing in the roaring
airport, put it this way: "My problem is I just don't agree
with the whole thing. When I first came over, I thought I
could accept some of the things. Then you get cynical.
Your friends get killed."

"You find you can't match the Vietnamese," he smiled cynically, "in patience or in apathy. Then you meet a few good Vietnamese and get a little hopeful."

"But it ends up--you don't care. Yet I'm a Marine. I'm well trained. So that doesn't stop me from doing my job."

Apparently large numbers of men here suffer from feelings of unreality--voiced over and over--about the war. To the men here, this is not a "life or death" war. They know their families are not threatened. There is a strange existential commercialism that hangs over it--and perhaps all this is typical of the frustrations of "limited war."

In the cool mountain town of Banmethuot, for instance, there was a Colonel Thomas Reid, the resident intellectual, who used to regale his friends with his interpretation of this war.

"This is a package deal," he would say. "You're told you're coming to Vietnam. You've got 365 days, with five days R & R out of the country and a couple of R & Rs in the country. Then you go home. It sounds fine. But then you get killed. The folks at home are angry and confused. That wasn't part of the package."

An Air Force pilot put it another way. "There is complete impersonality, especially among pilots," he said. "It's just a job to be done as well as possible. It seems unfair if you're killed. One night in Da Nang in the enlisted men's club, we were watching a show and outside you could hear the boom boom of the bombers. There was a feeling of unreality. It was all so strange."

Another part of the strangeness is how few Americans here talk with hatred of the Viet Cong or the North Vietnamese. It is certainly one of the first times in history that soldiers have admired the enemy more than they admire their allies.

One night in Tay Ninh, for instance, two officers, both of them dedicated to the basic commitment of the war, sat and talked with the frustration of so many officers here.

"The problem with this war is there's nobody to hate,"
one said. "Nobody liked the Japs and the Germans. Who
can hate Ho Chi Minh? I do hate him," he said, "But he's
hard to hate."

The other officer shrugged. "I don't even hate him,"
he said begrudgingly.

An Air Force captian put it this way. "In World War
II, you felt that if you failed, your homes and country were
at stake. Here you don't feel that way. It hasn't come
across to most men why they're really here."

"It's a never-never land. How can you get excited
about a place that doesn't really exist? We're not really here.
All our lives we've been trained for this moment. But when
it comes, you can't even identify the enemy."

"There are no caricatures like slant-eyed Japanese or
bull-necked Germans. Maybe this is an error. It's a good
psychological motivation to hate the enemy if he's depicted
as a monster. Here there's not much emotional involvement.
And in order to hate, you have to be emotionally involved."

January 17, 1969

For many GIs, disillusionment with the Vietnam war begins
with personal revulsion at the corruption of the South Vietnamese army and officialdom. Because they are Americans--
amazingly candid about everything--they talk about this all
the time.

"How can you have land reform when all the landowners
are the officials in Saigon?" a lieutenant colonel asks.

Or, as one 40ish colonel observed, "I came over here--
I thought there was something worth accomplishing. Now I
just want to serve my time and get out and get home. Every
day I go into the office of a Vietnamese major to get a pass
for my chauffeur. Every day his aide tells me, 'The major's
not here.' I see people going in with papers for him to sign
and coming out with them signed. Finally I just leave."

In some areas American helicopter pilots refused so

obdurately to pick up Vietnamese with their helicopters that
they were ordered to do so.

Recently, in Pleiku, Americans who go out on small
reconnaissance patrols of four and six people were integrated
with Vietnamese troops.   "The Vietnamese refuse to stand
guard at night," the Americans said.

A typical scene in this drama took place one night in
Saigon at one of the street-side bars, as the eerie red flares
shot up spasmodically around the city and the occasional boom
of artillery could be heard in the distance.

An Army officer was bent over his drink.   "The Vietnamese won't do anything," he said.   "The corruption is fantastic.   You're supposed to give a widow $200 and a decent
burial for her husband.   Instead, in my area, a Vietnamese
officer puts a couple of crates together and gives her $50.
She thinks that's a lot and he pockets the rest."

"And the Montagnards--no wonder the Montagnards hate
the Vietnamese.   We send things to them like soap.   The
Vietnamese officers cut the soap in half and give them half.
Why do we let them do it?   Because we want them to take
responsibility."   The last was said with irony.

"But what about the Viet Cong?" his companions asked.

"They're different," he continued.   "They have an idea.
They believe in something.   They have something to fight for.
They believe in equality.   They've created a unified society."

"You sound like you think we're on the wrong side,"
the other person interjected.

"I've sometimes wondered," the officer responded wryly.
"The thing is that I don't think communism is all bad.   It's
one way of organizing life, one way of doing things.   What
right do we have to tell these people how to live their lives?
What right do we have to be here?"

Still others find themselves personally upset when they
discover--often in contrast to what they had heard--how many
of the Vietnamese people actually are against them.

"My area is 95 per cent North Vietnamese," Corporal
Stanley Paige said.   "You go into the hills.   The people won't
tell you a thing.   The grunts really resent it."

"Somehow you have to have faith in your government.
You figure they know something you don't.   The officers
like it--sure they have a vested interest in it.   They want a
promotion."

"I go out and pick up civilians--any civilians--and we
put them in the chopper and bring them back to interrogate.
We take all their rice, so they hardly have enough left to
eat.   Here, you're in a state of suspended animation.   It's
a dehumanized life."

It is difficult to say exactly who the dissidents are in
Vietnam because they cut across all lines.   They also do
their job and do it well, regardless of their own personal
beliefs.   Much of the dissent--not surprisingly--is among the
more intellectual young officers.   These include many university men, in addition to those who aspire to becoming
"area specialists," the experts in one geopolitical area of the
world who advise the American military establishment.

It is these young officers who are leaving the service
in such large numbers that the Department of the Army is
deeply troubled.

Surveys which have been made of returning GIs also
mirror this dissent.   Leon Rappoport, a social psychologist
at Kansas State University, found in interviews that veterans
of heavy fighting in Vietnam came home disillusioned and hat-
ing the war.   Those with little or no combat experience felt
the involvement was justified.

What any of this means in the short or long run is
impossible to say.   The doubts have in no way affected the
men's jobs--though they could eventually lead to a kind of
"copping out" on the major decisions in American life.   Many
of these men say the experience of Vietnam has led to a deep
cynicism and skepticism about many of their country's motives
and actions.

Reprinted by permission of the author from the Chicago Daily
News, January 13-17, 1969.

Third Field Hospital, South Vietnam (May 27, 1970)

Two men, a father and a son, have learned firsthand that
this hospital is something of a miracle factory.

The episode that was to bring Spec. 4 Jeffrey Motyka
of 1st Cavalry Division (Air Mobile) to the Saigon-based medical complex began at an outpost just across the Cambodian
border. A tired Jeff carrying a heavy radio pack on his
back was heading for a bunker to awaken his perimeter guard
replacement. Suddenly the stillness and darkness were shattered by incoming mortars and rockets from Cambodian-based
NVA installations. One mortar hit less than 10 feet away and
Jeff never made it to his buddy's bunker.

Mortar fragments filled both legs. He attempted to
get up but without success and felt blood soaking his fatigues
Then began his inch-by-agonizing-inch crawl toward a tem-
porary underground command post to deliver the radio Jeff
knew was the lifeline for the other servicemen. That radio
meant the ability to summon gunships, medevac helicopters,
air strikes or whatever else a situation might require.

Mortars and rockets were coming in hellish quantities
and Jeff knew that he was only one of many hurt or even
dead. He pulled his wounded body over the ground and
pushed the radio ahead of him toward the hole that marked
the lieutenant's bunker. Jeff doesn't recall how he got to
the bunker opening, but he did, and he remembers seeing
the officer's hand reach out and pull the radio in, after whic
other hands reached out and also pulled in Jeff. This attack
took place the night of April 23, Vietnam time.

In the town of Plantation, Florida, Jeff's family would

soon be embarking on an ordeal of their own as they received
one of those dread telegrams from the Department of the Army.
The parents are Mr. and Mrs. John W. Motyka and there is
a younger brother Barry, 18, soon to graduate from Stranahan High School.   The father, a district sales director for
Youngs Drug Products Corp., had just returned from Jacksonville and a working session with Larry Houser who heads
the area made up of seven Southeastern states.   John was
tired from his trip and sat down briefly with wife Jeanne and
young Barry before making his way toward bed and much
needed sleep.

It was 10:30 p.m. when the bell rang and Jeanne went
to the door to see a young man standing there, telegram in
hand.   She took the yellow envelope and noted the stamp,
"Do Not Telephone."   Shaken and frightened, she knew she
could not bring herself to open it.   So she woke her husband.
The message told them of Jeff's injuries and gave them another
APO number to send mail.   There were many medical terms
in the telegram, but they did not confuse John Motyka.   He
had been a Navy corpsman in the submarine service in World
War II and knew just how gravely their son had been wounded.

After the first shock was over, John got busy notifying
the various members of the family because he knew that cards
and letters would mean a lot to Jeff.   Word went out to the
maternal grandparents, Mr. and Mrs. Walter McNaughtan of
Margate, Florida, and to John's own parents, Mr. and Mrs.
John J. Motyka of Phoenix, Arizona.   Mail was going to mean
a lot to that stricken young man 13,000 miles from home.   The
closing sentence in the telegram was a giveaway to John.   "Your
son has been seriously injured but is not at this time in imminent danger."   The father knew this really meant it was a
case of touch and go.

John then wrote a letter to Ed Hoffman, his friend and
national sales director for the New Jersey-based drug firm.
It was a letter that was to start a wonderful chain reaction
totally unexpected by any of the Motyka family.

On May 1 a telephone call came from the firm's president, John C. MacFarlane.   "John, you have a passport and
we have just made arrangements for you to go to Vietnam.
You're to fly to Los Angeles this afternoon where you'll be
met by Harold Halberstadt, our West Coast manager."

The father was stunned and even stammered a protest that he was no different from other parents whose sons had been hurt. MacFarlane cracked a mild little joke. "John, get out there, maybe you can set up a route in Vietnam." How his one suitcase and attache case got packed John doesn't know. He presumes Jeanne did it, but he was in a daze, and left to his devices, might have gone off without so much as a toothbrush. In Los Angeles he was handed a round trip ticket by Halberstadt along with some cash and credit cards, although nobody was sure if the credit could be used in Vietnam.

The stage now was set and the action about to transfer to Third Field Hospital. I had just returned from the I Corps area and was visiting the wounded. This day I was able to give a very sweet birthday gift, thanks to the women and Sunday school children of Lakewood Presbyterian Church in Jacksonville. They sent homemade fudge done up in fancily decorated cans (green matting with cutouts of chickens, ducks, and flowers, the work of the Sunday school set) and carefully stored away here just for birthdays. The first shipment consisted of 24 separate containers, each with a pound of fudge.

One man to whom I spoke told me, "I'm just lucky to be alive today, that's my best birthday present." I told him to wait a minute, that I'd be right back. I returned with a birthday card and the can of candy. He removed the lid and his eyes sparkled. "Holy smoke, real honest to gosh fudge! It's so good my jaws sort of ache with happiness. I haven't had any chocolate or homemade candy since I got out here."

Staff Sgt. Jim Sanders, the liaison officer for 1st Cav., one of that wonderful group of men who arrange everything from transfer of paychecks to notification of address change, told me, "Patches, I have a man here from Florida." He took me to the bedside of Jeff Motyka where the father also was sitting. I could sense the father's grave concern for his son, but I also knew the difficulties he would face as an utter stranger in Saigon. He had arrived May 3, having lost a day en route crossing the international dateline.

I and others at Third Field took John Motyka under our wings and a hectic week ensued--a week in which I even

found time to take John on a Saigon tour that included visits
to the bars to view the dainty Saigon tea girls. Tomorrow
I'll tell Jeff's progress and his father's acquaintance with
wartime Vietnam.

May 28, 1970

Skill, speed and genuine concern are the triple ingredients
which give our wounded the finest chance of full recovery
that any military force has ever known.

John Motyka of Plantation, Florida, a former Navy
corpsman, learned much as he visited with his wounded hero
son, Spec. 4 Jeff J. Motyka, Co. D 1st Battalion, 7th Cavalry
Division (Air Mobile). The father was here because his New
Jersey-based firm, Youngs Drug Products Corp., had provided the money for the trip, a gesture that was a complete
surprise to the Motyka family.

From Jeff the father got the full story of how lives
are saved by medical teamwork. Jeff had been seriously
wounded on the night of April 23 at a partially completed
fire support base near the Cambodian border. The perimeter,
begun only two days earlier, was still in a very makeshift
state at the time of the attack. Despite severe injuries Jeff
had only one thought in mind, to get the heavy radio he was
carrying into the hands of his lieutenant. Mortars and rockets
were still coming in, Jeff's legs were useless and gushing
blood, but he crawled along pushing the radio ahead of him.
He knew that radio was the camp's only means of calling in
military and medical help. His grim and successful effort
was to win him decorations. And that radio set in motion
the forces that enabled him to be a living hero instead of a
dead one.

I have often written of the fantastically fast aid given
our wounded and Jeff was to give me another firsthand example of it. It's another tribute to the field medics, medevac
chopper pilots, ambulance drivers, hospital medics, nurses,
surgeons and an array of lab and X-ray technicians. Together
they spell for the wounded the magic word--survival.

One of the finest of these setups comes under the name
of 68th Brigade and the Army Medical Command-Vietnam

(AMCVN) (Provisional) commanded by Brig. Gen. David E.
Thomas, M.D., surgeon general at the Long Bien Army Post
In giving a step-by-step story of how a wounded man is
cared for it is my hope that some comfort will be accrued to
those families who have or may receive that ominous telegram
from the Department of the Army.

Here then is Jeff's saga. As soon as he was pulled
into the shallow bunker, really no more than a hole, in which
the lieutenant had set up business and to which Jeff had
handed over that radio, the field medic went to work. The
blood-soaked fatigues and heavy combat boots were whipped
off. Plasma was given and there were quick injections to
guard against tetanus and other infectious possibilities. Already on the way were men of the 15th Medevac of 1st
Cavalry (don't call them dustoffs, this is a matter of 1st
Cavalry military etiquette!) Gunships, also summoned, were
already over the area to fend off further attack by the enemy
Many men of 1st Cav refer to themselves as an elite outfit,
their pride and morale are high, their esprit de corps is
tops.

In only 18 minutes after the call put in by the lieutenant for gunships and medevac crew Jeff was being placed on
a hospital gurney and being hurried along to the emergency
ward and from there to x-ray.

As Jeff told it to his father, "That field medic had me
stripped and wrapped in a poncho. When they unwrapped
me in the emergency ward there I was stark naked."

As soon as the diagnosis (with the aid of x-ray pictures) was complete, Jeff was wheeled into one of the operat
ing rooms at this the 24th Surgical Evacuation Hospital at
Long Bien, about 20 miles outside Saigon.

The surgeon told Jeff that a colostomy might be needed
if fragmentation had entered the intestinal tract. With almost
wizard skill he had discovered also that an artery had been
severed, but the bleeding had not been external, a factor
which could have been vital in Jeff's survival thus far. The
artery would get priority, the surgeon explained, and the
colostomy, if required, could be done later.

As the surgeon signaled the anesthetist he asked Jeff

where he was from.   When the reply was "Florida," the
doctor brightened.   "Well, what about that!   I'm from Gaines-
ville myself."   It gave Jeff a feeling of having found a real
friend in Capt.   Carl Thomas, the man who was about to put
him back together again.   Dr. Thomas smiled as he adjusted
his surgical mask and said cheerily, "Okay, buddy, just
relax and we'll have you fixed up in no time."

When Jeff awakened in the recovery room, he found
one leg in a splint, the other in a cast and both wrapped
in so much gauze as to appear three times normal size.   He
told me, "The Lord sure had His hand on me, Patches.   I
lucked out all the way from a first class field medic right
down to Dr. Thomas.   Didn't have to have the colostomy
either, the doc found the frags hadn't damaged my intestines.
He fixed the artery and the fractures and took some frags
from my stomach and backside.   I'm just real, real lucky."

While Jeff was still at 24th Surgical Evac he was awarded
the Bronze Star with V Device for Valor by Maj. Gen. E.B.
Roberts, commander of the 1st Cav. Division.   The general
had expected to deploy back to the States, but then the Cambodian orders came and the picture changed.   These orders
were ones long and impatiently awaited, the go-ahead to rout
out and destroy the caches and supply lines of the enemy
who have used Cambodia as a sanctuary.

Jeff spoke earnestly to his father and me about this,
"We should have hit him where it hurts by taking his food
and medical supplies as well as weapons and ammo.   They
have had large gun installations along that border and been
free to fire on us for a long time.   If this drive into Cambodia had come earlier there would have been far fewer dead
and wounded.   This is the only way to defeat the enemy,
Dad."

Then Jeff turned to me and said, "I hope your paper
prints this, Patches."   Men in beds on either side, both
wounded in the Cambodian campaign, added their endorse-
ments.   "That's a rog (short for roger), Patches, and quote
us so those people back home know what we really believed
in out here.   We're here and sure as hell know how things
ought to be done.   Back home there's a lot of sounding off
about things of which they know nothing and couldn't even
begin to understand."

A sergeant from Wisconsin added grimly, "You can quote me on that, too. We've needed this for a long time. I wish the folks back home would back up the President. He has made the first smart move we've seen out here in years. And the guys fighting this war--at least the ones I've met--are saying he has their vote. Now we just hope he doesn't back down to pressures from a bunch of ignorant jerks."

An ambulatory patient joined the discussion. "Don't these anti-war demonstrators know they're giving the enemy real comfort and support? If they think we're going to pull out they really hit us much harder. There are men getting hurt and killed out here because some creeps at home are waving VC flags and spitting on our own. To me these guys are traitors, there is no other word."

John Motyka had some twinges of guilt about his visit to his son. He feared some of the other patients might be rather envious of Jeff and wish their fathers could be there.

Staff Sgt. James Sanders was able to correct this idea. He told Motyka what I also knew, that the men were delighted for Jeff's sake. What's more they borrowed Jeff's Dad and agreed that the talks they had with him were the next best thing to having their own fathers beside them. And Motyka collected telephone numbers and messages to be delivered back home. He's now a man with unofficial ambassadorial status, but not without portfolio. His attaché case is loaded and he has his work cut out.

Motyka told me, "It's going to be rough to have to talk to those parents, but one thing I can tell them for certain is that their sick or wounded son is getting the best medical care in the world. I have never seen anything like it, and remember I'm an old Navy corpsman myself."

June 2, 1970

As John Motyka of Plantation, Florida neared the end of his week-long stay in Vietnam with his wounded son, there was to be a new parting of the ways--but this time on a happy note.

Spec. 4 Jeff Motyka of 1st Cavalry Division (Air Mobile)
was making wonderful progress thanks to the almost magical
teamwork that began at the Cambodian border fire support
base where he got zapped and which carried on through two
hospitals. Now he was ready for a third move, this time to
a hospital in Japan after which he'll transfer to a Stateside
hospital close to his home.

Father and son were cheerful and confident now. For
the father it was a lot different from the way he, his wife
Jeanne and younger son Barry felt the night they received
the detailed telegram from the Department of the Army in
which they were informed that Jeff had fractures in both legs,
fragmentation wounds in abdomen, hips and arms, and a
severed artery. Through the generosity and kindness of
John MacFarlane, president of Youngs Drug Product Corp.,
Motyka had been given the trip to Vietnam to be with his
son. It had been a revelation to the father as he saw for
himself the speed, efficiency and unstinting dedication which
go into the care of our wounded. He learned that there is
no clock-watching, no clinical coldness in this care.

John Motyka was a man closer to coming unglued than
he himself realized. Worry, fear, 23 hours in the air, the
time-disorientation caused by crossing the International Dateline and losing a day, plus all the problems of lodging, cur-
rency restrictions and drinking water that is more chemicals
than anything else, had all taken their toll.

This now was the morning of the sixth day and Jeff
was being transferred by ambulance to the 21st Casualty
Staging Center, U.S. Air Force, at Ton Son Nhut air base
just outside Saigon. This, too, is a complete hospital unit
fully staffed by Air Force doctors, nurses and medics. From
this staging center Jeff would go to Japan for convalescence
in an Army, Air Force or Navy hospital. After that it would
be back to the U.S.A.

John Motyka stayed away from Third Field on this particular
morning. He didn't want to be in anyone's way as patients
were brought from the wards, transferred to litters and then
placed on racks in the Air Force ambulances. I watched
John and noted the many signs of weariness. In addition to
being with his own son he had made the rounds of the wards
where he chatted with the men and took down names, telephones

and addresses of their folks at home to whom he promised to
deliver eyewitness news of how each man was doing. He had
given much of himself to these other men and had assured
them that the vast majority of Americans were with them heart
and soul. The men, deeply appreciative, said that it was
the next best thing to having a visit from their own fathers.

Many of these men had been wounded in the Cambodian
campaign, yet they begged John to get over the message to
the people at home that this action was the only logical one
which could have been taken and that the move should have
been made long ago. John listened and promised he would
get the word back to as many people as possible. It amazed
him to hear the commendations these wounded men had for
the President, for the stand he had taken on Cambodia. The
less seriously wounded men wanted only one thing, to recover
sufficiently to get back to their outfits.

At noon John and I collected a huge bag of mail which
had come for Jeff from his company and the folks at home.
We hurried over to the staging area with it and when it was
placed in Jeff's lap I had only one regret, that I wasn't able
to catch the expression on his face and keep it forever on
a photograph. It told the story we all know to be true, the
biggest morale factor for any fighting man is mail and plenty
of it.

A voice rang out, "Hello, Patches, how are you, you
old war horse?" It was Lt. Leonard Rodriguez of Blythe,
California, who is with 1st Cavalry Division headquarters.
I'd been expecting Len and knew he was there on a special
mission. John and I hurried back to Jeff because the young
infantryman was about to receive another decoration.

Len solemnly read the citation that goes with the Army
Commendation Medal. Decorations were certainly accumulating
for Jeff, he'd already been awarded the Bronze Star with V
device for valor, the Purple Heart and the Combat Infantry
Badge, this last designating a man who has served 30 con-
secutive days at least in the combat bush areas. Jeff had
also been decorated with the Cross of Gallantry by the Republic of Vietnam. When Len pinned on the newest insignia
of honor, John stepped away from Jeff's bed and went off
a short distance. He didn't want Jeff to see the tears in his
eyes. After regaining his composure the father returned to
say goodby to Jeff whose takeoff time was drawing near.

I had no worries about the hero son, he was making
fine progress. And for Jeff it would mean return soon to
civilian life. In a few hours Jeff would be in Japan, in the
morning the father would be winging back to Florida.

But right now what John Motyka needed was some rest.
I led him back to my little hootch in the alley across from
Third Field. He needed little urging to lie down, he was
utterly exhausted.

Jeff, for whom the war was over, had told me his personal history. He graduated in 1966 from Stranahan High
School in Fort Lauderdale and went to the University of
Florida in 1967-68. He left after one year to volunteer for
service because he felt deeply committed to fighting the
threat of communism. He was proud of his status as an infantryman and arrived in Vietnam Dec. 20. He attended 1st
Cav's 1st Team Academy at Bien Hoa. By New Year's Day
he was at Quan Loi where he was assigned to Charlie Alpha
Combat Assault Co. He has been in the field ever since.
When he gets home Jeff thinks he'd like to resume his college
training, but wonders sadly if there are any peaceful campuses left where a man can just settle down to study and
work.

Next morning at the civilian section of Ton Son Nhut
I was to witness a most unusual procedure. John Motyka
not only was checked through immigration, health and customs
in just 10 minutes, but was treated with deference and courtesy. I merely held out a photograph of John's wounded son
and said that the father had been there visiting him. At
the immigration desk there were expressions of sympathy for
Jeff's injuries and one official said, "Sir, maybe Vietnam
people do not show thank-you, but we do thank you and
your son and your country for helping us. Without you we
would be with big boot on our back."

In a land where dawdle and sneer had long seemed
the inflexible rule, I had witnessed a miracle.

Condensed from a five-part Series in the Jacksonville (Florida)
Journal May 27-June 2, 1970. Reprinted by permission of the
author.

CHAPTER VII

Im March 1971 Gloria Emerson was at B Med, a field medical
unit near Khe Sanh, where a new base had been built. Casualties were coming into the base from an operation called
Lam Son 719, the disastrous South Vietnamese invasion of
Laos. The South Vietnamese officers did not want foreign
reporters to cover the assault, because they believed the
foreign press wrote only bad things about them. Only good
news was given at the press briefings. One day Emerson
listened as a cheerful South Vietnamese officer told the press
that the day's operations had captured two hundred cooking
utensils, two tons of writing paper and two thousand caged
chickens and ducks belonging to the enemy. The officer
looked offended when one of the reporters cynically asked
him who had counted the chickens and ducks.

At B Med, Emerson wrote, the hostility between the
Americans and the South Vietnamese was intense. The South
Vietnamese vented their resentment on the press, often refusing to speak to them. In turn, the Americans loathed the
ARVN, calling them cowards. Emerson reserved her own
loathing for the South Vietnamese doctors at B Med. According to her, they spent their time drinking and napping inside the tents while outside the wounded were lying on the
ground awaiting the evacuation helicopter.

Emerson's sympathies were with the ARVN soldiers,
who were demoralized and desperate, the victims of their
confused and corrupt government, and the seemingly endless
war. Emerson's friend and interpreter Nguyen Ngoc Luong
translated as the ARVN survivors of the Laos invasion told
her at length of the desperation of the failed assault, of
hysterical scrambles to get aboard evacuation helicopters, of
propaganda radio broadcasts on which the North Vietnamese
tried to shame them for fighting alongside the Americans.

They told of having to leave wounded comrades behind.   According to Emerson, Lam Son 719 was the death of the army of South Vietnam, although total collapse was still four years away.

Emerson traveled throughout South Vietnam, interviewing pilots at Phu Cat Air Base, veterans who had fought with the Viet Minh against the French, and anti-government, anti-American South Vietnamese students in Saigon.   In Danang she interviewed children who had been arrested as Viet Cong spies.   The head of the police chided Emerson not to turn the interviews into an anti-war story, but to stress how the Viet Cong exploited children.   Emerson agreed that the frightened children had indeed been exploited, but to her the important part of the story was that they were being held in dreadful prisons, that the Americans knew fully well what the conditions were in the prisons, and that they were, after all, children.

Everywhere Emerson went in South Vietnam she saw disillusionment and despair.   Her animosity towards the American officers grew.   "I did not like or trust the professional U.S. Army officers I met during two years in Vietnam,"[1] she wrote after she had returned to the United States.   To her they were all stunted and simple-minded liars who lied about body counts, military targets, the morale of the troops, and the fact that we were not winning the war.   Their stupidity, she wrote, was summed up in the statement made to her by a young lieutenant who pointed out that even if the war wasn't coming out exactly the way the Americans might have liked, she certainly had to admit that the United States had developed a superior weapons system.

Emerson's attack on the U.S. professional officer, published shortly after she returned to the United States, elicited cries of outrage from readers.   They protested that her characterization of the officers was stereotyped, pointing out that obviously all Army officers were not wild-eyed cretins, any more than all enlisted men were wise and articulate.   Unperturbed, Emerson stuck to her assertion that professional soldiers liked war, while most enlisted men did not.

Emerson herself most assuredly did not like war, and her critics said that she had lost her sense of perspective.   She wrote, for instance, that the sanest and most sensible

G.I.'s she met in South Vietnam were members of a platoon
who went out on patrol, hid in the bushes, and smoked mari-
juana. But she was criticized most severely because of an
incident which occurred during the October 1971 South Vietnamese elections.

        She had talked to South Vietnamese students who had
decided that the best way to protest President Thieu's one-
man election was to attack the Americans who kept Thieu in
office. Their plan was to drive through Saigon looking for
American military vehicles, and then toss fire-bombs into the
vehicles. Emerson went along with the students on their
fire-bombing mission. She apparently did not protest against
the students' intentions, although she wrote that she prayed
that no American military vehicle would pass. Fortunately,
when a fire-bomb was finally thrown at a passing jeep, the
student's aim was bad, and the bomb merely glanced off the
Jeep's windshield. The experience left Emerson shaken, but
did not dent her anti-war fervor. Learning of the incident
later, New York Times correspondent Homer Bigart criticized
Emerson for what he considered a serious breach of journalistic ethics. Bigart himself was then criticized for deploring
Emerson's ethics when journalists often went along on bombing missions against the Viet Cong and North Vietnamese.
It is an indication of the fuzziness of the issues at this point
that the difference between an American journalist going on
an American bombing mission and an American journalist going on a mission to bomb Americans did not occur to Bigart's
critic.

        According to Emerson, South Vietnamese intelligence
officers suspected that she was associated with the Viet Cong.
They had seen her talking to Viet Cong prisoners and giving money to a pregnant seventeen-year-old prisoner who
had been a Viet Cong nurse. By the time she left Vietnam
in February 1972 Gloria Emerson's bitterness for the professional military and hatred of the war in Vietnam could not
be contained. She wrote:

                Nothing is simple here for the Americans or the South
                Vietnamese. The blame and the guilt, the guilt and
                the blame, and always the surprise that it turned
                out as miserably as this, covers us all. [2]

        In Paris on her way back to the United States, Emerson

met a Vietnamese man who was with the peace delegation.
The man was from South Vietnam, a representative of the
Communist Provisional Revolutionary Government (PRG), which
was the official name given the Viet Cong.   For the first time
Emerson found herself talking to a Vietnamese who was free
to express the Viet Cong point of view.   He spoke to her
about the Americans who were protesting the war.   "They
must love their country," he said.   Then he advised her,
"Love your country as we love ours.   If you do not, you
cannot change it."[3]   Emerson returned to New York thinking
that she could leave the Vietnam War behind her and get on
with her life.   As it turned out, she was wrong.

One of Emerson's last assignments in South Vietnam had
been coverage of the October 1971 presidential election, in
which Thieu's name was the only one on the ballot.   Emerson
wrote how frustrated many of the people of South Vietnam
were over President Thieu's one-man election, but there was
little they could do.   One woman told her that she had burned
her voting card, because it did not matter whether she voted
or not.   Luong and Emerson went to several polling places
on election day, October 3.   The South Vietnamese were so
used to foreign observers at their elections that no one took
notice of Emerson.   She was bemused, wondering what American reaction would be if a Vietnamese delegation turned up
at the polls in New York or Minneapolis.

The election had also been covered by UPI's Margaret
Kilgore.   Kilgore had found South Vietnam increasingly depressing as, during the final months of her tour of duty,
correspondents were being killed or captured with "almost
uncanny regularity."[4]   Four correspondents had been killed
in Laos in 1971, nine were killed in Cambodia and seventeen
were missing there.   Kilgore's bureau chief told her that he
was almost afraid to answer the telephone for fear of more
bad news.   Kilgore herself was under fire at least once during her tour of duty.   In January 1971 she had flown with
a group of correspondents to a site just south of the de-
militarized zone.   The South Vietnamese government was con-
ducting one of its periodic returns to the north of North
Vietnamese prisoners-of-war.   The correspondents were to
be ferried by helicopter to a spot where they could watch
the prisoner exchange.   A ceasefire was supposed to be in
effect, but the correspondents found themselves under fire
as the helicopters were about to land.   Unable to land, the

helicopters hovered ten feet above the ground. The correspondents jumped into a swamp and then ran 100 yards to
the safety of a Red Cross convoy on the road. "It was the
longest 100 yards I ever ran," Kilgore said.[5]

Meanwhile, in Phnom Penh, Cambodia, Kilgore's UPI
colleague Kate Webb had been appointed bureau chief. She
had been promoted the hard way, when her friends Frank
Frosch, the former bureau chief, and Kyoichi Sawada were
killed in October 1970. Sitting and smoking in her office
one evening, Webb was joined by Chea Ho, a free-lance photographer who told her that there was due to be a big battle
on Highway 4 the next day. Webb was silent, remembering
the last big battle on Highway 4, during which two photographers had been wounded. She thought at first not to go,
but the next day when news came of a new offensive, she
changed her mind. It was April 7, 1971.

Webb and her interpreter Chhimmy Sarath were checking the kilometer marker on the highway about fifty miles
outside Phnom Penh when gunfire burst from all sides, accompanied by the roar of mortars. Webb and Sarath dove
into a ditch, where they were soon joined by Eang Charoon,
a Cambodian cartoonist; Toshiichi Suzuki, a Japanese newsman; Tea Kim Heang, a Cambodian free-lance photographer,
and Kong Vorn, who was Suzuki's interpreter. They all
scrambled from the ditch and began to run through the jungle.
Webb felt more silly than frightened. She was conscious of
the fact that she made a faintly ridiculous figure, wearing
white jeans and a short-sleeved sweater, and carrying her
purse.

The next day they were captured by a North Vietnamese
patrol. Tied together, the six prisoners were marched throug
the jungle while American observation planes droned overhead.
Webb found herself grimly amused at the amount of activity
which the observation planes did not observe. The prisoners
were forced to give up their shoes, and their feet were soon
bruised and lacerated. Although they were eventually given
rubber sandals, their feet were badly injured by the time
they reached the North Vietnamese mountain camp. There
they were given medication, placed together in a hut, and
interrogated. It was apparent that the North Vietnamese
believed their assertions that they were journalists. They
asked Webb why she worked for the "American Imperialists,"

since she was not an American.   They asked who she thought
would win the war.   She replied: "I am not a clairvoyant.
I do not know who will win the war.   If I did, I'd write
that story and leave and stop reporting."[6]

Webb found herself patiently explaining how UPI worked;
how it could be American but not connected to the American
government.   She realized that the North Vietnamese did not
really trust the press and found it difficult to comprehend
how anyone could be neutral during a war.

Like Michele Ray, Kate Webb was given a custom-made
black "pyjama" suit like those worn by the Viet Cong.   Also
like Ray, Webb was struck by the realization that the suit
was probably the largest that the tailor had ever made.   Unlike Ray, however, Webb clung to her own filthy clothing
and would be wearing it when she was finally released.   It
occurred to her that there was one distinct disadvantage to
the black outfit.   From the air, she would just be one more
black figure scrambling for cover.   "If someone shot me now,"
she thought, "I'd be in the U.S. body count.   No one would
investigate the black figure sprawled on the ground."[7]

Like others who had been captured before them, Webb
and the others found that their major enemy during their
three-week captivity was boredom.   "That's why all prisoner-
of-war movies are unreal," she later wrote, "They can't film
long minutes of boredom."[8]   Breaks in the boredom were
provided by occasional air attack scares, by interrogation
sessions, and by the visits of the young medic who came to
treat their feet.   One day they were given a questionnaire
to answer.   Webb was perplexed by a question which asked
whether she had seen atrocities committed.   She recalled a
burned village she had seen, but she had not known who
perpetrated the massacre.   She remembered the thousands
of civilians who had been killed by the North Vietnamese in
Hue during Tet.   But she knew that she was supposed to be
writing about American and South Vietnamese atrocities, and
if she tried for balance by writing about how both sides were
committing atrocities, she might be endangering all of the
prisoners' lives.   Finally she wrote a careful sentence about
the killings at My Lai and the Cong Son tiger cages.   They
were atrocities, but known to the world already.

Caught in the dilemma of whether she should follow her

conscience and perhaps provide the North Vietnamese with propaganda material, Webb next faced the task of writing a statement to be broadcast over Radio Hanoi. She finally decided to simply write what she actually believed, and let the world make of it what they would. She wrote that she had been well treated by the Liberation Armed Forces in Cambod and that they had provided adequate food and medical treatment. She also wrote that she, like the members of the LAF believed that withdrawal of American forces from South Vietnam would be an important step towards peace. Since the withdrawal was already underway, she felt that the state ment did not place her in one "camp" or the other.

During her captivity Webb became friendly with some of the North Vietnamese soldiers and later wrote of them sym pathetically. She compared the plight of the North Vietnamese soldier in Cambodia with that of the American soldier in South Vietnam. She wrote that they were:

> People caught in a war ... fighting so long they
> didn't know what to say about peace, because peace
> was unreal ... and now they were learning the adde
> loneliness of fighting in a place where no one spoke
> their language, the loneliness of the G.I. in Vietnam

Webb suffered from a malarial fever and pain in her battered feet, but suffered the most distress when she discovered she needed a tampon, and couldn't make the North Vietnamese understand her problem. She cursed the reality which kept interfering with her desire to be a jungle heroine Finally, with the aid of Suzuki, she was able to explain her need and was provided with a field dressing and some white parachute silk.

Two weeks after Webb and the others had been captured, advancing Cambodian troops had found several bodies including one identified as a Caucasian woman. The woman, who had been shot in the chest, was identified by a Cambodian army captain as Kate Webb and was cremated on the spot in accordance with Cambodian military custom. It was reported in the American press that the body which had bee found was almost certainly Webb.

At virtually the same moment that reports of her death were appearing in the American media, Kate Webb walked out

of the jungle with her five companions.   They had been told
that they would be released, given back their valuables, and
taken back to Highway 4.   In the early dawn of May 1, they
changed back into their civilian clothes and started down
the highway.   Webb fashioned a white flag out of some of the
white parachute silk and took the lead, waving her white
flag.   When they finally saw Cambodian troops on the road
ahead they had no way of knowing if they were friendly troops
or Khmer Rouge.   The Cambodian officer stared at Kate Webb
in amazement as they walked up.   "Miss Webb," he exclaimed,
"You're supposed to be dead!"[10]

Like Elizabeth Pond, Kate Webb wondered why they
had been released, when so many correspondents were dead
or still missing in Cambodia.   She learned that many people,
including Prince Sihanouk and U Thant of the United Nations,
had been involved in efforts to rescue them.   But she finally
concluded that they had been spared because they had been
captured by North Vietnamese who had realized the propaganda value of releasing captured foreign journalists, and
that it was significant that they, and especially Toshiichi
Suzuki, had known enough of Vietnamese customs not to an-
tagonize their captors inadvertently.

Webb spent a brief time in Hong Kong recuperating from
her damaged feet and from malaria, and returned to her position as UPI bureau chief in Phnom Penh in September 1971.
She told Newsweek that she was thankful to have had the
opportunity to have had a glimpse of the "other side," but
added, "I still don't lean toward one side or the other in
this war.   My reaction is a woman's reaction: how very sad
it all is, what a bloody awful waste."[11]

Although the war was "winding down" from the American point of view, and fewer journalists were assigned to
cover the war, there were still journalists coming to Vietnam,
and many of them were women.   As in the past, some of the
women came simply to be with men who were covering the
war.   One such was Marina Warner, who came in 1971 to join
her husband William Shawcross of the Times of London, and
"got herself accredited as a war correspondent in order to
travel freely (or as freely as possible)."[12]   Although not a
journalist on assignment, Warner was a writer, and she kept
copious notebooks while in South Vietnam.   Some of the material in the notebooks later turned up in her novels, such

as In a Dark Wood. But some of the material she published
as articles the following year in Spectator.

Warner, born in 1946 in London, was an Oxford graduate who had already received the London Daily Telegraph
Young Writer of the Year Award in 1970. Her stories from
South Vietnam were varied. She wrote on orphans of the
war, on bargirls, and on the ethics of other journalists. In
her story on journalists she wrote of their sitting around
in the Hotel Royal in Saigon discussing the day's stories
over drinks. She wrote of the machismo--or was it masochism--
which led journalists into bloody and dangerous situations.
She wrote that the journalists did not really want the Americans to withdraw from South Vietnam, because the end of
the war would mean the end of a good story.

> However impassioned he is against the American
> presence in Vietnam--and many pressmen are--he
> does not really want the Americans to withdraw com-
> pletely because it is their actions that makes Vietnam
> a story of international concern. So the same criti-
> cism that many writers make against the Americans--
> that they care little or nothing for the interests of
> the Vietnamese people--can be levelled at the press.[13]

In another story Warner wrote about the "poor little
bastards of Vietnam,"[14] the more than 100,000 orphans of
the war. Somewhere between 15,000 and 50,000 of these
children had American fathers. In spite of formidable red
tape, some of the children had been adopted by Vietnamese
families, and some had been adopted by foreigners. But for
the majority, their fate was to remain in the overcrowded orphanages, or to make a pitiful living on the streets hawking
newspapers and shining shoes.

Much of Warner's writing before she went to Vietnam
dealt with religious symbolism and its relationship to feminism.
She continued this interest while in Vietnam. It was on a
research trip to Tay Ninh to visit the site of the sacred Black
Goddess that she found herself on Highway 13 as the village
of Trang Bang was napalmed by "friendly" forces. Warner
watched in horror as wounded women and children ran down
the road, including a terrified, naked little girl whose photograph later became a symbol of the kinds of mistakes America
was making in Vietnam. Warner stood in the road longer than

was necessary, exposing herself to danger, feeling that if
she could have been hurt herself it might help to alleviate
her guilt.

Two women who had made earlier trips to Vietnam returned in 1972.   One was Oriana Fallaci, who returned in
December to interview President Nguyen Van Thieu.   Thieu
told Fallaci that he knew that it was not in his best interests to disagree openly with the Americans, but admitted that
he had told the Americans that his government would not
agree to a compromise which submitted to North Vietnamese
remaining in South Vietnam.   He told her that he did not
look for victories, all he wanted was for the war to end.
But when asked how long he thought the war would last, he
said that it was difficult to put a time limit on wars fought
with guerrillas, whom he referred to as "hooligans."   "If I
could bring the war to North Vietnam, as militarily I would
like, then you could ask me that question and get the right
answer," he told her.[15]   Fallaci's sympathetic interview with
Thieu presented him as as religious man who was philosophical
about his tortuous relations with the Americans.   After interviewing Thieu, Fallaci left South Vietnam again, saying as
she left that she had no desire to return, nor any desire to
ever again report a war.   "The last time I flew into Tan Son
Nhut," she wrote, "I felt real nausea."[16]

Also returning to South Vietnam after an absence of
nearly five years was Frances Fitzgerald.   When she returned
in 1971 to cover the elections, she spent time visiting sites
she had seen on her first trip.   It was a sad experience.
She looked for one of the villages she had visited in 1966,
and found that it had been bombed into oblivion by U.S.
forces.   "America had damaged Vietnam very badly when I
was first there," she wrote, "But it's astonishing how much
more suffering has been caused since then."[17]   She visited
Camranh Bay, where the Americans had spent millions of
dollars dredging a deep-water port.   Now it was abandoned,
the harbor entrance choked with sand.   At Kontum, which
had been the "permanent" U.S. Army base in the central
highlands, Fitzgerald found only rusty barbed wire and a
water-logged baseball fielder's mitt.   The futility of the war
overwhelmed her.

Fitzgerald returned to the United States to work for
the presidential campaign of George McGovern, who was

pledged to withdraw American troops from Vietnam and end
the war. In mid-1972 her book, Fire in the Lake, was published and catapulted her to fame. Fitzgerald was praised
for insights into Vietnamese society and into the war itself.
The book became a bestseller, perhaps, suggested one reviewer, because it "somehow manages to get under the skin
of this ugly war which has left so many Americans feeling
bewildered and morally bankrupt."[18]

Fitzgerald took the title of her book from the I Ching:
the Book of Changes, an ancient Chinese collection of linear
signs to be used as oracles.

> Fire in the Lake; the image of Revolution
> Thus the superior man
> Sets the calendar in order
> and makes the season clear.[19]

Fitzgerald contended that just as the philosophy of the
I Ching is difficult for the Western mind to comprehend, the
society and attitudes of the Vietnamese had remained incomprehensible to the Americans. She concluded that fundamental
differences between Eastern and Western culture and thought
had doomed the American-South Vietnamese alliance from the
start. The war was futile from the beginning, she wrote,
and therefore, as thousands died and no end was accom-
plished, the war was immoral.

Reviews of Fire in the Lake were generally ecstatic.
Even the conservative National Review, while calling the book
"all the old snake oil smoothly bottled anew,"[20] grudgingly
admitted that no other book on Vietnam had yet been written
with the power and conviction of Fitzgerald's book. In March
1973 Fitzgerald was awarded the George Polk Memorial Award
for her Vietnam coverage, and in May 1973 Fire in the Lake
was awarded the Pulitzer Prize.

Fitzgerald made another trip to Vietnam in February
1973, at a time when a cease fire was theoretically in effect.
In fact, fighting had continued almost constantly between the
Viet Cong (now called the PRG--Provisional Revolutionary
Government) and the forces of the South Vietnamese government. On January 17, 1973 peace agreements had finally
been signed in Paris. To all appearances the war was over,
but, as Fitzgerald wrote, "the signing of the Paris Peace

Accord did not change a great deal in Vietnam--it certainly
did not end the war."[21]

The PRG invited foreign journalists based in Saigon
to cross into its zones of control. The Saigon government
agreed in principle with the right of foreign reporters to
enter the PRG zones, but in practice reporters who did so
were harassed, interrogated, and threatened. Nevertheless,
in February Fitzgerald took advantage of this opportunity to
interview members of the PRG. With David Greenway of the
Washington Post, Fitzgerald drove south from Can Tho to a
region which was controlled almost entirely by the North
Vietnamese and the Viet Cong, which she referred to as the
NLF (National Liberation Front.) Fitzgerald wrote:

> For an American reporter, even the attempt to enter
> the liberated zones brought revelation: it was to
> see for the first time the invisible geography of the
> war. In certain places in South Vietnam, the NLF
> zones were half a mile or less from American-built
> roads and GVN (i.e., South Vietnamese government)
> outposts. [22]

Fitzgerald and Greenway had no trouble making contact
with the PRG and were greeted as guests, fed almost constantly and sung songs of the resistance. They were given
a briefing on South Vietnamese government cease-fire violations in the province, and told by the PRG that its aim was
to bring democracy, liberty, and happiness to South Vietnam.

Propaganda this may have been, but in fact Fitzgerald
found that the civilians in the province strongly supported
the PRG. "The fact is," she wrote, "after thirty years of
war ... the people in those areas that first supported the
revolution continue to do so today."[23] She found that many
people were bitter about the South Vietnamese government's
violations of the cease-fire. The villagers reported that
government troops harassed them, committed rape and theft,
while PRG soldiers did not. The villagers told Fitzgerald
that they were puzzled how two armies which were both Vietnamese could behave so differently.

Leaving the PRG, Fitzgerald and Greenway failed in
their attempt to evade South Vietnamese government forces
and were arrested. They were interrogated as to where

they had been and what they had seen, and were told that
they must give up their film. Greenway shouted at the interrogator, playing the part of an irate American tourist until
finally the two journalists were rescued by an American Foreign Service officer.

When she returned to the United States Fitzgerald tried
to get Vietnam out of her system by taking assignments in
Cuba, Syria, and Lebanon, but in late 1974 she went back
to Vietnam. This time she traveled to Hanoi. She was somewhat surprised to find no signs of war in Hanoi; no air raid
alerts, no troops, and no anti-aircraft guns. Fitzgerald
spent nineteen days there, talking with officials, artists,
workers, and intellectuals. She found the people both curious and friendly. In a conversation with a man who was an
editor and a member of the Communist Party Central Committee, Fitzgerald found that he was knowledgable not only about
American politics, but about American culture as well. He
told Fitzgerald that he felt that the role Vietnam was playing
in world history was to help change the balance of forces in
the world. The North Vietnamese told Fitzgerald that the
end of the war was imminent, and that it would bring an
end to the American military presence in Southeast Asia.
She was told that reunification of the country was inevitable,
even if it took as long as ten years, and that the North Vietnamese were hopeful that eventually normal relations with
the United States could be established.

Returning again to the United States, Fitzgerald tried
to free herself from Vietnam and begin other projects. But
she realized that she would not really be free to concentrate
on another book until the war was actually over. Similarly
Gloria Emerson had discovered that while she may have left
Vietnam, she had not been able to leave the war behind.

Back in New York, Emerson was irritated by the inane
questions people asked her about her experiences in Vietnam.
Her friends told her to try to put the war behind her, but
she could not. With each piece she published on the war,
she received mail from veterans who shared her horror and
aversion, and who could not forget. She began to travel
throughout the United States, collecting evidence of the damage the war had done to the American people. The result
was Winners and Losers: Battles, Retreats, Gains, Losses
and Ruins From a Long War. The book is an agonized ca-

tharsis, which at least one reviewer found moving because
of the evidence it offered of the way the war had affected
Emerson herself.

Although her own opinion is always evident, Emerson
tried for balance in the book by including interviews with
a number of Americans who supported the war, including a
blinded veteran who told her how proud he was to have
served in Vietnam, and a father who assured her that his son
had died in the cause of freedom. But mostly it is an angry,
anti-war book. Most of the veterans, war resisters, and
survivors of those who died in Vietnam who were interviewed
by Emerson were furious and embittered. In Winners and
Losers Emerson concluded that the Vietnam War had left an
entire generation of Americans scarred and permanently
damaged, whether or not they were actually in Vietnam.

As the war spluttered to its conclusion, only a handful
of journalists remained in the Saigon press corps. In 1971
the press corps lost a six-year veteran and the war lost one
of its strongest supporters when Patches Musgrove was forced
to return to the United States with heart disease. Musgrove
had been active up until the day before her collapse at LZ
Cates. After her collapse she was told by doctors that she
would have to return to the United States for surgery. With
the departures of Musgrove, Gloria Emerson, and Margaret
Kilgore, there were no women correspondents in Vietnam on
regular assignment. During the final years of the war, however, two French women photographers covered the war in
Cambodia. They were Françoise Demulder and Christine
Spengler. When Cambodia fell to the Khmer Rouge, Demulder
returned to South Vietnam, and was there to cover the fall
of Saigon in 1975.

But Vietnam had been replaced in the United States
as the number-one news story. By mid-1974 there were
only thirty-five accredited correspondents in South Vietnam
as the American media concentrated on the Watergate scandal
and the resignation of President Richard Nixon. It was
barely front-page news when the North Vietnamese launched
a major offensive in South Vietnam in December 1974. By
March 1975 both Danang and Hue had fallen to the North
Vietnamese and Saigon had been surrounded. In April U.S.
armed forces began the final evacuation of American military
and civilian advisers, U.S. citizens, and some Vietnamese.

On April 21 President Thieu resigned, turning the government over to Vice President Tran Van Huong, who in turn
resigned in favor of a "neutralist," Duong Van Minh.   On
April 30, Minh surrendered, and Saigon was occupied by the
North Vietnamese and Viet Cong.   In a final, panicky scramble,
helicopters plucked Americans and Vietnamese from the roof
of the U.S. embassy in Saigon.   On May 7 U.S. President
Gerald Ford declared that the war was over.

THE END IS THE BEGINNING _____ Frances Fitzgerald

It is now exactly twenty-five years since the United States
first entered the war in Indochina with a gift of military aid
to the French. As the end draws near it is clear that the
course of the war has had all the rigidity of a fugue: there
are variations, but each event refers back to others in history, and the end is the beginning. In March the Communist
troops seized control of the central highlands of South Vietnam; they had done the same in 1954 as they drove the
French from the country. As it happened the ARVN commander of the highlands military region had fought with the
French at Dien Bien Phu. As the offensive progressed Nguyen
Van Thieu began to act more and more like Ngo Dinh Diem
in the last months of his life: he refused all compromise,
isolated himself more and more from his generals and waited
passively, as it were, for a miracle. Ambassador Graham
Martin clung to Thieu the way Ambassador Frederick Nolting had clung to Diem, offering no way for the Vietnamese
to change the government by peaceful means and thus each
day increasing the risk of assassination for Thieu, who waited
until it no longer mattered to resign.

Like his four predecessors, President Ford could have
ended the war with a political compromise. The stakes were
perhaps, lower but the way out was a good deal easier for
him than it was for them. The North Vietnamese and the
PRG had designed it that way in the political articles of the
Paris peace accord. An ambush on three sides being so often
their strategy, they kept the offer of a cease-fire and a
political settlement open until the very end. But Ford refused that offer. He asked the ARVN to die at Xuan Loc
the way the Eisenhower administration had asked the French
to die at Dien Bien Phu, holding out a promise of military
aid the way Nixon in 1954 had held out a promise of atom
bombs. (Not one atom bomb, not three, but two.) Nothing,
it seemed, but total defeat and the collapse of an army would
do.

How to explain these repetitions of history? How to
explain the rigid repetitiveness of American policy over
twenty-five years? Quite clearly, the policy of support for
the war was not a simple mistake based on a misreading of
the Indochinese. As the Pentagon papers show, not one of
the five Presidents who supported intervention had the confidence that the war could be won. Certainly Ford and Nixon,
if not Johnson and Kennedy as well, saw the end, however,
far off. Their intelligence analysts erred on tactical matters,
but they tended to be right about the essentials. They even
made correct predictions about psychological events such as
the Vietnamese reaction to an American withdrawal. The
protection of Americans from angry mobs of "allied" soldiers
and civilians figured in the Pentagon's contingency planning
since 1965. American officials, of course, rarely dwelled on
these gloomy predictions in public. And in a sense it was
not Da Nang, the city, that fell some weeks ago, but the
world of illusion they had created about the war. Many believed in the illusions, but it was with no real hope of success that five administrations proceeded on a course that led
to the death of 55,000 Americans and the near-destruction
of three Indochinese societies.

American policy is inexplicable in terms of Indochina
alone, and indeed American officials often explained it in other
ways. For twenty years or so they described it variously as
an effort to stop communism, to contain China or to deter
national liberation movements all around the world. With
détente and the opening of relations with China, these ex-
planations tended mysteriously to appear in reverse. All of
a sudden the United States was actually helping China by
continuing the war; alternatively it was helping the Soviet
Union against China in Southeast Asia. President Nixon and
Secretary Kissinger, however, took a new tack. As they
explained it, the reasons for the war were intangibles: they
were questions of "face" and "credibility" and the image of
the United States around the world. With the beginning of
the current offensive, Kissinger and Ford revived one of the
oldest of the explanations--the domino theory--while at the
same time adding a series of new ones: the Indochina war
was, it seemed, "linked" to almost every foreign policy objective the United States had in the world with the result
that the fall of Saigon might eventually mean the fall of Israel
Portugal, and so on. To take all of this new rhetoric seriously is, of course, to imagine that Kissinger lives in some

strange, metaphysical landscape where symbolic battles are
fought over the future of civilization itself. To take it
seriously is to believe that Kissinger looks at Indochina with
the detachment of a schizophrenic.

The detachment, of course, is real. The rigidity and
the brutality of American policy in Indochina has entirely to
do with the fact that no American President has ever really
cared what happened to the Indochinese. What is question-
able is whether any other official explanation for the war is
correct, whether in fact any administration pursued the war
for genuine reasons of foreign policy. Conceivably Eisenhower, Kennedy and Johnson did, at least in part. But by
linking the fall of Saigon to American "credibility" everywhere on earth, the Nixon and Ford administrations, guided
by Henry Kissinger, seemed to detach themselves from all
the other objectives of their foreign policy. As time passed
it became more and more clear that their theories were but
another kind of cover-up and that the war continued because
a few cynical men wished to prove themselves right and to
retain their old authority with the American public. They
did not realize, of course, that it was too late--that Americans had rejected their theories and no longer cared. Isolated as Nguyen Van Thieu, they continued to play all of
the old games with greater desperation. In the last few weeks
of the war Kissinger, at least, indicated that he was ready
to sacrifice not only more Vietnamese lives but much of American foreign policy in his battle with Congress.

THREE-WEEK CAPTIVITY _____ Kate Webb

I was behind the lines on the other side of the Indochina
war for just over three weeks, as prisoner and a reporter.
I say the Indochina war rather than Cambodia because our
captors were Vietnamese--from the South and the North--
and they spoke to us more about Vietnam than about Cambodia.

They never tired of talking. Throughout, I found them
an odd mixture of toughness and thoughtfulness.

They were homesick, listened to the Hanoi radio on
their transistors and said they were working within a frame-
work of "arrangements" with the Cambodian Communists.
They talked of being stationed at the toughest battle spots,
and they described the improvement of the Cambodian "liberation army" in the same way American military briefers in
Saigon point to the success of Vietnamization.

What I was able to see, of course, was only a glimpse.
Nine of the twenty-four days--or rather nine of the nights--
we spent walking with the guards, a bobbing column of
shadows in the jungles of southern Cambodia. Two weeks
were spent confined in a space a quarter of the size of the
Hong Kong hotel room where this is being written.

Our hands went up as we suddenly encountered the
muzzles of two AK-47 assault rifles at 11:30 A.M. on April 8
on a Vietcong trail.

What we had already seen while dodging through Communist lines for almost 24 hours in the midst of heavy fighting was more than I had seen firsthand of this "other side"
in four years in Indochina.

Telephone lines, we had noticed, were strung between
their deep, well-fortified bunkers. Their trails wind through

dense jungle but are clearly defined once you learn the mark-
ers of knotted grass and broken branches.   They twist and
curve and double back in a way that seems senseless to the
outsider until you think of the bombing and strafing.

The front-line soldiers move in ones, twos and small
groups until they are ordered to regroup or retire to the
rear.   It is eerie to lie hidden and eavesdrop on them, their
AK-47s slung over their shoulders, laughing and chattering.

Their men and women wear thick rubber sandals and
light blue, brown and green cotton uniforms.   Their floppy
hats and pith helmets are designed to shade from the sun,
not protect from enemy fire.

Tied individually and roped together in a human chain,
we began walking in the afternoon of the day of our capture,
our only daylight march.   With me in the chain were Toshiichi
Suzuki of Nihon Denpa News, a Japanese newsfilm agency;
Chhim Sarath, the U.P.I. driver-interpreter; Tea Lim Heang,
a free-lance photographer; Kong Vorn, Suzuki's driver; and
Eang Charoon, a Cambodian newspaper cartoonist.

With six guards pushing us swiftly along a winding
jungle trail, it was the worst of our many walks, which were
never short.   We were still parched with thirst from our day
of trying to elude the Communists.

The trail was one we had crossed several times during
that day, and it led back to the Kirirom road branching off
from Das Kanchor, the Cambodian outpost that had been our
hoped-for rendezvous point with Government troops.

The guards stopped and hacked branches from the
trees around us.   With difficulty we each held one with our
bound hands.   Like walking trees, we set off down the
roadside.

American observation planes droned low over our heads.
"If you run from the planes, we will shoot," the guards warned
us.   "Just stop when we tell you."

Suzuki translated the Vietnamese commands.

They have to see us, I thought.   The planes were

droning over almost at treetop level. We would stand motion-
less for an instant on their approach, not even moving into
the forest, then move on as the aircraft were directly overhead. Even with my white jeans and two of the others with
white shirts, the pilots apparently did not see a thing. I
found myself laughing.

It seemed about two hours before the first rest stop.
We lay against a roadside bank. There were yells from
nearby trees and soldiers appeared. They stood over us,
cocked their rifles and prodded us. Our shoes and Suzuki's
glasses were ripped off and the soldiers retied the men with
wire, tighter this time. My bonds were left alone.

One guard walked away and the other sat smoking. I
motioned my head at a soldier's canteen and asked for water.
The soldier laughed and clicked his AK breech again. Too
tired to care, I closed my eyes. "American," I heard the
soldier say. "No, no. Anglaise, English," Sarath insisted.

They carry their water in the jungle in ponchos tied
by each end to a wooden pole. There must have been two
gallons, and we drained it as the guards stood by laughing.

We shuffled on until dusk. We discarded our tree
branches, no longer caring about the planes. Finally we
stopped. Soldiers appeared from the forest and grouped
around. I had four cigarettes left and smoked two, which
the soldiers lit for me. The other prisoners were taken behind a nearby tree.

Trucks moved on the road and into the forest with
shaded headlights. I again found myself grimly amused at
what observation planes could not observe.

A Cambodian wearing a bright blue shirt and civilian
trousers appeared from somewhere and soon the other five
captives were brought back. They whispered that they had
simply undergone some questioning by the Vietnamese.

The Cambodian, prompted by Vietnamese, announced
that we were prisoners of the Cambodian liberation forces.
He said we were not to fear for our lives and would be taken
a short way to another place. He said the liberation armed
forces were "humane."

Our ropes were replaced with green plastic-covered wire. Mine, I noticed, were looser than the others. Tied in a chain and warned again not to run from the planes, we marched off into the night.

I remember little of that walk except that we had no shoes. We were passed by shadowy groups of troops, girls with pony-tail hair styles. Four litters moved past like shadows, their bearers running at a shuffling trot. Two litters were closed, carrying dead. Groans and screams came from the other and a guard told us it was a malaria case.

We were moving deep into the mountains and an artillery barrage started. We were herded into a three-man bunker. The guards stayed outside.

Our party moved across creek beds always uphill. Sometime in the middle of the night we stopped at a military camp that had flimsy shelters over deep bunkers.

A Vietnamese, speaking English with extreme difficulty, questioned me. We were to hear the same questions often during the coming days. This night the others were questioned separately, in the dark and closely watched by their guards.

Then they brought us a basket of rice and thin pork-fat soup, our first meal in about forty hours, but I couldn't get it down.

Next day we were given the breakfast that was to become our staple diet--rice with fatty pork in a salt sauce. The soldiers ate the same. We were questioned again and they fingered through our belongings. We offered them odd trinkets, but they refused them.

Early the same evening we moved again. They gave us shower shoes they said were taken from the bodies of dead paratroopers on Highway 4, which we crossed that night. We walked about a mile down the center of the road in the moonlight. It was littered with burned-out trucks and there was the smell of burned bodies.

The bombing was heavy that night. We stopped at

another camp. The bombs crashed only fifty to one hundred
yards away, but the soldiers, some of them women, stood
around casually smoking cigarettes and talking. They laughed
at our fear of the planes.

An officer about sixty, pale and very thin, conducted
an exhausting but civilized interrogation for about two hours.
I was told not to fear being killed.

We were clad in "liberation" uniforms, me in black pajamas and the others in deep leaf green. We spent long hours
being interrogated by our captors--and we in turn interviewed
them. We listened to the Hanoi radio or chatted with the
guards who sat night and day outside our hut.

We sometimes lost track of the days and never saw our
faces in a mirror. I made a crude sundial out of a stick in
the ground. We gauged when our twice-daily meals would
come by when the cows walked past.

The monotony was broken only during our conversations
with the officers and casual chats with our guards.

One night the guards gave Suzuki and me half a coconut
shell filled with rank, fiery rice wine. It was the only night
we slept well.

There were daily visits from the camp doctor, a cheerful
young kid with a shock of black hair, who lanced my feet
and cleaned the open wounds of one of the others. He hande
out pills for fever and stomach upsets and warned us against
becoming seriously ill because, he said, nothing could be don
about it.

I found the daylong interrogation tough and worrying.

Why were you following the Lon Nol troops?

Why do you work for the American imperialist?

You cannot be a neutral observer in this war. Everyone is on one side or the other.

We do not believe you put yourself in dangerous militar
situations if you are not C.I.A. Why would you risk your
life if you were not?

I tried to put as much humor as I could into my answers. They quipped in return, but I was never certain what was serious and what was not.

"Do you realize," said an interrogator, "you are a prisoner of war, that one shot through the head could finish you, just like that?"

"I'm in your hands," I said, grinning. "That's up to you now, there's nothing I can do about it."

The tough guerrilla life weakened us all--myself most of all--but even the Cambodians captured with us. We all lost weight, some had stomach upsets, and I had recurring fevers.

In the last week release was often hinted, but we were not certain until the day of an elaborate release ceremony.

Two nights of walking, our march to freedom, were tough. We were weak and feverish. The guards urged me on, and one lent me his Ho Chi Minh sandals.

We were released along a lonely stretch of Route 4, about forty miles from Pnom Penh. It was before dawn. We hurriedly shook hands with the Vietnamese and whispered farewells. "Tell the truth about us," our guards said, and melted into the dark.

New York Times (May 13, 1971). Reprinted by permission of United Press International.

CHAPTER VIII

AFTERMATH

Even though President Gerald Ford declared that, as far as America was concerned, the Vietnam War was over, for many Americans it was not over, and some have said that it will not be over as long as they are alive to remember it. The scars that the war had left were deep. For the first time, American veterans returning from war were not fêted as heroes. Some, in fact, were reviled, and made to feel guilty that they had been in Vietnam. Some veterans said that the worst part of the war was returning to the United States and being made to feel ashamed of having served in Vietnam. Bitterness over the war was only beginning to fade ten years after it ended, when the creation of the Vietnam War Memorial in Washington D.C. and some attempts to honor the returned veterans had begun to help heal the wounds. In the meantime, many veterans who had served in Vietnam were found to be suffering from a psychological disorder which doctors named Post Traumatic Stress Disorder (PTSD), and which was said to be due to the inability of the returned veterans to adjust properly to their return to the United States and to the ambiguous attitude many Americans had towards the war.

Women veterans have also suffered from PTSD, although it was not until 1982 that the U.S. Veterans Administration acknowledged this fact by setting up the "Working Group on Women Vietnam Veterans." In fact, according to Shad Meshad of the Veterans Administration, women veterans often have a more acute problem, since they usually do not feel free to express their anger and frustration and instead compound the stress by holding in their rage and behaving in an "appropriate" manner. The symptoms of PTSD have been reported by female nurses and other military personnel who served in Vietnam, but the women who were there as war correspondents have, for the most part, not reported that

they suffered from the disorder. An exception is Patches
Musgrove, who underwent treatment for PTSD ten years after
leaving Vietnam.

Musgrove did not leave the war behind her when she
returned to the United States. She devoted much of her time
after the war's end to the defense of the men who fought
there. Musgrove remained staunch in her support of the
troops in Vietnam, many of whom continued to correspond
with her, but had little of a positive nature to say about
many of the officers she encountered during the war. She
reserved most of her contempt for the highest ranking officers, and was disappointed when the settlement of General
Westmoreland's 1984 libel suit against CBS prevented her
from giving testimony.

Similarly, Elaine Shepard wrote in 1981 of her desire
to support and help the veterans. "Brave men returned
home to indifference or treatment normally accorded infected
animals," Elaine Shepard wrote. "It bit into me deeply.
Morale, even in best of times, is a delicate flower among
troops."[1]

Gloria Emerson, and, to a certain extent, Frances Fitzgerald were also unable to leave the war behind them. Fitzgerald, as will be seen, became embroiled in the continuing
controversy over press coverage of the war. And, in April
1985, on the tenth anniversary of the war's end, Emerson
wrote:

> Do you know what I'd do? I'd chain all of (the poli-
> ticians) to that haunting Vietnam memorial and have
> them read--slowly--every name aloud. Then the
> war would end for me.[2]

But most of the women correspondents who served in
Vietnam have been able to put the war behind them. Perhaps this is because, as they often stated, they saw themselves as "observers," there simply to do a job. Three of
the women who were emotionally involved with the war because of their ardent anti-Communism--and who presumably
would have been appalled by the war's conclusion--did not
survive to see the American retreat from Saigon. It will
never be known what Marguerite Higgins, Dickey Chapelle,
and Philippa Schuyler would have had to say about the aftermath of the war.

Most of the women who served in Vietnam as war correspondents had had their fill of war, and did not continue
to cover conflicts. Two exceptions were photographers Françoise Demulder and Catherine Leroy, who both went on to
cover the civil war in Lebanon in 1975. Leroy stayed eighteen
months in Lebanon and found it more horrible than Vietnam.
She tried to cover both sides of the bloody conflict, but soon
found it too dangerous to pass from one side to the other.
She was nearly killed more than once and later said, "for
the few of us who covered the whole course of the civil war,
it was the worst place ever."[3]

Several of the women who covered the war changed career
after leaving Vietnam. Both Kate Webb and Margaret Kilgore
found post-war careers in public relations. Looking around
her posh, carpeted office in a Century City skyscraper, Kilgore allowed in 1981 that it was a better life than that of a
foreign correspondent. Webb remained with UPI and took
assignments in Hong Kong, Indonesia, Singapore, and the
Philippines before settling in Indonesia to pursue a career in
public relations and free-lance journalism. Fiction writing,
which had been their careers before they took a turn as war
correspondents, continued to be the choice of Marina Warner
and Martha Gellhorn. Both lived in Great Britain, although
Gellhorn is an American by birth. She preferred Great Britain, she said, because she thinks Americans are "provincial,
conceited, immensely self-forgiving ... and sober-sided."[4]

However, most of the women who had been journalists
in Vietnam remained journalists. Oriana Fallaci continued to
specialize in provocative interviews, and continued also with
her propensity for being newsworthy herself. In 1970 she
interviewed Iran's Ayatollah Khomeini. Out of respect for
Khomeini as a religious leader, Fallaci wore a traditional
Persian chador, the floor-length garment and veil worn by
Muslim women. Half-way through the interview, Khomeini
pointed out that she didn't really have to wear the chador,
since it was reserved for "good and proper" women. Miffed,
Fallaci pulled off the chador and Khomeini stood up without
a word and stalked out the door. In 1981 another of Fallaci's
interviews made news when she called Libyan leader Moammer
Khadafy a "cretin, a poor thing whose intelligence does not
surpass that of a chicken."[5] Later she announced that she
also considered him crazy and dangerous and that she would
have killed him during the interview if she had had the nerv

When her 1980 "novel" A Man, received critical acclaim, Fallaci admitted that the book was neither truth nor fiction.
A Man is based upon Fallaci's long relationship with Greek resistance leader Alexandros Panagoulis, but Fallaci admitted that she did not stick strictly to the truth.   Fallaci stated that she used the same technique--"truth truer than truth"[6]-- in her journalism. She hates objectivity--does not believe in it--and includes not only her own opinions, but also her sentiments, in what she writes.

Georgie Anne Geyer, Elizabeth Pond, Frances Fitzgerald, and Gloria Emerson all remained in the field of journalism after leaving Vietnam. Geyer became a columnist for the Universal Press Syndicate, and a frequent participant on television's Washington Week in Review. She continued to be a foreign correspondent, with a specialization in Latin America. Elizabeth Pond, still with the Christian Science Monitor, went to South Korea. In 1974 she was expelled from South Korea by its government for writing articles which, in their opinion, lacked "accuracy, objectivity, and balance."[7]   The Monitor stood by its correspondent, declaring that her reporting from South Korea had been a fair and accurate portrayal of events in that country. Pond then went to Europe, reporting for the Christian Science Monitor, mostly out of Bonn, Germany. Neither Geyer nor Pond returned to the subject of the Vietnam War, but the same cannot be said of Fitzgerald and Emerson.

Frances Fitzgerald finally began work on her second book, America Revised, a critique of American History textbooks, as soon as the war in Vietnam was over. But the war had not shaken its grip on her. Although she declared in 1980 that the war's end in 1975 had liberated her, she said in the same year that she was almost as obsessed by the problem of refugees in Cambodia as she had been by the war in Vietnam. She was working at that time for Oxfam, the Oxford Famine Relief Agency. And, in 1982, she became embroiled in the controversy that broke out after CBS Reports broadcast a documentary called "The Uncounted Enemy: A Vietnam Deception," the program that inspired General Westmoreland's libel suit.

The television program, with reporter Mike Wallace, presented evidence that General Westmoreland and others in the U.S. military had suppressed information about the size of

enemy forces during the year before the Tet offensive in
1968. The show itself created little controversy, save among
those actually involved in the alleged cover-up, including
General Westmoreland. An article in TV Guide called the CBS
program a "smear," and accused CBS of lapses in accuracy
and journalistic techniques. In a rebuttal article, Fitzgerald
pointed out that TV Guide had not professed to know whether
the charges against Westmoreland were truthful or not, and
that they had therefore failed to prove a "smear." Her conclusion was that the article was written not in defense of
accurate journalism, but in defense of General Westmoreland
and President Ronald Reagan, both good friends of TV Guide's
publisher Walter Annenberg.

In her article Fitzgerald outlined the titanic battle between the CIA and MACV which had taken place in the months
preceding the Tet offensive. The CIA had insisted that
nearly half a million North Vietnamese and Viet Cong guerrillas were in South Vietnam at that time, and MACV had insisted that the figure was about half that number. Furthermore MACV was officially reporting that fewer than 8,000
North Vietnamese were infiltrating South Vietnam over the
Ho Chi Minh Trail every month. Five CIA intelligence officers interviewed stated that the number was closer to 25,000
every month. Fitzgerald reiterated that the "true" figures
were kept from Congress, the press, and the public, although it is her conclusion that they were known to President Johnson.

Fitzgerald's article was furiously attacked by TV Guide
staff writer Don Kowet, who cited her factual error in iden-
tifying Daniel Graham as the Chief of Intelligence in Vietnam
in late 1967 and who took exception to her use of the word
"trivial" to describe CBS's alleged journalistic lapses. Fitzgerald was also challenged by the same Daniel Graham, who
took exception to virtually everything in her article. He
wrote:

> Frances Fitzgerald is of course entitled to her view that
> U.S. involvement in Vietnam was wicked and to her
> hostility toward the people who dutifully conducted
> the war. She is not, however, entitled to her own
> facts. [8]

According to Graham, there was no official disagreement

about the number of troops committed to the Tet offensive
by North Vietnam. In response, Fitzgerald serenely replied
that she had been writing about the months in late 1967 leading up to the offensive, and Graham was writing about the
actual offensive in early 1968, and that he therefore had not
addressed the charges made by CBS. As the trial of Westmoreland's libel case progressed, evidence was presented that
there was, at the very least, confusion among the military as
to the number of guerrillas and North Vietnamese in South
Vietnam before Tet. In the end, Westmoreland settled the
case out of court.

In 1984 Fitzgerald again wrote about Vietnam, in an
article on lessons to be learned from the war. She wrote:

> Vietnam was not a quagmire, in the sense that we
> stumbled into it and were sucked down and unable
> to get out despite our own efforts; though this is
> the textbook, and I think probably the cinematic
> version of the war. In fact the United States created
> the war. And if you count from the time of the
> Geneva agreements in 1954, that creation took over
> a decade. It took enormous amounts of time, expense
> and the energies of a great many people. There is
> nothing easier than to avoid future Vietnams. [9]

Like Fitzgerald, Gloria Emerson continued to write about
the Vietnam War. She could not, would not, did not want
to forget, nor did she want anyone else to. Reviewers of
Winners and Losers had commented on the "intensity of Emerson's own feelings,"[10] and called her "possessed by the memory of the war."[11] But writing the book did not lessen her
fervor. She did not deny that the intensity of her experience
had changed her completely. She could not get used to having people she met trivialize the war by asking her what she
wore, what she ate, whether she had actually seen people die.
"People are baffled by the way I've carried on about the war
since I came back from Vietnam," she told an interviewer in
1977. "But," she added, "I shan't let them forget Vietnam.
I'll live to be 100, and I'll keep talking about it till I die."[12]
Both her friend and former interpreter Nguyen Ngoc Luong
and a United Nations delegate from Vietnam invited Emerson
to revisit the country. Although she would have liked to
visit Luong, now living in Saigon (re-named Ho Chi Minh
City) with his wife and child and working for Associated

Press, Emerson declined.   There were too many ghosts in
Vietnam for her, she wrote.   She would not return.

Five years after the fall of Saigon, in April 1980, Emerson wrote about recalling the lessons of the Vietnam War.
In the intervening years there had been the exodus of the
so-called "boat people," refugees from Communist Vietnam.
There had been the Vietnamese invasion of Cambodia to expel the Khmer Rouge.   But she wrote that mistakes made by
the government of Vietnam must not be used as an excuse
for the years of suffering and horror inflicted upon Vietnam
by the United States.   She wrote:

> This last week of April, if nothing else is done, it
> might be a fitting time to remember what the war cost
> us, not only the millions of gallons of fuel used every
> day to keep on with the killing and bombing, but
> who among us was chosen to take the terrible risks
> and never asked why.[13]

In spite of her statement that she would never go back
to Vietnam, Emerson did return to Southeast Asia.   In 1980
she went to Thailand on assignment for Geo magazine to write
about Cambodian refugees.   Filled with horror to be once
again reporting "unimaginable tales of suffering," Emerson
says, "I just prayed, 'God, get me out of this.'   And She
did."[14]

In one of the refugee camps Emerson kissed a feverish
child.   As a result she contracted meningococcal meningitis,
and ended up in a Bangkok hospital.   She decided that there
was a kind of justice in her finally sharing some small part
of the pain of the people whose suffering she had recorded
for so many years.   She concluded that she was not sorry
that she had kissed the child.

In February 1983 both Emerson and Fitzgerald were on
the program of a conference on the press and the Vietnam
War held at the University of Southern California in Los
Angeles.   The conference, called "Vietnam Reconsidered:
Lessons from a War," was one of the first attempts at dis-
passionate analysis of the war.   The only other woman correspondent on the program was photographer Judith Coburn,
who had been a correspondent in Vietnam for the Village
Voice and the Far Eastern Economic Review, and who was on

the faculty of the USC School of Journalism. Attending the conference--and finding it slanted towards the dovish side in her opinion--was Patches Musgrove. Musgrove's misgivings notwithstanding, the conference attempted an even tone by bringing together many of the major journalists who had covered the war, representatives of the military, the Vietnam veterans, the CIA, the antiwar movement, and the South Vietnamese government--although Nguyen Cao Ky was a no-show. Also invited was Mrs. Nguyen Ngoc Dung, an official of the new Socialist Republic of Vietnam, but she was not allowed to travel to Los Angeles and was forced to address the conference via radio.

The conference proved to be tempestuous. On the first day of the conference, as Gloria Emerson emotionally read her piece on the children who had been arrested as Viet Cong, a crowd of more than one hundred demonstrators--mostly Vietnamese Refugees--marched and chanted anti-Communist slogans outside the auditorium. Later, during a panel discussion on CIA involvement in South Vietnam, Keyes Beech admitted that he, and other journalists he had known in Vietnam, had used the CIA as one of their sources of information. Morley Safer of CBS then suggested that Beech had been used by the CIA. Beech's outraged reply was that a good journalist used any and all sources, and he made it quite clear that he did not consider Safer a good journalist. At still another panel program, after scholars Ngo Vinh Long and Michael Huynh suggested that the war had been over long enough for the United States to consider normalizing relations with the government of Vietnam, they were loudly attacked from the audience. Shouting denunciations and obscenities in two languages, members of the local Vietnamese community let it be known that they did not think it would ever be the right time to normalize relations between the two countries. Mrs. Nguyen Ngoc Dung's radio message was likewise greeted with shouts and hoots from the Vietnamese in the audience, most of whom were refugees from her government. Clearly, in the minds of many who attended the conference, the war was not over.

One of the most emotional sessions came when distressed Vietnam veterans, who considered the use of the defoliant Agent Orange and its possible effect on people who served in Vietnam to be the most important issue that had come out of the war, complained that not enough attention was being

given to their plight. The session on Vietnam veterans on
the final day of the conference was chaired by Gloria Emerson, long an advocate of veterans' rights. Emerson began
by saying that she would keep remarks short because some
of the men on the panel had been waiting fifteen years to
speak their mind. It was evident that Emerson identified
deeply with the veterans.

Emerson reminded the audience that there was no one
particular type of Vietnam veteran, in spite of the stereotype of the crazed victim of PTSD so favored by the media.
She said that the stereotype was a way to deceive and pacify
people and allow them to distance themselves from veterans.
She pointed out that many of the men who fought in Vietnam
came from working class families, while members of the middle
and upper classes were often able to defer their service.
She said:

> I think the veterans themselves will tell you some of
> the difficulties that they had in a society that so
> willingly relinquished them, but it would be deceit-
> ful of me, a correspondent in Vietnam ... if I did
> not tell you that Vietnam illuminated many aspects of
> America I had never really understood ... it illumin-
> ated nothing quite as clearly as the American caste
> system. [15]

Furthermore, Emerson pointed out, for the ones who
survived, no heroes' welcome awaited them back in the United
States. The G.I. Bill for Vietnam veterans was inferior to
that for World War II veterans, she said. She found treatment in Veteran's Administration hospitals appalling. In
every way, the Vietnam veteran was despised and ill-treated.
Emerson said that it was incorrect to suggest that the anti-
war movement had been an elitist group which had treated
the G.I. as a pariah. She pointed out that the anti-war
movement had grown stronger when the Vietnam veterans
had joined it. Of course, she admitted, not all Vietnam
veterans opposed the American role in Vietnam. And, she
reminded the audience, it was important to remember that
veterans of other armies also feel pain. She told a story of
two Vietnamese brothers who had told her how they and their
older brother had suffered psychological problems which were
very much like PTSD.

At first Emerson's remarks were warmly received by the audience. The panel discussion which followed Emerson's introductory remarks was an emotional one, which featured veterans who spoke of exposure to Agent Orange, of the uncaring inadequacies they had encountered in the Veteran's Administration, and of the hostile attitudes they had faced when they had returned to the United States. So emotional were the young veterans that panelist James Stockdale, a retired Admiral who had spent eight years as a prisoner in North Vietnam, declared that nothing he had suffered seemed to be as acute as the suffering of the veterans who had spoken before him. The difference, he said, was that he and the other prisoners had not lost their confidence and faith in the rightness of the war, and had comforted each other in their captivity. They had not suffered the staggering loss of self esteem which tortured the other veterans.

If the panelists had been emotional, they were surpassed by the men and women who spoke during the question and answer session which followed. As the veterans told of their suffering and stress, some of them began to single out the media as villains who had created the stereotypical image of the crazed Vietnam veteran. One veteran accused the "famous faces" among the reporters of distracting attention from real issues such as veterans' rights. Stung by the attack from those she considered her allies, Emerson responded:

> I was a reporter for two-and-a-half years in Vietnam ... I'm not a famous face but I worked for the New York Times. Here's the big joke. It was I who had the idea of letting you (the audience) speak. Not one of the veterans on the panel suggested it![16]

In another altercation a Chicana accused Emerson of not allowing her to speak on the subject of Mexican-Americans in Vietnam. From the audience a man shouted that Emerson wanted to co-opt the entire program, and that it was time that she retired and let the veterans speak for themselves. Even though it was obvious that anguish and the excitement of finally having a forum was distorting the veterans' attitudes, the encounters must have been painful for Emerson, who was such a fervent defender of the veterans. One of the panelists pointed out to the audience that there would not even have been a veterans' panel without Emerson's suggestion.

Speaking to a far less hostile audience on the closing night of the conference, Frances Fitzgerald focused on the lessons to be learned from the Vietnam War. Avoiding future Vietnams would be easy, Fitzgerald said. "It's extremely easy not to intervene in the internal affairs of small, third-world countries," she pointed out. "And, of course, if any administration forgets the lessons of Vietnam, it has only to look to the lessons of the Soviet Union in Afghanistan."[17]

Detailed lessons could be drawn from the Vietnam experience, Fitzgerald went on. One such lesson would be that it is possible to create a leader, like Ngo Dinh Diem, but his purposes will not necessarily be your purposes. From President Kennedy, Fitzgerald said with tongue in cheek, could be learned the lesson not to have too clever speech writers, because people will remember what you said.

Finally, Fitzgerald said, the lesson to be learned from the Vietnam war was that:

> ... the past is not simply for historians ... The past and the future are balanced in the present.... You can have control over the future only to the extent that you are deeply and firmly attached to your own history.[18]

While it presented diverse opinions about the Vietnam War, and possibly the first public forum for the frustrated and aggrieved veterans, the USC conference did little to settle the issue of the role of the media in Vietnam. In fact, on the final evening of the conference, the controversy over the role of the media in the Vietnam War was evident as the New York Times' Harrison Salisbury's statement that the "new right" had created the myth of " ... a valiant American fighting force lost by a stab in the back of treacherous newspapermen and TV cameras...."[19] was immediately followed by Keyes Beech condemning the "merciless, relentlessly negative, staggeringly lopsided reporting of the war."[20]

Because of this controversy, which is likely to continue as long as the war is discussed by people who were involved in it, the media coverage of the Vietnam War assumes an importance dispproportionate to that of coverage of other wars. In an article written nearly ten years after the end of the war, Thomas B. Morgan wrote:

> For most Americans the Vietnam War was media ...
> it is so easy ... to lump together war correspond-
> ents--not to mention any other journalists--as 'media.'
> They become an abstraction, rather than a collection
> of men and women with individual identities. [21]

Certainly the women who formed part of the Vietnam
press corps had highly individual identities.   In fact, the
only attribute they seemed to share was a high degree of
individualism.

Individual women registered individual reactions to the
one experience they all shared in common--that of being a
female playing a male game.   For the most part women correspondents agree that they were treated "differently" than
their male colleagues in Vietnam.   But what a difference is
to be found in individual interpretations of what "differently"
meant!

For a very few of the women, blending in with the military was easy.   Dickey Chapelle, for instance, had long
since won the argument about the absence of ladies' rooms
by the time she got to Vietnam.   If the subject of latrines
ever came up during her tours of duty in Vietnam, she did
not mention it in her correspondence.   Of course, by the
time she got to Vietnam, Chapelle had been accepted by the
Marines as one of the guys.   Her courage and determination
not to be offered special treatment because she was female
were well known to the military.

Similarly, Marguerite Higgins, who had waged many a
battle against regulations such as the one that had forbidden
women to board a naval flagship during the Korean War, had
an established reputation as a war correspondent when she
came to cover the war in Vietnam.   Moreover, she was married
to a general, and was respected by the military.   The same
can be said of Patches Musgrove, who had many friends among
the military in Vietnam.   None of these women mentioned any
hostility or condescension being directed towards them as
woman correspondents in Vietnam.   Musgrove encountered
some difficulty with the highest level of officialdom, but her
problems had more to do with her disregard of bureaucracy
than with her sex.

On the other hand, Gloria Emerson encountered not only

the old latrine story, but reported attitudes which ranged
from patronization to outright hostility from the military.
Of course, Emerson was openly hostile to the military in return. She believed that commanding officers became nervous
when around women correspondents for reasons that had
nothing to do with latrines. It was Emerson's belief that
women reporters made the officers nervous because women,
unable to conjure up the proper military attitude toward war,
often asked questions in tones which indicated disapproval.
When an officer suggested to Emerson that she simply didn't
understand the weaponry or tactics or why men sometimes
liked living in the bush, she had to agree that he was quite
correct. She didn't understand.

Paternalism was also reported by Beverly Deepe. She
found American commanders extra-protective and too chival-
rous in dealing with women correspondents. She reported
that often she was ordered back to base camp when she tried
to visit front-line units. She reported that one Marine captain explained to her that men got killed all the time, but it
would be an insult to the commander if a woman got killed
while with his unit. It cannot be ignored, however, that
some of the women correspondents found this paternalistic
attitude comforting. Catherine Leroy, for instance, reported
that being the only woman among a large number of men gave
her a certain illusion of security. Michele Ray positively
basked in the admiration of the soldiers. So did Elaine Shepard. Helen Gibson wrote:

> I was treated by the military, both American and
> Vietnamese, with almost embarrassing deference.
> The Americans particularly were, from private to
> general, terribly polite and because I was female,
> they always seemed pleased to have me around--it
> was difficult not to get very spoilt. [22]

Georgie Anne Geyer also believed that being a female
was not a problem for a reporter in Vietnam. She wrote:

> I've covered revolutions in Latin America but this is
> my first war. I was surprised to find no barriers
> to women reporters here. I've been out in the field
> almost every week since I've been here but I've
> never been told not to go anywhere because I'm a
> woman. The troops and officers probably treat me

a little bit nicer but they make you feel that you're
a morale booster rather than a burden.[23]

In fact, Geyer believed that women had an advantage
in understanding the psychology of societies like South Vietnam because, having been dependent themselves, women could
better understand dependent countries and people.

Like Geyer and Gibson, Kate Webb, Elizabeth Pond, and
Marlene Sanders also insisted that being female caused them
no problems in Vietnam. Webb has stated that "sex makes
no difference to any kind of reporting."[24] What matters is
the quality of the reporting. Sanders said plainly that she
has never been in a situation where being a woman was a
problem. And Pond has written that, not only was the fact
that she is female no handicap in Vietnam, but in fact her
sex may have saved her life when she was captured in Cambodia. Pond believed that the Cambodians might have shot
the journalists immediately if one of them had not been a
woman.

Even as far back as the Korean War, Marguerite Higgins
had noted that the disadvantages of being a woman correspondent, such as high visibility and the general disapproval
of military brass, could be balanced against the rewards of
being female. She wrote:

> The advantages balance the disadvantages. In Korea
> the mere fact that for a time I was a unique phenom-
> enon meant that my work attracted unusual attention.
> So I received far more national acclaim and publicity
> than many of my male colleagues who did just as fine
> or better.[25]

This advantage did not necessarily occur in Vietnam,
where there were far more women in the press corps. For
women reporters without Higgins' reputation, the fact that
they were female did nothing to help them get their stories
published. In some cases it did help them to get the stories
in the first place, though. Jurate Kazickas, for instance,
believed that the G.I.'s reacted to her in a different way
than they did to her male colleagues. Lonely G.I.'s would
talk to her at length. Pilots would offer her a lift because
they wanted to have an attractive woman passenger, thus
providing her with access sometimes denied to the male reporters.

Nevertheless, she said, these advantages must be weighed
against the advantages enjoyed by male reporters, such as
access to the "males only" officer's clubs and the fact that
they did not have to constantly battle the paternalism of the
military.

There is no doubt that the lot of the woman correspondent
has improved since the days when they were absolutely forbidden access to combat. In Vietnam there were individual
officers who balked at having a woman correspondent under
fire, but there was no official policy forbidding them access.
(Of course, the Vietnam experience was unique in that access
to the war, for both male and female reporters, was remark-
ably easy.) Then, too, there have been wide-ranging changes
in American societal roles for women since the Vietnam War.
Women reporters have been routinely assigned dangerous assignments in the Middle East and in Central America in recent
years. Women such as free-lance photographer Susan Mei-
selas, journalist Anne Nelson, television field producer Ellen
McKeefe have received assignments in El Salvador and Nicar-
agua. Said McKeefe: "We've got women all over the place.
They've realized we can be in there with the best of them."[26]

Of course, the battles in Central America are not even
as "official" from the point of view of the United States government as was the war in Vietnam. And it might also be true
that the employers of these women reporters were reacting
more from a desire to comply with Affirmative Action regula-
tions--as was suggested by Washington Post reporter Joanne
Omang--than from a conviction that women reporters should
cover combat. Whatever the reason for their presence, however, women war correspondents are no longer an oddity.
It is unlikely that these women will be set aside in footnotes
or in chapters with cute titles. "Ladies on the front lines"
are no more. Now there are only war reporters, and some of
them are women.

CHAPTER NOTES

Introduction

1. Gloria Emerson, "Hey, Lady, What Are You Doing Here?" McCalls, Vol. 98, August 1971, p. 108.

2. Dickey Chapelle, What's a Woman Doing Here? New York: Wm. Morrow & Co., 1962, p. 53.

3. Marguerite Higgins, War in Korea. New York: Doubleday, 1951, p. 100.

4. Gloria Emerson, "Hey Lady, What are You Doing Here?" op. cit., p. 108.

5. M. L. Stein, Under Fire: The Story of America's War Correspondents. New York: Julian Messner, 1969, p. 229.

6. Kelly Smith Tunney, Interview, New York, 1984.

7. Ibid.

8. Kate Webb, Letter to Author, 1980.

9. Gloria Emerson, Letter to Author, 1980.

10. Gloria Emerson, "Hey Lady, What Are You Doing here?" op cit., p. 108.

11. Jurate Kazickas, Interview, Washington, D.C., 1980.

12. Gloria Emerson, "Arms and the Woman," Harpers, Vol. 246, April 1973, p. 40.

13. Oriana Fallaci, Interview with Robert Scheer, Playboy, Vol. 28, No. 11, November 1981, p. 97.

Chapter I

1. Dickey Chapelle, What's a Woman Doing Here? New York: Wm. Morrow & Co., 1962, p. 282.

2. Dickey Chapelle, "The Fighting Priest of South Vietnam," Reader's Digest, Vol. 83, July 1963, p. 200.

3. Dickey Chapelle, What's a Woman Doing Here? op. cit., p. 77.

4. Ibid., p. 126.

5. Ibid., p. 137.

6. Ibid., p. 217.

7. Ibid., p. 254.

8. Dickey Chapelle, "I Roam the Edge of Freedom," Coronet, Vol. 52, February 1961, p. 136.

9. Ibid., p. 139.

10. Dickey Chapelle, Letter to Chester Williams, April 29, 1962.

11. Dickey Chapelle, "Helicopter War in South Viet-Nam," National Geographic, Vol. 122, November 1962, p. 733.

12. Marguerite Higgins, "Why the Buddhist Fury?" New York Herald Tribune, August 27, 1963, p. 10.

13. Ibid.

14. Marguerite Higgins, News is a Singular Thing. Garden City, New York: Doubleday, 1955, p. 114.

15. Ibid.

16. Ibid., p. 218.

17. Marguerite Higgins, War in Korea. Garden City, New York: Doubleday, 1951, p. 107.

18. Ibid., p. 16.

19. Marguerite Higgins, Our Vietnam Nightmare. New York: Harper & Row, 1965, p. ix.

20. Marguerite Higgins, "The Diem Government, Pro and Con," New York Herald Tribune, September 1, 1963, p. 1.

21. Marguerite Higgins, "On the Spot," Newsday, January 31, 1964.

22. Beverly Deepe, "Vietnam: The New Metal Birds," Newsweek, Vol. 60, October 29, 1962, p. 38.

23. Glenn MacDonald, Report or Distort? New York: Exposition Press, 1973, p. 101.

24. Beverly Deepe, "The Fall of the House of Ngo," Newsweek, Vol. 62, November 11, 1963, p. 28.

25. Eugene Lyons, "Suzanne Labin: Joan of Arc of Freedom," American Legion Magazine, Vol. 73, December 1962, p. 19.

26. Ibid., p. 51.

27. Suzanne Labin, as quoted in Report or Distort? op. cit., p. 58.

28. Suzanne Labin, Vietnam Assessment. Saigon: Vietnam Council on Foreign Relations, 1969, p. 23.

29. Beverly Deepe, "South Vietnam: The Break-even Point," Newsweek, Vol. 62, December 2, 1963, p. 57.

Chapter II

1. Frances Fitzgerald, Fire in the Lake. Boston: Little Brown, 1972, p. 342.

2. Marguerite Higgins, "On the Spot," Newsday, March 4, 1964.

3. Marguerite Higgins, "Ugly Americans of Vietnam," America, Vol. III, October 3, 1964, p. 376.

4. Marguerite Higgins, "No Club for Cookie Pushers," NEA Journal, Vol. 54, March 1965, p. 15.

5. Ibid.

6. Marguerite Higgins, Our Vietnam Nightmare. New York: Harper and Row, 1965, p. 287.

7. Marguerite Higgins, "On the Spot," Newsday, November 10, 1965.

8. Marguerite Higgins, Excerpts from Our Vietnam Nightmare, Newsday, December 11, 1965, p. 32.

9. M. L. Stein, Under Fire: The Story of America's War Correspondents. New York: Julian Messner, 1969, p. 223.

10. Marguerite Higgins, News is a Singular Thing. Garden City, New York: Doubleday, 1955, p. 56.

11. Carl Mydans, "Girl War Correspondent," Life, Vol. 29, October 2, 1950, p. 51.

12. Marguerite Higgins, Excerpts from Our Vietnam Nightmare, Newsday, op. cit., p. 32.

13. Dickey Chapelle, "Water War in VietNam," National Geographic, Vol. 129, February 1966, p. 280.

14. Dickey Chapelle, "Vietnam: Win, Lose or Draw," The Face of War: Vietnam. Earle Hawley, ed. North Hollywood, CA: M. Luros, 1965, p. 24.

15. Ibid.

16. Elaine Shepard, The Doom Pussy. New York: Trident Press, 1967, p. 247.

17. Dickey Chapelle, "Searching Vietnam for Victor Charlie," The National Observer, November 8, 1965, p. 9.

18. Ibid., p. 1.

19. Jim Lucas, "We Loved This Gal ... This Spitfire," Scripps-Howard News, January 1967, p. 6.

20. Elaine Shepard, Letter to Author, February 1981.

21. "Maggie in the Congo," Newsweek, Vol. 57, April 3, 1961, p. 82.

22. Elaine Shepard, The Doom Pussy. op. cit., p. 24.

23. Ibid., p. 102.

24. "Self Reliance in Saigon," Time, Vol. 85, January 8, 1965, p. 38.

25. Ibid.

26. Beverly Deepe, "Red Ambush Smashes Reeling Viet Force," The New York Herald Tribune, January 5, 1965, p. 3.

27. Susan Sheehan, Ten Vietnamese. New York: Alfred A. Knopf, 1967, p. xii.

28. Ibid., p. 204.

29. Madeleine Riffaud, "North Vietnam: Two Months, Two Thousand Kilometers During the Escalation," L'Humanité, October 18, 1966, p. 2.

Chapter III

1. Keyes Beech, "Some Observations on Vietnam," in William Kennedy, "Press Coverage of the Vietnam War, Draft Report," Carlisle Barracks, Pennsylvania: U.S. Army War College. Strategic Studies Institute, 1979, Appendix A, p. A-1.

2. "Femininity at the Front," Time, Vol. 88, October 28, 1966, p. 74.

3. Ibid.

4. Denby Fawcett, "American Girl in Saigon Finds Life Is No Lark," Honolulu (Hawaii) Advertiser, June 1, 1966, p. 1.

5. "Femininity at the Front," op. cit.

6. Ibid.

7. Patches (Helen) Musgrove, Interview, Orange, California, 1985.

8. Ibid.

9. Ibid.

10. Ibid.

11. Glenn MacDonald, Report or Distort? New York: Exposition Press, 1973, p. 83.

12. Michele Ray, The Two Shores of Hell. New York: McKay, 1968, p. xvii.

13. Ibid., p. 29.

14. Ibid., p. 60.

15. Ibid., p. 30.

16. Jorge Lewinski, The Camera at War: A History of War Photography from 1848 to the Present Day. New York: Simon and Schuster, 1980, p. 26.

17. "Marlene Sanders," in Greta Walker, Women Today. New York: Hawthorn, 1975, p. 116.

18. Martha Gellhorn, "A New Kind of War," Reprinted from The Manchester Guardian, Manchester, England: Manchester Guardian and Evening News, 1966, p. 15.

19. Martha Gellhorn, "Suffer the Little Children," Ladies Home Journal, Vol. 84, January 1967, p. 57.

20. Martha Gellhorn, "A New Kind of War," op. cit., p. 7.

21. D. D. Buck, Review of Fire in the Lake, Library Journal, Vol. 97, June 15, 1972, p. 2169.

22. Robert Friedman, "Frances Fitzgerald Is Fascinated with Failure," Esquire, Vol. 94, July 1980, p. 52.

23. Ibid.

24. Philippa Schuyler, Good Men Die. New York: Twin Circle Publishing Co., 1969, p. 214.

25. Philippa Schuyler, Who Killed the Congo? New York: Devin-Adair Co., 1962, p. vi.

26. Philippa Schuyler, Good Men Die, op. cit., p. 56.

27. Ibid., p. 57.

28. Ibid., p. 70.

29. Philippa Schuyler, "Ray of Hope: Koreans," Manchester (New Hampshire) Union Leader, October 26, 1966, p. 24.

30. Philippa Schuyler, Good Men Die, op. cit., p. 220.

31. Philippa Schuyler, "What's Wrong in VietNam," Manchester (New Hampshire) Union Leader, October 21, 1966, p. 5.

32. Philippa Schuyler, Good Men Die, op. cit., p. 131.

33. Ibid., p. 132.

34. Ibid., p. 161.

35. Ibid., p. 214.

36. Madeleine Riffaud, "North Vietnam: Two Months, Two Thousand Kilometers During the Escalation," L'Humanité, October 27, 1966, p. 2.

37. Ibid.

Chapter IV

1. Linda Grant Martin, "Angels of VietNam," Today's Health, Vol. 45, August 1967, p. 17.

2. Jurate Kazickas, Interview, Washington, D.C., 1980.

3. Oriana Fallaci, Nothing and So Be It. Garden
City, New York: Doubleday, 1972, p. 30.

4. Jurate Kazickas, Interview, Washington, D.C.,
1980.

5. Oriana Fallaci, Nothing and So Be It, op. cit.,
p. 96.

6. Ibid., p. 8.

7. George P. Hunt, "A Tiny Girl with Paratrooper's
Wings," Life   Vol. 64, February 16, 1968, p. 3.

8. Michele Ray, The Two Shores of Hell. New York:
McKay, 1968, p. 86.

9. Ibid., p. 166.

10. Ibid., p. 201-202.

11. "Out of the Woods," Newsweek, Vol. 69, February
20, 1967, p. 89.

12. Michele Ray, The Two Shores of Hell, op. cit.,
p. 215-216.

13. Georgie Anne Geyer, Buying the Night Flight.
New York: Delecorte Press, 1975, p. 276.

14. Ibid., p. 65.

15. Elizabeth Pond, Letter to Author, 1981.

16. Philippa Schuyler, "Getting a Story the Hard Way,"
Manchester (New Hampshire) Union Leader, March 31, 1967,
p. 8.

17. Ibid.

18. Philippa Schuyler, "Vietnam, A Sea of Futility:
We've Got to Win it Now!" Manchester (New Hampshire)
Union Leader, May 2, 1967, p. 12.

19. William Loeb, "Brilliant Shines Her Star," Manchester (New Hampshire) Union Leader, May 11, 1967, p. 17.

20. Phillip Knightley, The First Casualty. New York:
Harcourt Brace Jovanovich, 1975, p. 418.

Chapter V

1. William Kennedy, "Press Coverage of the Vietnam
War: The Third View, Draft Report," Carlisle Barracks,
Pennsylvania: Strategic Studies Institute, U.S. Army War
College, 1979, p. 44.

2. Kate Webb, as quoted in Phillip Knightley, The
First Casualty. New York: Harcourt Brace Jovanovich,
1975, p. 418.

3. Catherine Leroy, "Soldiers of North Vietnam Strike
a Pose for the Camera," Life, Vol. 64, February 16, 1968,
p. 24.

4. Ibid., p. 26.

5. Orianna Fallaci, Nothing, and So Be It. Garden City, New York: Doubleday, 1972, p. 159.

6. Orianna Fallaci, Interview with Stephen Banker, Women's Audio Exchange, Washington, D.C., 1980.

7. Elizabeth Pond, "Cadreman Echoes Cong Terms," The Christian Science Monitor, January 4, 1968, p. 2.

8. Beverly Deepe, "Hanoi's Goal: Reds Aim to End Vietnam War in 1968--On Own Terms," The Christian Science Monitor, July 10, 1968, p. 1.

9. Beverly Deepe, "South Viet Control Battered," The Christian Science Monitor, February 6, 1968, p. 4.

10. Beverly Deepe, "Viet Propaganda Battle Seesaws," The Christian Science Monitor, February 8, 1968, p. 4.

11. Georgie Anne Geyer, Buying the Night Flight. New York: Delacorte Press, 1983, p. 278.

12. Georgie Anne Geyer, "Two Weeks That Softened Saigon," Chicago Daily News, December 3, 1968, p. 3.

13. Helen Gibson, Letter to Author, April 1985.

14. "Susie Kirk," Women's Wear Daily, October 9, 1968, p. 4.

15. "Liz Trotta," Women's Wear Daily, October 9, 1968, p. 4.

16. Ibid.

17. Liz Trotta, "Hey, Fellows, Chet & David Have Sent a Woman," TV Guide, Vol. 17, April 19, 1969, p. 8.

18. James Fallows, "Mary McCarthy: The Blinders She Wears," Washington Monthly, February 1977, p. 56.

19. Susan Sontag, Styles of Radical Will. New York: Farrar, Straus & Giroux, 1969, p. 259.

20. Gemma Cruz Araneta, Hanoi Diary. Manila: Self-published, 1968, p. vi.

Chapter VI

1. Elizabeth Pond, "Viet Tide Is with the U.S.," The Christian Science Monitor, July 7, 1969, p. 7.

2. Elizabeth Pond, "Vietnamese Politics: Longer Term," Article written for the Alicia Patterson Fund, October 1969.

3. Elizabeth Pond, "The Chau Trial III: Aftermath," Article written for the Alicia Patterson Fund, October 1970.

4. Elizabeth Pond, "Out From Cambodian Captivity," The Christian Science Monitor, June 22, 1970, p. 2.

5. Elizabeth Pond, "Profile of Journalists' Captors: 'We Are Part of the Revolution'," The Christian Science Monitor, June 24, 1970, p. 4.

6. Elizabeth Pond, "Freed Journalists' Question: 'Why Us?'," The Christian Science Monitor, June 26, 1970, p. 17.

7. Elizabeth Pond, "The Chau Trial III: Aftermath," op. cit.

8. "Beverly Deepe," Women's Wear Daily, October 9, 1968, p. 4.

9. Georgie Anne Geyer, "Our New G.I.: Graft, Corruption in Saigon Disgusting to Many Yanks," Chicago Daily News, January 17, 1969, p. 1.

10. Barbaralee Diamonstein, Open Secrets. New York: Viking Press, 1972, p. 114.

11. Gloria Emerson, Winners and Losers: Battles, Retreats, Gains, Losses, and Ruins from a Long War. New York: Random House, 1976, p. 8.

12. Gloria Emerson, "A Young Refugee Mourns His Lost Bicycle," The New York Times, May 11, 1970, p. 21.

13. Gerry Kirk, "As Seen by Gloomy Gloria," National Review, Vol. 23, April 20, 1971, p. 426.

14. Gloria Emerson, "Soldiers Arriving in Service in Vietnam Find Little Cheer in Nixon's Plan to Step Up Withdrawals," The New York Times, October 23, 1970, p. 12.

15. Margaret Kilgore, "The Female War Correspondent in Vietnam," Quill, Vol. 60, May 1972, p. 10.

16. Elaine Shepard, "An Appeal from the Forest of Darkness," Twin Circle, December 20, 1970, p. 11.

17. Margaret Kilgore, "The Female War Correspondent in Vietnam," op. cit., p. 11.

Chapter VII

1. Gloria Emerson, "Arms and the Woman," Harpers, Vol. 246, April 1973, p. 34.

2. Gloria Emerson, "Hey, Lady, What Are You Doing Here?" McCalls, Vol. 98, August 1971, p. 108.

3. Gloria Emerson, Winners and Losers: Battles, Retreats, Gains, Losses, and Ruins from a Long War. New York: Random House, 1976, p. 5.

4. Margaret Kilgore, "The Female War Correspondent in Vietnam," Quill, Vol. 60, May 1972, p. 12.

5. Ibid.

6. Kate Webb, On The Other Side. New York:
Quadrangle Books, 1972, p. 109.
7. Ibid., p. 83.
8. Ibid., p. 101.
9. Ibid., p. 94.
10. Ibid., p. 153.
11. "Kate Webb's Story," Newsweek, Vol. 77, May 24,
1971, p. 60.
12. Marina Warner, Letter to Author, August 1985.
13. Marina Warner, "The Bitch Route Thirteen,"
The Spectator, July 1, 1972, p. 10.
14. Marina Warner, "Poor Little Bastards of Vietnam,"
The Spectator, August 12, 1972, p. 262.
15. Oriana Fallaci, "An Interview with Thieu," New
Republic, Vol. 168, January 20, 1973, p. 21.
16. "The Fallaci Treatment," Newsweek, Vol. 81, January 22, 1973, p. 84.
17. "Reporter at a Fire," Newsweek, Vol. 80, August
7, 1972, p. 62c.
18. Michael Mok, "Frances Fitzgerald," Publishers
Weekly, Vol. 202, October 16, 1972, p. 16.
19. I Ching: The Book of Changes. Translated by
Richard Wilhelm/Cary Baynes. Princeton, New Jersey: Princeton University Press, 1950, p. 190.
20. David Brudnoy, "The New Anti-Vietnam Bible,"
National Review, Vol. 24, September 29, 1972, p. 1069.
21. Frances Fitzgerald, "Vietnam: Reconciliation,"
Atlantic, Vol. 233, June 1974, p. 14.
22. Frances Fitzgerald, "Vietnam: Behind the Lines
of the 'Cease-Fire' War," Atlantic, Vol. 233, April 1974, p. 8.
23. Frances Fitzgerald, "Vietnam: Reconciliation,"
op. cit., p. 14.

Chapter VIII

1. Elaine Shepard, Letter to Author, February 1981.
2. "Gloria Emerson," Newsweek, Vol. 67, April 15,
1985, p. 67.
3. Jorge Lewinski, The Camera at War: A History
of War Photography from 1848 to the Present Day. New York:
Simon & Schuster, 1980, p. 183.
4. Mary Blume, "Gellhorn on the Warpath," Los Angeles
Times, March 16, 1980, Calendar, p. 56.

5.   Oriana Fallaci, "Fallaci on Khadafy," Los Angeles
Herald Examiner, October 14, 1981, p. All.

6.   Lucinda Franks, "Behind the Fallaci Image," Saturday Review, Vol. 8, January 1981, p. 21.

7.   "South Koreans Bar Monitor Reporter; Unfairness
Alleged," The Christian Science Monitor, June 6, 1974, p. 2.

8.   Daniel O. Graham, "Discussion of June 26, 1982
Frances Fitzgerald Article," The Nation, Vol. 235, August
7-14, 1982, p. 98.

9.   Frances Fitzgerald, "Lessons From a War," Intervention, Vol. 1, No. 1, Spring 1984, p. 24.

10. Walter Clemons, "Lest We Forget," Newsweek,
January 10, 1977, p. 67.

11. John F. Baker, "Gloria Emerson," Publishers
Weekly, Vol. 211, January 10, 1977, p. 8.

12. Ibid.

13. Gloria Emerson, "Recalling the Lessons of Vietnam,"
Los Angeles Times, April 27, 1980, Part V, p. 6.

14. Thomas B. Morgan, "Reporters of the Lost War:
Good Woman of Saigon," Esquire, Vol. 58, July 1984, p. 59.

15. "Vietnam Reconsidered: Lessons From a War,"
Conference held February 6-9, 1983, University of Southern
California, Session XI: "The War and the Veterans," Febru-
ary 9, 1983.

16. Ibid.

17. "Vietnam Reconsidered: Lessons From a War,"
op, cit., Session XIII, "Lessons from a War," February 9,
1983.

18. Ibid.

19. Ibid.

20. Ibid.

21. Thomas B. Morgan, "Reporters of the Lost War,"
op. cit., p. 49.

22. Helen Gibson, Letter to Author, April 1985.

23. "Georgie Anne Geyer," Women's Wear Daily, October 9, 1968, p. 4.

24. Kate Webb, Letter to Author, April 1980.

25. Marguerite Higgins, News is a Singular Thing.
New York: Doubleday, 1955, p. 213.

26. Leslie Bennetts, "Nerve Under Fire," Vogue, Vol.
173, November 1983, p. 440.

SELECTED BIBLIOGRAPHY

Included are biographical and autobiographical materials on the women in this book, examples of their correspondence from the Vietnam War, and materials which pertain to their careers as was correspondents.

BOOKS

American Women Writers. N.Y.: Frederick Ungar Publishing Co., 1980.

Araneta, Gemma Cruz. Hanoi Diary. Manila: Self-published, 1968.

Army Times. American Heroes of Asian Wars. N.Y.: Dodd, Mead, & Co., 1968.

Author Speaks: Selected Publishers Weekly Interviews 1967-1976. N.Y.: R.R. Bowker Co., 1977.

Beasley, Maurine and Sheila Silvers. Women in Media: Documentary Source Book. Washington, D.C.: Women's Institute for Freedom of the Press, 1977.

Braestrup, Peter. Big Story: How the American Press and Television Reported and Interpreted the Crisis of Tet 1968 in Vietnam and Washington. Boulder, Colo.: Westview Press, 1977. 2 vols.

Burchett, Wilfred. Vietnam: Inside Story of the Guerrilla War. N.Y.: International Publishers, 1965.

Chapelle, Dickey. What's A Woman Doing Here? N.Y.: Morrow, 1962.

Charlton, Michael and Anthony Moncrieff. Many Reasons Why:
    The American Involvement in Vietnam. N.Y.: Hill & Wang,
    1978.

Chen, John Hseuh-Ming. Vietnam: A Comprehensive Bibliog-
    raphy. Metuchen, N.J.: Scarecrow Press, 1973.

Contemporary Authors: A Bio-bibliographical Guide to Current
    Authors and Their Works. Detroit: Gale Research Co.,
    First Revision 1967, New Revision 1981.

Current Biography: Who's News and Why. N.Y.: H. W.
    Wilson Co., 1940--.

Diamonstein, Barbaralee. Open Secrets. N.Y.: Viking,
    1972.

Dictionary of Literary Biography Yearbook: 1982. Detroit:
    Gale Research Co., 1983.

Dudman, Richard. Forty Days With the Enemy. N.Y.:
    Liveright, 1971.

Emerson, Gloria. Winners and Losers: Battles, Retreats,
    Gains, Losses and Ruins From a Long War. N.Y.: Ran-
    dom House, 1976.

Fallaci, Oriana. Interview with History. (Tr. by John
    Shepley) N.Y.: Liveright, 1976.

Fallaci, Oriana. Nothing, and So Be It. (Tr. by Isobel
    Quigley) N.Y.: Doubleday, 1972.

Fitzgerald, Frances. Fire in the Lake. Boston: Little Brown
    1972.

Fleming, Alice. Reporters at War. N.Y.: Cowles Book Co.,
    Inc., 1970.

Gelfman, Judith. Women in TV News. N.Y.: Columbia Uni-
    versity Press, 1976.

Gellhorn, Martha. The Face of War. N.Y.: Simon and
    Schuster, 1959.

Gellhorn, Martha. A New Kind of War. Manchester, England: Manchester Guardian and Evening News, 1966.

Geyer, Georgie Anne. Buying the Night Flight. N.Y.: Delacorte, 1983.

Halberstam, David. The Making of a Quagmire. N.Y.: Random House, 1964.

Hawley, Earle, Ed. The Face of War: Vietnam, The Full Photographic Record. North Hollywood, CA: M. Luros, 1965.

Higgins, Hugh. Vietnam. 2nd Ed. London: Heinemann Educational Books. 1982.

Higgins, Marguerite. News is a Singular Thing. N.Y.: Doubleday, 1955.

Higgins, Marguerite. Our Vietnam Nightmare. N.Y.: Harper & Row, 1965.

Higgins, Marguerite. War in Korea: The Report of a Woman Combat Correspondent. N.Y.: Doubleday, 1951.

Hohenberg, John, ed. The Pulitzer Prize Story. N.Y.: Columbia University Press, 1959.

Jakes, John. Great War Correspondents. N.Y.: G. P. Putnam's Sons, 1967.

Jakes, John. Great Women Reporters. N.Y.: G. P. Putnam's Sons, 1969.

Kert, Bernice. The Hemingway Women. N.Y.: W. W. Norton & Co., 1983.

Knightley, Phillip. The First Casualty. N.Y.: Harcourt Brace Jovanovich, 1975.

Krementz, Jill. The Face of South Vietnam. (Text by Dean Brelis) N.Y.: Houghton, 1968.

Labin, Suzanne. Sellout in Vietnam? Arlington, VA: Crestwood Books, 1966.

Leroy, Catherine and Tony Clifton. God Cried. London:
    Quarter, 1983.

Lewinski, Jorge. The Camera at War--A History of War
    Photography From 1848 to the Present Day. N.Y.:
    Simon & Schuster, 1980.

McCarthy, Mary. The Seventeenth Degree. N.Y.: Harcourt
    Brace Jovanovich, 1974.

McCarthy, Mary. Vietnam. N.Y.: Harcourt Brace & World,
    1967.

MacDonald, Glenn. Report or Distort? N.Y.: Exposition
    Press, 1973.

Marzolf, Marion. Up From the Footnote: A History of Women
    Journalists. N.Y.: Hastings House, 1977.

Mathews, Joseph J. Reporting the Wars. Minneapolis: Uni-
    versity of Minnesota Press, 1957.

May, Antoinette. Witness to War: A Biography of Marguerite
    Higgins. N.Y.: Beaufort Books, 1983.

Minor, Dale. The Information War. New York: Hawthorn
    Books, Inc. 1970.

Musgrove, Patches (Helen). Vietnam: Front Row Center.
    Santa Ana, CA: Patches Publishing, Inc., 1986. (2
    volumes)

Nolan, Keith W. Battle for Hue: Tet, 1968. Novato, CA:
    Presidio Press, 1984.

Notable American Women. Volume IV, The Modern Period.
    Cambridge, Ma.: The Belknap Press of Harvard Univer-
    sity Press. 1980.

Overseas Press Club of America. How I Got That Story.
    David Brown & W. Richard Bruner, eds. N.Y.: E. P.
    Dutton & Co., 1967.

Parshalle, Eve. Kashmir Bridge-women. Los Angeles: Ox-
    ford Press, 1965.

Pelger, John. Heroes. London: Jonathan Cape, 1986.

Pfeffer, Richard M. No More Vietnam?: The War and the Future of American Foreign Policy. N.Y.: Harper & Row for the Adlai Stevenson Institute of International Affairs, 1968.

Ray, Michele. The Two Shores of Hell. (Translated by Elisabeth Abbott) N.Y.: McKay, 1968.

Riffaud, Madeleine. Au Nord Viet-nam (Ecrit Sous Les Bombes) Paris: Rene Julliard, 1967.

Riffaud, Madeleine. Dans Les Maquis "Vietcong." Paris: Rene Julliard, 1965.

Salisbury, Harrison, ed. Vietnam Reconsidered: Lessons from a War. N.Y.: Harper & Row, 1984.

Schilpp, Madelon Golden and Sharon M. Murphy. Great Women of the Press. Carbondale, IL: Southern Illinois University Press, 1983.

Schuyler, Josephine. Philippa: The Beautiful American. Privately Printed for the Philippa Schuyler Memorial Foundation, 1969.

Schuyler, Philippa. Good Men Die. N.Y.: Twin Circle Publishing Co., 1969.

Schuyler, Philippa. Who Killed the Congo? N.Y.: Devin-Adair Co., 1962.

Sheehan, Susan. Ten Vietnamese. N.Y.: Alfred A. Knopf, 1967.

Shepard, Elaine. The Doom Pussy. N.Y.: Trident Press, 1967.

Shepard, Elaine. Forgive Us Our Press Passes. Englewood Cliffs, NJ: Prentice-Hall, 1962.

Sontag, Susan. Styles of Radical Will. N.Y.: Farrar, Straus & Giroux, 1969.

Stein, M. L. <u>Under Fire: The Story of American War Cor-</u>
<u>respondents.</u> N.Y.: Julian Messner, 1969.

<u>Twentieth Century Authors, 1st Supplement.</u> N.Y.: Wilson,
1955.

Walker, Greta. <u>Women Today.</u> N.Y.: Hawthorn, 1975.

Warfel, Harry R. <u>American Novelists of Today.</u> N.Y.:
American Book Co., 1951.

Webb, Kate. <u>On The Other Side: Twenty-three Days With</u>
<u>the Viet Cong.</u> N.Y.: Quadrangle Books, 1972.

Zasloff, Joseph J. & Allen F. Goodman, eds. <u>Indochina in</u>
<u>Conflict: A Political Assessment.</u> Lexington, MA: Lexing-
ton Books, 1972.

PERIODICALS

"After Cambodian Detention Correspondents Freed." (Elizabeth Pond) <u>The Christian Science Monitor.</u> June 17, 1970,
p. 1.

"And Now There Are Ten." (Kate Webb) <u>Time</u> 97:33 May 3,
1971.

Baker, John F. "Gloria Emerson." <u>Publishers Weekly</u> 211:8-9
January 10, 1977.

Bates, Helen. "Musgrove: War No Longer Worth Cost."
<u>Jacksonville</u> (Florida) <u>Journal,</u> September 1, 1970, p. 24.

Bennett, Leslie. "Nerve Under Fire." <u>Vogue</u> 173:440-441+
November 1983.

"Beverly Deepe." <u>Women's Wear Daily,</u> October 9, 1968, p. 4

Blume, Mary. "Gellhorn on War Path." <u>Los Angeles Times,</u>
March 16, 1980, Calender Section, p. 56.

Brittain, Victoria. "Child Victims in Vietnam." <u>The Times</u>
(London) June 5, 1972, p. 13.

Carlson, Timothy and Woody Hochswender. "Vietnam Reconsidered: Lessons from a War. USC Conference Looks Back." Los Angeles Herald Examiner, February 8, 1983, pp. A-1 and A-7.

"Cathy Leroy." Women's Wear Daily, October 9, 1968, p. 4.

Chamberlain, John. "Chancy Treaty: Bridge Building." Los Angeles Herald Examiner, March 8, 1967, p. B-2. (Elaine Shepard)

Chapelle, Dickey. "The Fighting Priest of South Vietnam." Reader's Digest 83:194-200 July, 1963.

_____. "Helicopter War in South Vietnam." National Geographic 102:723-754 November 1962.

_____. "I Roam the Edge of Freedom." Coronet 52:129-141 February, 1961.

_____. "On Okinawa, A Rehearsal for War." The National Observer November 1, 1965, p. 1.

_____. "Searching Vietnam for Victor Charlie." The National Observer November 8, 1965, p. 1.

_____. "Water War in Vietnam." National Geographic 129:273-296 February, 1966.

_____. "With the Paratroops." Reader's Digest 80:292-298 February 1962.

Clifton, T. "The Fallaci Treatment." Newsweek 81:83-84 January 22, 1973.

"Close-up" (Marlene Sanders) Seventeen 32:48 September 1973.

"Coming Home" (Vietnam Reconsidered Conference) The Nation 236:196-7 February 19, 1983.

"Dateline Saigon: War of Words." Newsweek 62:98-99 October 7, 1963. (Beverly Deepe)

"Death Reported: Catherine M. Webb." Newsweek 77:82 May 3, 1971.

"Dedicated Reporter."   Scholastic 88:19 February 4, 1966.
   (Marguerite Higgins)

Deepe, Beverly.   "Blitz Erodes U.S. Position in Vietnam."
   The Christian Science Monitor February 3, 1968, p. 1.

_____. "Cong Raids Take High Political Toll."   The Christian
Science Monitor February 5, 1968, p. 1.

_____. "Dateline, Saigon: War of Words."   Newsweek 62:98-
99 October 7, 1963.

_____. "Defeat, Victory and Pressure on Vietnam."   Newsweek
62:45-46 November 4, 1963.

_____. "The Fall of the House of Ngo."   Newsweek 62:27-31
November 11, 1963.

_____. "Frictions Stir Viet Cong."   The Christian Science
Monitor July 6, 1968 p. 1.

_____. "Hanoi's Goal."   The Christian Science Monitor July
10, 1968 p. 1.

_____. "Hardly a Hamlet Feels Safe."   The Christian Science
Monitor February 7, 1968 p. 1.

_____. "Inner War: Battle for the Masses."   The New York
Herald Tribune January 5, 1965, p. 3.

_____. "Red Ambush Smashes Ruling Viet Forces."   The
New York Herald Tribune January 5, 1965, p. 3.

_____. "Reds Mustered in Saigon."   The Christian Science
Monitor July 11, 1968, p. 1.

_____. "Saigon Effectiveness Seen Crucial To War."   The
Christian Science Monitor January 2, 1968, p. 5.

_____. "South Viet Control Battered."   The Christian Science
Monitor February 6, 1968, p. 4.

_____. "South Vietnam: The Break-even Point."   Newsweek
62:57-58 December 2, 1963.

_____. "Training by Hanoi Sagging." The Christian Science Monitor July 5, 1968 p. 1.

_____. "Viet Cong Officers Reconnoiter Saigon 'ala James Bond'." The Christian Science Monitor July 9, 1968 p. 5.

_____. "Viet Propaganda Battle Seesaws." The Christian Science Monitor February 8, 1968 p. 1.

_____. "Vietnam: Getting to Know the Nhus." Newsweek 62:33-39 September 9, 1963.

_____. "Vietnam: The New Metal Birds." Newsweek 60:37-38 October 29, 1962.

_____. "Vietnam's Future: 'All Bets Are Off'." Newsweek 62:35-36 August 26, 1963.

_____. "War in the Pagodas: Who Is the Enemy?" Newsweek 62:35-38 September 2, 1963.

"Dickey Chapelle Dies in Viet Nam." The Overseas Press Club Bulletin. November 6, 1965 pp. 1-3.

"Dickey Chapelle Killed in Vietnam." The New York Times November 4, 1965 p. 1+.

"Died: Philippa Schuyler." Time 89:112 May 19, 1967.

Dreifus, Claudia. "Frances Fitzgerald Interview." Newsday February 17, 1980.

Emerson, Gloria. "About Oriana." Vogue 170:334+ November 1980.

_____. "Arms and the Woman." Harpers 246-34+ April 1973. See also letters and Emerson reply June 1973 pp. 99-100.

_____. "Facts Invented for a General's Medal." The New York Times October 21, 1970, p. 3.

_____. Gloria Emerson's Vietnam Diary." Vogue 159-74+ January 1, 1972.

_____. "Hey, Lady, What Are You Doing Here?" McCalls 98:61+ August 1971.

_____. "Recalling the Lessons of Vietnam: Five Years After Saigon's Fall, America Is Still Divided." Los Angeles Times April 27, 1980, Pt. V, pp. 1 and 6.

_____. "Soldiers Arriving for Service in Vietnam Find Little Cheer in Nixon's Plan to Step Up Withdrawals." The New York Times October 23, 1970, p. 12.

_____. "Tailor Relives Ordeal at Con Son." The New York Times July 19, 1970, p. 14.

_____. "A Young Refugee Mourns His Lost Bicycle." The New York Times May 11, 1970, p. 21.

Fallaci, Oriana. "Interview with a Vietcong Terrorist." Look 32:36+ April 16, 1968.

_____. "Interview with Thieu." New Republic 168:16-25 January 20, 1973.

_____. "Interview with Two American POW's." Look 33:30-32 July 15, 1969.

_____. "On Khadafy." The Los Angeles Herald Examiner October 14, 1981, p. A-11.

Fawcett, Denby. "American Girl in Saigon Finds Life Is no Lark." Honolulu (Hawaii) Advertiser June 1, 1966, p. 1.

"Femininity at the Front." Time 88:73-74 October 28, 1966.

Ferguson, Charles W. "Americans Not Everyone Knows: Philippa Duke Schuyler." The PTA Magazine 61/62:12-14 December 1967.

"Fine Print." Time 70:70 November 25, 1957. (Marguerite Higgins)

Fitzgerald, Frances. "Annals of War." New Yorker 48:36+ July 1, 1972, 48:34+ July 8, 1972, 48:33+ July 15, 1972, 48:53+ July 22, 1972, and 48:56+ July 29, 1972.

_____. "Duc Lap." The New York Times Magazine September 4, 1966, p. 5.

_____. "The End Is the Beginning." New Republic 172:7-8 May 3, 1975.

_____. "How it Is Now With the People of My Lai." The New York Times May 4, 1973, p. 37.

_____. "Journey to North Vietnam." New Yorker 51:96+ April 28, 1975.

_____. "Lessons From a War." Intervention 1:24-27 Spring 1984.

_____. "The Long Fear: Fresh Eyes on Vietnam." Vogue 149:110+ January 1, 1967.

_____. "The Power Set: The Fragile but Dominating Women of VietNam." Vogue 149:154-205 February 1, 1967.

_____. "The Struggle and the War." Atlantic 220:72-82 August 1967.

_____. "The Tragedy of Saigon." Atlantic 218:59-67 December 1966.

_____. "Vietnam: Behind the Lines of the 'Cease-Fire' War." Atlantic 233:4+ April 1974.

_____. "The Vietnam Numbers Game." The Nation 234:776-778 June 26, 1982. See also discussion 235:98+ August 7-14, 1982.

_____. "Vietnam: Reconciliation." Atlantic 233:14+ June 1974.

_____. "Vietnam: The Cadres and the Villagers." Atlantic 233:4+ May 1974.

_____. "Vietnam: The People." Vogue 149:174-175 May 1967.

Folden, Roy. "Union Leader War Reporter Killed." Manchester (New Hampshire) Union Leader May 10, 1967, p. 1+. (Schuyler)

"Frances Fitzgerald." Time 100:61 August 28, 1972.

"Frances Fitzgerald." Newsweek 69:58 February 13, 1967.

"Frances Fitzgerald." Newsweek 80:62+ August 7, 1972.

"Frances Fitzgerald Wins 1967 Overseas Press Club Award
    for Best Interpretation of Foreign Affairs for Articles on
    Vietnam in the Atlantic." The New York Times April 23,
    1968, p. 29.

Franks, Lucinda. "Behind the Fallaci Image." Saturday Re-
    view 8:18-22 January, 1981.

Friedman, Robert. "Frances Fitzgerald is Fascinated with
    Failure." Esquire 94:48-54 July, 1980.

Friedman, Stanley. "Dickey Chapelle: Two Wars and Four
    Revolutions." Ms 4:24-27 April, 1976.

Garrett, W. E. "What Was a Woman Doing There?" (Dickey
    Chapelle) National Geographic 129:270-271 February, 1966.

Gellhorn, Martha. "Suffer the Little Children." Ladies' Home
    Journal 84:57+ January, 1967.

"Georgie Anne Geyer." Women's Wear Daily October 9, 1968
    P. 4.

Geyer, Georgie Anne. "Cambodia's Careful Political Balance
    Tilts." Chicago Daily News December 14, 1968 p. 2.

_____. "Deep Down, Prince Sihanouk Likes U.S." Chicago
    Daily News December 28, 1967 p. 1.

_____. "Graft, Corruption in Saigon Disgusting to Many Yanks."
    Chicago Daily News January 17, 1969 p. 1.

_____. "Hanoi Plotting 'Last-gasp' Attack?" Chicago Daily
    News August 16, 1968 p. 2.

_____. "Our New G.I.: He Asks Why." Chicago Daily News
    January 13-17, 1969. (Five part series.)

_____. "Red Cadres Target: Viet Spies Dealt Blow." Chicago
    Daily News October 29, 1968, p. 2.

_____. "Saigon's Swift Avenging Angels." Chicago Daily News
    October 28, 1968, pp. 3 and 4.

_____. "Souls 'Lost' in War a Tragedy in Vietnam." Chicago Daily News August 14, 1968, p. 2.

_____. "Thieu Seeking 'Coalition' of Peace Envoys." Chicago Daily News November 23, 1968, p. 2.

_____. "Two Weeks that Softened Saigon." Chicago Daily News December 3, 1968, p. 3.

_____. "U.S. Rebuilds the Viet Village it Bombed." Chicago Daily News July 26, 1968, p. 2.

_____. "Viet Cong Girl Tells Her '2nd Thoughts'," Chicago Daily News August 3, 1968, p. 6.

_____. "Viet Spies Dealt Blow." Chicago Daily News October 28, 1968, p. 2.

"Gloria Emerson." Newsweek 105:67 April 15, 1985.

"Gloria Emerson Wins LIU Polk Award." The New York Times February 17, 1971, p. 2 and March 25, 1971, p. 3.

"Gnat of Hill 881." Time 89:42 May 12, 1967 (Catherine Leroy)

"Goring the Egotists." Time 92:48 November 29, 1968 (Oriana Fallaci)

Higgins, Marguerite. "No Club for Cookie Pushers." NEA Journal 54:15 March 1965.

_____. "On the Spot." Newsday. Various dates in 1963 and 1964. (Regularly appearing column.)

_____. "Our Vietnam Nightmare." (Condensation of book.) Newsday December 11, 1965, p. 12+.

_____. "Saigon Summary." America. 110:18-21 January 4, 1964.

_____. "Ugly Americans of Vietnam." America 111:376-382 October 3, 1964.

_____. "Vietnam: Fact and Fiction." The New York Herald Tribune August 26-September 1, 1963. (Six-part series.)

Howard, Jane. "Frankie's Fire." <u>Life</u> 73:51+ October 27, 1972. (Frances Fitzgerald)

Hunt, George P. "A Tiny Girl with Paratrooper's Wings." <u>Life</u> 64:3 February 16, 1968. (Catherine Leroy)

"I'll Do Anything." <u>Newsweek</u> 69:58 February 13, 1967 (Frances Fitzgerald)

"<u>Journal</u>'s Musgrove Reaccredited." <u>Jacksonville</u> (Florida) <u>Journal</u> June 20, 1968, p. 1.

"Kate Webb." <u>Women's Wear Daily</u> October 9, 1968, p. 4.

"Kate Webb's Story." <u>Newsweek</u> 77:59-60 May 24, 1971.

Kazickas, Jurate. "Opinion on Men at War." <u>Mademoiselle</u> 64:124+ March 1967.

_____. "Vietnam Vignettes." <u>Eugene</u> (Oregon) <u>Register-Guard</u> May 1, 1969.

Kilgore, Margaret. "The Female War Correspondent in Vietnam." <u>Quill</u> 60:10-12. May, 1972.

Kirk, Gerry. "As Seen by Gloomy Gloria (Emerson)." <u>National Review</u> 23:426. April 20, 1971.

Klingensmith, Peg. "Patches Musgrove--A Tender Heart in Combat Boots." <u>Orange County Illustrated</u> 14:53. December, 1975.

Knight, Christopher. "Vietnam Pictures Tell a Story of Repulsion and Attraction." <u>Los Angeles Herald Examiner</u>, February 7, 1983, pp. C-1 and C-5.

"Lady at War." <u>Time</u> 87:61, January 14, 1966. (Marguerite Higgins)

Lamb, David. "Vietnam Correspondents Gather for Reunion." Los Angeles <u>Times</u>, November 23, 1986, Sec. I, p. 22+.

"Last Word." (Marguerite Higgins) <u>Time</u> 56:53. July 31, 1950.

Leroy, Catherine. "A Tense Interlude." Life 64:22-27.
    February 16, 1968.

_____. "This is That War." Look 32:25-32. May 14, 1968.

_____. "Up Hill 881 with the Marines." Life 62:40-44A. May
    19, 1967.

Levin, Phyllis Lee. "Fire in the Mind: Frances Fitzgerald."
    Vogue 161:108-111 January 1973.

"Liz Trotta." Women's Wear Daily, October 9, 1968, p. 4.

Loeb, William. "Brilliant Shines Her Star." Manchester (New
    Hampshire) Union Leader May 11, 1967, p. 1+. (Philippa
    Schuyler)

_____. "Philippa Schuyler Thanks You." Manchester (New
    Hampshire) Union Leader September 19, 1968, Editorial.

_____. "This Reporter Has Brains and Courage." Manchester
    (New Hampshire) Union Leader March 27, 1967, p. 1+.

Lucas, Jim. "We Loved this gal ... this spitfire." Scripps-
    Howard News January 1967, p. 6-7. (Dickey Chapelle)

Lyons, Eugene. "Suzanne Labin: 'Joan of Arc of Freedom'."
    The American Legion Magazine 73:19+. December, 1962.

Lytle, Douglas. "Vietnam Reconsidered." USC Daily Trojan.
    February 7, 1983, p. 2.

"Maggie." (Marguerite Higgins) Newsweek 67:83. January
    17, 1966.

"Maggie in the Congo." (Marguerite Higgins) Newsweek 57:
    82. April 3, 1961.

"Marguerite Higgins Dies at 45." The New York Times. Jan-
    uary 4, 1966, p. 27.

"Marguerite Higgins Obituary." Editor and Publisher 99:67.
    January 8, 1966.

"Marguerite Higgins Obituary." Publisher's Weekly 189:108.
    January 17, 1966.

"Marguerite Higgins RIP." National Review. 18:60-61. January 25, 1966.

"Marietta Tree and Her Two Daughters." (Frances Fitzgerald) Vogue 151:177. May, 1968.

"Marlene Sanders: The Other Woman in Network News." Broadcasting 91:105. November 8, 1976.

Martin, Linda Grant. "Angels of Viet Nam." Today's Health 47:17+. August, 1967.

_____. "Keeping Up with the Tran Quan Lacs." New York Times Magazine. August 20, 1967, p. 22-23.

_____. "The Thirty-seven Year War of the Village of Tananhoi. The New York Times Magazine, October 29, 1967, p. 30+.

_____. "When Crisis is a Way of Life." Mademoiselle 64:172+ November 1966.

"Michele Is Missing." (Michele Ray) Time 89:58. February 3, 1967.

Miller, E. "Marlene Sanders: Closeup." Seventeen 32:48. September, 1973.

"Miss Schuyler Dies as Copter Crashes in Viet." (Philippa Schuyler) Manchester (New Hampshire) Union Leader. May 10, 1967, p. 1.

"Miss Schuyler Rites Thursday." (Philippa Schuyler) Manchester (New Hampshire Union Leader. May 16, 1967, p. 1.

"Missing U.P.I. Correspondent Freed by Enemy in Cambodia." (Kate Webb) The New York Times. May 1, 1971, p. 5.

Mok, M. "Frances Fitzgerald." Publisher's Weekly 202:16-17 October 16, 1972.

Morgan, Thomas B. "Reporters of the Lost War." Esquire 102:49-60 July 1984.

Musgrove, Helen (Patches). "GI's Join Fight on Her Expulsion." Jacksonville (Florida) Journal May 21, 1968, p. 10

_____. "Patches' Role in Gurney Viet Probe." Jacksonville
(Florida) Journal December 2, 1970, p. 24.

_____. "She Wins the Popcorn War." Jacksonville (Florida
Journal June 20, 1968, p. 32.

_____. "War Reporter Expelled Without Trail." Jacksonville
(Florida) Journal May 20, 1968.

_____. "Wounded Florida GI's Dad Sees for Himself." Jackson-
ville (Florida) Journal May 27, 1970 to June 2, 1970. Six-
part Series.

Mydans, Carl. "Girl War Correspondent." Life 29: 51-56
October 2, 1950. (Marguerite Higgins)

"Out of the Woods." Newsweek 69: 88-89 February 20, 1967.
(Michele Ray)

"Overseas Press Club and News Guild Give Prizes." The
New York Times April 11, 1968, p. 39. (Frances Fitzgerald
and Catherine Leroy)

Penn, Patricia. "A Small Town in Vietnam." New Statesman
79: 764-765 May 29, 1970.

"Philippa Schuyler, Pianist, Dies in Crash of a Copter in Vietnam." The New York Times May 10, 1967, p. 5+.

"Philippa Schuyler, RIP." National Review 19: 559 May 30,
1967.

"Philippa's Death on Eve of Return." (Philippa Schuyler)
Manchester (New Hampshire) Union Leader May 10, 1967,
p. 1.

"Pianist, Author Dies in S. Vietnam Crash." The Washington
Post May 10, 1967, Sec. A, p. 18. (Philippa Schuyler)

"Playboy Interview: Oriana Fallaci." Playboy 28: 77-108
November 1981.

Pond, Elizabeth. "Cadreman Echoes Cong Terms." The Christian Science Monitor. January 4, 1968, p. 1.

_____. "Civilian Tickets Attract Viet Voters." The Christian Science Monitor. August 28, 1967, p. 2.

_____. "Freed Journalists' Question: Why Us?" The Christian Science Monitor. June 26, 1970, p. 1.

_____. "Last Days of Captivity." The Christian Science Monitor. June 25, 1970, p. 1.

_____. "Officer's View: 'Viet Tide Is with U.S.'" The Christian Science Monitor. July 7, 1969, p. 1.

_____. "Out from Cambodian Captivity: 'Don't Shoot, We Are International Journalists.'" The Christian Science Monitor. June 22, 1970, p. 1.

_____. "Profile of Journalists' Captors: 'We Are Part of the Revolution.'" The Christian Science Monitor. June 24, 1970, p. 1.

_____. "Soft Circle Sifts Out Viet Cong." The Christian Science Monitor. July 11, 1969, p. 14.

_____. "Typical Day in Captivity." The Christian Science Monitor. June 23, 1970, p. 1.

_____. "Viet Interlude: Sampan Society Poles On." The Christian Science Monitor. July 5, 1969, p. 4.

_____. "Vietnamese Chant Political Speeches." The Christian Science Monitor. August 26, 1967, p. 4.

_____. "Vietnamese Observer Pessimistic on War." The Christian Science Monitor. July 2, 1968, p. 1.

_____. "Vietnamese Sort Out Senatorial Candidates." The Christian Science Monitor. August 3, 1967, p. 2.

"Pride of the Regiment." Time 56:63-64. September 25, 1950. (Marguerite Higgins)

Randolph, John. "The Little Marine and His New Boots."

The Washington Post. March 24, 1968, Sec. B, p. 1.
(Jurate Kazickas)

"Released: Catherine M. (Kate) Webb." Newsweek 77:95
May 10, 1971.

"A Reporter's Death." Newsweek 66:52 November 15, 1965.
(Dickey Chapelle)

Riffaud, Madeleine. "North Vietnam: Two Months, Two
Thousand Kilometers During the Escalation." L'Humanité
October 18, 26, 27, 1966. Translated by JPRS (RMP
Micro Library Ed. Vol. V #5 JPRS #38832)

Robinson, Douglas. "Press Club Gives Awards for 1965."
The New York Times April 23, 1966, p. 32. (Dickey Chapelle)

Rowes, Barbara. "Lovers, Colleagues, Family, Literati: All
Hail Author Frankie Fitzgerald." People Weekly 12:91-97
December 3, 1979.

Sabouret, Anne. "Michele Costa Gavras." Elle. September
1983, pp. 76-77. (Michele Ray)

Salazar, S. L. "Where Action Is, GG Woman Is There."
Orange County News October 22, 1986, p. 1. (Patches
Musgrove)

Sanford, David. "Two Women: The Lady of the Tapes."
Esquire 83:102-105 June 1975. (Oriana Fallaci)

Sanders, Marlene. "Women in TV News--Where We've Been
and Where We're Going." TV Quarterly XVIII (1)49-56
Spring 1981.

Schuyler, Philippa. "Beloved War Leader." Manchester (New
Hampshire) Union Leader October 27, 1966, pp. 36 and 13.

_____. "Failure in Vietnam: Nation Bitter, Confused." Man-
chester (New Hampshire) Union Leader March 27, 1967,
p. 17+.

_____. "Free China Is Ready for War: Apocalypse in Red
China." Manchester (New Hampshire) Union Leader March
2, 1967, p. 9+.

_____. "The Marines' Civic Action." Manchester (New Hampshire) Union Leader October 24, 1966, pp. 30 and 7.

_____. "Ray of Hope: Koreans." Manchester (New Hampshire) Union Leader October 26, 1966 pp. 56 and 24.

_____. "VC Resemble Mafia." Manchester (New Hapshire) Union Leader October 28, 1966, pp. 30 and 15.

_____. "The Viet Cong Casualties." Manchester (New Hampshire) Union Leader October 22, 1966, pp. 20 and 13.

_____. "Vietnam: A Sea of Futility: Does Anyone Really Care?" Manchester (New Hampshire) Union Leader Apr8il 12, 1967, p. 17+.

_____. "Vietnam: A Sea of Futility: Getting a Story the Hard Way." Manchester (New Hampshire) Union Leader. March 31, 1967, pp. 8+.

_____. "Vietnam: A Sea of Futility: Land of Country People." Manchester (New Hampshire) Union Leader. April 28, 1967, pp. 28 and 10.

_____. "Vietnam: A Sea of Futility: May Be Too Late to Win." Manchester (New Hampshire) Union Leader. April 14, 1967, pp. 24+.

_____. "Vietnam: A Sea of Futility: Pleasures of War Zone." Manchester (New Hampshire) Union Leader. April 27, 1967, pp. 18+.

_____. "Vietnam: A Sea of Futility: War and Culture in Hue. Manchester (New Hampshire) Union Leader. May 1, 1967, pp. 30 and 18.

_____. "Vietnam: A Sea of Futility: We Chose Wrong Friends Manchester (New Hampshire) Union Leader. April 6, 1967, pp. 9+.

_____. "Vietnam: A Sea of Futility: We've Got to Win It Now." Manchester (New Hampshire) Union Leader. May 2, 1967, pp. 24 and 12.

_____. "Weapons of the Viet Cong." Manchester (New Hampshire) Union Leader. October 25, 1966, pp. 28 and 11.

_____. "What's Wrong in Viet Nam?" Manchester (New Hampshire) Union Leader. October 21, 1966, pp. 30 and 5.

"Self Reliance in Saigon." Time 85:38 January 8, 1965. (Beverly Deepe.)

Sestanovich, Stephen. "Still Burning: New Republic 192: 39-41 April 29, 1985. (Frances Fitzgerald)

Shaw, Susan. "First Lessons at Vietnam Conference." USC Daily Trojan February 7, 1983, p. 1.

Sheehan, Susan. "The Enemy." The New Yorker. 42:62+ September 10, 1966.

_____. "Le Quang." The New Yorker. 42:137+ November 5, 1966.

_____. "Letter from Abroad: A Vietnamese Woman." McCalls 94:48+ March 1967.

Shepard, Elaine. "An Appeal from the 'Forest of Darkness'." Twin Circle. December 20, 1970, pp. 3 and 11.

_____. "The Best We Have ... And Their Beautiful Patriotism." Olney (Illinois) Daily Mail (Reprint from Twin Circle) August 21, 1973, p. 4.

_____. "The Elite 'Dirty Thirty'." Twin Circle. December 13, 1970, p. 3.

_____. "The Gentle Leatherneck." Twin Circle. June 13, 1971, pp. 1 and 11.

_____. "Green Beret Weds: Life Has a Flavor." Twin Circle January 18, 1970, pp. 3 and 11.

_____. "Philippa Schuyler: Angel of Mercy, Glorious Talent." Twin Circle. August 10, 1969, pp. 3 and 12.

_____. "They Have Seen the Doom Pussy." Twin Circle. September 7, 1969, pp. 3 and 11.

"South Koreans Bar Monitor Reporter; Unfairness Alleged." (Elizabeth Pond) The Christian Science Monitor. June 6, 1974, p. 2.

Specht, Wayne, Sgt.   "Among Shuttle Visitors Was Truly
    Special Person."   Desert Wings (Edwards Air Force Base)
    May 5, 1983, pp. 9 and 11.   (Patches Musgrove)

"Spellman Takes Part at Mass for Philippa."   Manchester
    (New Hampshire) Union Leader May 17, 1967.   (Philippa
    Schuyler)

Stewart, Bob.   "Writer Thrills Students with Her Action Story.
    Palm Beach (Florida) Daily News April 25, 1968, p. 1.
    (Elaine Shepard)

Stolley, Richard.   "Oriana Fallaci."   Life 66:36-39 February
    21, 1969.

"Susie Kirk."   Women's Wear Daily.   October 9, 1968, p. 4.

"This Time, Korea."   Newsweek 36:54-55 July 10, 1950.   (Mar-
    guerite Higgins)

Trotta, Liz.   "Hey, Fellows, Chet and David Have Sent a
    Woman."   TV Guide 17:6-10, April 1969.

"2000 at St. Patrick's Attend Requiem for Philippa Schuyler."
    The New York Times May 19, 1967, p. 39.

"The U.S. vs. The Generals."   Time 85:32 January 1, 1965
    (Beverly Deepe)

Viorst, Judith.   "Three Women."   (Frances Fitzgerald) Red-
    book 144:44-51, March, 1975.

"War Reporters Are Honored in Pentagon."   (Dickey Chapelle
    and Philippa Schuyler) Editor and Publisher 105:11, De-
    cember 2, 1972.

Warner, Marina.   "The Bitch Route Thirteen."   Spectator
    July 1, 1972, pp. 9 and 10.

_____.   "Poor Little Bastards of Vietnam."   Spectator August
    12, 1972, pp. 262-263.

Webb, Kate.   "Kate Webb Tells of Her 3-Week Captivity."
    The New York Times, May 13, 1971, p. 10.

_____. "While Captive in Cambodia, War Reporter Kept Diary."
The New York Times. May 14, 1971, p. 10.

"Who's Who at the Monitor: Tokyo Correspondent." The
Christian Science Monitor June 6, 1972, p. 19. (Elizabeth
Pond)

Wiley, Charles. "Dickey Chapelle, RIP." National Review
17:1066 November 30, 1965.

"Woman at War." Time 86:54 November 12, 1965. (Dickey
Chapelle)

"Woman Honored for War Reports." The New York Times
April 14, 1962, p. 22. (Dickey Chapelle)

"Woman War Reporter." Scholastic. 58:17 May 9, 1951 (Marguerite Higgins)

                            THESES

Brumagin, Vicki Lee. "A Study of Women in American Journalism from 1696 to 1972." MA Thesis, California State University, Northridge, 1972.

Burchfield, Stephanie. "The New Journalism of Oriana Fallaci."
MA Thesis, California State University, Northridge, 1984.

Ellis, Frederick R. "Dickey Chapelle: A Reporter and Her
Work." MA Thesis, University of Wisconsin, 1968.

Lewis Kathleen H. "Maggie Higgins." MA Thesis, University
of Maryland, 1973.

Morgan, Margaret Knox. "Women in Photojournalism." MA
Thesis, University of Missouri, 1962. (Dickey Chapelle)

Raudy, John Hill. "The Price of News: American War Correspondent Casualties. MA Thesis, Texas Tech University,
1977. (Dickey Chapelle)

Yang, Punley Huston. "War News Coverage: A Study of Its
Development in the United States." MS Thesis, Kansas
State University, 1968.

UNPUBLISHED MATERIALS

Kennedy, William V. "Press Coverage of the Vietnam War: The Third View." Draft Report. Carlisle Barracks Pennsylvania: Strategic Studies Institute, U.S. Army War College, 1979.

Leneweaver, Sandra. "A Preliminary Look at Women Journalists During World War II." Paper presented at the West Coast Journalism Historians Conference, Arizona State University, March 2, 1979.

Pond, Elizabeth. "The Chau Trial I: Prologue." Article written for the Alicia Patterson Fund, March 1970.

_____. "The Chau Trial II: Denouement." Article written for the Alicia Patterson Fund, April-July 1970.

_____. "The Chau Trial III: Aftermath." Article written for the Alicia Patterson Fund, October 1970.

_____. "Portrait of a Revolutionary, Part I and Part II." Articles written for the Alicia Patterson Fund, September 1970.

_____. "Student Protest." Article written for the Alicia Patterson Fund, April 1970.

_____. "Sunday in Saigon." Article written for the Alicia Patterson Fund, January 1970.

_____. "Vietnamese Politics: Longer Term." Article written for the Alicia Patterson Fund, October 1969.

_____. "Vietnamese Politics: Short-Term." Article written for the Alicia Patterson Fund, September 1969.

Webb, Kate. "On the Other Side of the War." United Press International. Selections, 1971. Available from UPI.

SELECTED BOOK REVIEWS

Chapelle, Dickey. What's a Woman Doing Here? Reviewed by:

Arndt, J.A. Christian Science Monitor, February 21, 1962,
    p. 7.

Poore, Charles. "Books of the Times." The New York
    Times, February 1, 1962, p. 29.

Reynolds, Quentin. "She Shot the Gunfire." Saturday
    Review 45:29. May 12, 1962.

Emerson, Gloria. Winners and Losers: Battles, Retreats,
    Gains, Losses and Ruins From a Long War. Reviewed by:

Bigart, Homer. New Republic 176:70-72, January 22, 1977.

Brugger, Robert J. "Few of Us Who Were There Can Claim
    Innocence." Virginia Quarterly 53:522-525. Summer
    1977.

Bryan, C.D.B. "By War Possessed." Saturday Review.
    4:22-23 May 5, 1977.

Clemons, Walter. "Lest We Forget." Newsweek 89:67.
    January 10, 1977.

Morrow, Lance. "Fury and Intelligence." Time 109:81-82
    January 24, 1977.

Young, Marilyn. "Critical Amnesia." The Nation 224:406
    April 2, 1977.

Fallaci, Oriana. Nothing and So Be It. Reviewed by:

Majkut, P. T. Best Seller 32:12 April, 1972.

Parton, Margaret. Saturday Review 55:75 March 18, 1972.

Quinn, Sally. Book World. March 19, 1972, p. 12.

Fitzgerald, Frances. Fire in the Lake. Reviewed by:

Bernal, Martin. "What Is it About the Vietnamese?" New
    York Review of Books 19:24 October 5, 1972.

Buck, D. D. Library Journal 97:2169 June 15, 1972.

Buckley, Kevin. "Reporter at a Fire." Newsweek 80:62-62b. August 7, 1972.

Brudnoy, David. "The New Anti-Vietnam Bible." National Review 24:1068-1070 September 29, 1972.

Duffy, Martha. "The Big Attrit." Time 100:61-62 August 28, 1972.

Gellhorn, Martha. The Face of War. Reviewed by:

Mitgang, Herbert. New York Times Book Review. March 22, 1959, p. 10.

Nicolson, Nigel. New Statesman. 58:517 October 17, 1959.

Weeks, Edward. Atlantic. 203:83 March 1959.

Geyer, Georgie Anne. Buying the Night Flight. Reviewed by:

Davidon, Ann M. "Woman of the World." Progressive 47:55-56 May 1983.

Grossman, Elizabeth. New York Times Book Review. January 30, 1983, p. 16.

Rosenberg, Merri. Columbia Journalism Review 22:62 Jan/Feb 1983.

Wall, James M. "The Night Flight: A Personal Journey." Christian Century. 100:35-36. January 19, 1983.

Higgins, Marguerite. Our Vietnam Nightmare. Reviewed by:

Clarke, J.J. Best Seller 25:370 December 15, 1965.

Dudman, Richard. Saturday Review. 48:34 November 27, 1965.

Kearney, V.S. America. 114:23 January 1, 1966.

Higgins, Marguerite. War in Korea. Reviewed by:

Marshall, S.L.A. "Almost Alone at the Front." Saturday Review. 34:20 April 21, 1951.

McCarthy, Mary. The Seventeenth Degree. Reviewed by:

  Fallows, James. "Mary McCarthy--the Blinders She Wears."
    Washington Monthly 8:55-63 February 1977 (Reprinted
    from 6:5-17 May 1974)

Ray, Michele. The Two Shores of Hell. Reviewed by:

  Camenson, H.S. Library Journal. 93:2492 June 15, 1968.

  Dudman, Richard. Saturday Review. 51:36 June 15, 1968.

  Mecklin, J.M. New York Times Book Review. June 30,
    1968, p. 3.

May, Antoinette. Witness to War: A Biography of Marguerite
Higgins. Reviewed by:

  Rifkin, Ira. "Correspondent Lived Her Life on World's
    Front Lines." Los Angeles Daily News. December 11,
    1983, LA Life Section, p. 30.

Sheehan, Susan. Ten Vietnamese. Reviewed by:

  Young, Gavin. "They Live in a War-torn World." New
    York Times Book Review. April 16, 1967, p. 16.

Shepard, Elaine. The Doom Pussy. Reviewed by:

  "The Gal's Dainty, but the Book Ain't." The Miami (Flor-
    ida) Herald. February 12, 1967.

  Kirwan, J.D. National Review. 19:318. March 21, 1967.

Sontag, Susan. Styles of Radical Will. Reviewed by:

  Capouya, Emile. Saturday Review. 53:29 May 3, 1969.

  Gilman, Richard. New Republic. 160:23 May 3, 1969.

Included in the index are references to women war correspondents in Vietnam and in other conflicts, media for which women correspondents reported, and books on Vietnam written by women correspondents. References to male journalists, to other media, and to events in the Vietnam war are limited to their association with women correspondents.